PELICAN BOOKS

Politics and Power in the U.S.A.

David McKay is Senior Lecturer in Government and Executive Director of the European Consortium for Political Research at the University of Essex. He was educated at the universities of Hull, Essex and Wisconsin and has been teaching at Essex since 1973. His publications include *Housing and Race in Industrial Society* (1977), *The Politics of Urban Change* (co-authored, 1979), *Planning and Politics in Western Europe* (editor, 1982), *The New British Political System* (co-authored, 1983), *American Politics and Society* (revised edition, 1985) and *Domestic Policy and Ideologies* (1988).

He is a frequent visitor to the United States and has held appointments at Cornell University and at the University of California. David McKay is also past Chairman of the American Politics Group of the British Political Studies Association, and he is currently working on theories of American political development.

DAVID McKAY

Politics and Power in the U.S.A.

PENGUIN BOOKS

PENGUIN BOOKS

Published by the Penguin Group
27 Wrights Lane, London W8 5TZ, England
Viking Penguin Inc., 40 West 23rd Street, New York, New York 10010, USA
Penguin Books Australia Ltd, Ringwood, Victoria, Australia
Penguin Books Canada Ltd, 2801 John Street, Markham, Ontario, Canada L3R 1B4
Penguin Books (NZ) Ltd, 182–190 Wairau Road, Auckland 10, New Zealand

Penguin Books Ltd, Registered Offices: Harmondsworth, Middlesex, England

First published 1987
Reprinted 1988

Typeset, printed and bound in Great Britain by
Hazell Watson & Viney Limited
Member of BPCC plc
Aylesbury, Bucks, England
Typeset in Linotron Melior

Contents

Preface

The major motive behind the writing of this book is that both within and outside the United States it is surprisingly difficult to find information and comment on U.S. events which is not in some way modified or distorted by strictly American values and perspectives. When European television reports an American story, more often than not American rather than European experts are summoned to comment. The generally high quality and quantity of American news reporting invites exploitation by the foreign media. Even in the academic world it is impossible to ignore Americans' views of their own society and polity. As a result non-Americans tend to be over dependent on U.S. scholarship, and confine themselves either to writing essentially non-controversial textbooks, or to providing a broader readership with unstructured reflective essays. This book is neither of these. As with texts, it has a clear didactic purpose: it seeks to inform the reader about contemporary American politics. But it also takes a particular, critical position in relation to the way in which the United States is governed today. Few answers or solutions to America's domestic and international problems are offered. Instead, the objective is to provide both Americans and non-Americans with a uniquely British or European perspective on the ways in which the American political system has adapted to what can only be called the monumental changes of the last forty years.

I owe a debt of thanks to numerous individuals and institutions on both sides of the Atlantic, but I am particularly grateful to the publisher's readers and to John Owens, who read the whole manuscript with great care. All the errors that remain are, of course, mine. I must reserve a pantheon of praise for Anne Slowgrove who typed, corrected and retyped the manuscript quite expertly. Finally, I must thank the

Department of Government, University of Essex, for providing such an amenable working environment for so many years.

David McKay
University of Essex,
Colchester
February 1986

CHAPTER ONE

Studying American Politics
in America's Century

By almost every measure – economic power, military might, cultural influence – this is America's century. Twice, U.S. military power has rescued the Old World from disaster. Since 1945 the American economy has been first the saviour and more recently the locomotive of the world economy. Modern capitalism – from production-line manufacturing and mass ownership of consumer goods to the latest in micro-technology – is an essentially American phenomenon. Fashion in music, literature, art, architecture and inter-personal relations has been shaped more by developments in the United States than anywhere else. American politics, too, have been exported to the rest of the world. By example, imi-tation and by force, states almost everywhere have adopted American notions of republicanism and democracy. By the mid 1980s it was common to argue that the U.S. was winning the battle for global influence against its ideological rivals, communism and socialism. Yet in the economic, military and political arenas, most of the world was beginning to feel uncomfortable about the changing nature of American power. In part this was because, as the next chapter will show, U.S. economic power was declining in relative terms. But the dis-quiet extended beyond questioning America's capacity to lead, to a sense that American society and its polity were themselves less than ideal examples for the rest of the world.

For the student of American politics, the shifting status and fortunes of the U.S. can be a serious obstacle to objective analysis. The briefest glance at what is a vast literature on the subject shows just how much perceptions have changed over a very short period. During the 1950s most commentators were self-congratulatory in approach. By the late 1960s and early 1970s the mood had shifted to one of moral outrage at America's apparent inability to deal with social injustice, imperialism and corruption in government. Later, in the 1970s, how effective government was at handling the economy and solving the energy crisis became the main theme. By Ronald Reagan's second term something of the self-congratulatory style had returned – although it was hardly dominant. Indeed, as many critics as supporters of the new 'economic realism' were active in defence of their positions.[1]

In spite of these shifts in mood and emphasis, the outside observer of American politics cannot help but notice certain enduring features of the system that help facilitate a more historically balanced sense of what is going on at any one time. Political fragmentation has always been a part of American politics. Congress is internally fragmented; presidential/-congressional liaison is rarely without tensions and misunderstandings. The federal system, with its myriad governments and what amounts to fifty-one distinct constitutional structures, is the very essence of fragmentation. There is an absence of any overarching authority in the political system. Presidents may be at the political apex, but compared with many chief executives they are uncommonly constrained by Congress, public opinion and even their own executive establishment. The political parties are not in a position to provide a focus of leadership by obliging mass memberships to remain loyal to particular ideologies which are then translated into political power. Parties may be weaker now than twenty or thirty years ago, but they have never played the centralizing ideological role associated with many European parties.

The relative weakness of the U.S. central state is linked to an aversion among Americans to inclusive or all-embracing ideologies. Adherence to socialism, fascism or communism is unacceptable to most. Indeed it is downright un-American, for, as Chapter Three will show, Americans have their own ideology – a complex mixture of anti-statism, freedom, equality and democracy – which has endured throughout the history of the republic. This resilience is the most remarkable feature of 'Americanism'. Time after time in history the country has been bombarded by major economic and social changes which, in other states, would have brought revolu-

tion or disintegration. Consider the following. Massive immigration, especially from 1870 onwards, all but transformed
the ethnic and religious character of America. The resulting
population growth was accompanied by (and was a cause of)
truly dramatic industrialization. If in 1870 U.K. manufacturing output was 100, in the U.S. it was fifty-one. Again assign-
ing the base figure of 100 to the U.K., in 1913 American output
had soared to 235.[2]

America's industrial slums and poverty – not to mention
exploitation by a ruthless capitalism – were just as bad as in
other countries. Then, during the 1930s, the bubble burst in
a much more damaging way than in most comparable countries. In addition to high unemployment among farmers and
industrial workers, the American middle class was badly hit.
By 1933 40 per cent of existing mortgage debt was in default,
and in 1931 alone a staggering 2,298 banks had failed.[3] Only
prompt action by the Roosevelt administration prevented a
total collapse of capitalism.

The Second World War brought a recovery which lasted
until the 1970s. Since 1973, however, the economy's fortunes
have been fluctuating once again – not in the manner of the
1930s, but in a sufficiently unpredictable way to cause deep
concern. Post-war social and political shocks have been as
severe as ever, however. Racial segregation and injustice in
the South, urban riots, Vietnam, Watergate and political
assassinations have all taken their toll. Yet not once throughout all these dramatic economic and social changes have
basic American values been fundamentally challenged, and
not once has the viability of the American regime been in
question.

While few doubt the resilience of the American ideology –
or the American idea – and most accept that the U.S. continues to display a remarkable ability to adapt to change,
anxiety about the efficiency and responsiveness of political
institutions is a recurring theme in American history. As
implied earlier, this concern has been growing in very recent
years, and there is evidence that the new 'crisis' is qualitatively different from all previous crises. Three major changes
have occurred which have no precedent in American history;
how U.S. political institutions and processes have adapted

to these changes is the theme of this book and each will be discussed at length in later chapters. First, America's role in the world has been transformed since 1941. As the next chapter will show, in economic and military terms the U.S. has assumed the status of *hegemon* – albeit one in relative decline since the early 1970s. Virtually everything that happens in American domestic politics has repercussions beyond America's borders. Similarly, events overseas – from oil production levels to Japanese industrial management and the latest crisis in the Lebanon – affect Americans and their political system. As we will see, this new interdependence has subjected political institutions to enormous stress.

Second, the U.S. has acquired all the trappings of the modern central state, whether the citizenry like it or not. An enormous military establishment, an incomplete but growing welfare state and myriad rules and regulations governing most aspects of society all require some degree of central co-ordination and control. Yet both institutionally and ideologically such centralized power remains alien to the traditional American way of doing things. In our discussion of Congress, the presidency, the courts and federalism this contradiction appears time and again.

Third, while acknowledging that coalition-building has always been difficult in the American system, a new social fragmentation has made the job of political mobilization even more difficult over the last twenty years. Again, there is no precedent for this in American history. Region, ethnicity and social class have always played some role, usually via the political parties, in overcoming the institutional fragmentation characteristic of American government. Today these cues are much less effective as agents of political change. Instead, we find ourselves in the era of political personalities and of discrete issues. Media-based, politics is a fluid and ephemeral world where political allegiances and the salience of particular issues change quickly and unpredictably. In such a context, the redistribution of resources from haves to have-nots – never an easy task in the United States – has become increasingly difficult to achieve. This is the theme of Chapter Three and is also relevant to our discussion of Congress, the presidency, the courts and interest groups.

Few doubt that these three changes are testing American political institutions as they have never been tested before. We are not, as some have argued, in the midst of a crisis of political alienation,[4] but the sense that the present institutional structure is simply not adequate, or cannot cope, has been growing. Chapter Nine will present a scorecard of plus and minus points, and will discuss what reforms, if any, might help to produce a more effective polity.

In addition to the business of assessing the performance of political institutions this book also attempts to inform the reader regarding the basic structure and functions of American government. It assumes little or no prior knowledge of the subject, and helps guide the reader through the central institutions of Congress, presidency, courts and federalism, as well as providing insights into the functioning of parties and interest groups. At all times, however, basic facts are presented in the context of the three fundamental changes discussed above. Naturally, attention will tend to be focused on the record of the recent administrations and particularly those led by Ronald Reagan. Certainly there can be no doubt that our three changes helped bring about the election and re-election of a president who set out to break what had been a fifty-year consensus on the need for middle-of-the-road politics. Did Ronald Reagan break the political mould? Indeed can any president stop the movement towards a shiftless, almost leaderless politics of issues and shallow personalities? Before we answer these questions, let us return to that change which has probably had more effect on U.S. politics than any other this century – the transformation of America's economic and military role in the world.

CHAPTER TWO

The Declining Hegemon

There was a time when books on American domestic politics made little reference to the rest of the world. Until 1941, indeed, the U.S. was so insulated from world events that such references were largely unnecessary. After the Second World War the United States assumed the status of a hegemonic power whose domestic political arrangements had profound effects on relations with virtually every nation on earth. This accepted, it was common during the 1970s to argue that the period of American dominance was over. Following the election of Ronald Reagan, however, the United States attempted to reassert its influence over economic and foreign affairs. The period of total hegemony may be over, but the U.S. remains easily the most significant economic and military power on earth. During 1983 and 1984 the dollar appreciated almost wildly in relation to other currencies as investors rushed to take advantage of high American interest rates. At the same time the Western economies – including Japan – looked to the U.S. for a lead to guide them out of recession. So America remains the industrial locomotive in spite of recent advances in the performance of the West European and Japanese economies. In military and foreign affairs the United States continues to hold the key to an uncertain future. Except for the immediate Soviet and Chinese spheres of interest, every corner of the world is affected directly or indirectly by American military power. From the South Atlantic to Western Europe, the Middle East, South Asia and Japan, what American politicians and military men say can have a crucial impact on literally billions of lives.

Yet the 1980s are clearly different from the 1950s and 1960s. The last twenty years have seen dramatic changes both in the United States and in the rest of the world. It is these changes which have placed such awesome demands on

American leaders – demands which increasingly cannot or will not be met. To question the capacity of the U.S. to lead need not involve engaging in a polemic against the United States or even in a critique of the substance of U.S. relations with the world. By happenstance – some would say by misfortune – America found itself in a position of world hegemony in the mid-1940s. It was a role long resisted by the Americans before the war but accepted, at first with reluctance but eventually with equanimity and even enthusiasm, during the dangerous post-war years. As the British found during the nineteenth century, it is the fate of *hegemons* to be feared but reluctantly respected. Later, during the 1920s and 1930s, the British discovered that *hegemons* in decline are feared but despised. In many respects the U.S. finds itself in an analogous position in the 1980s – although American decline is both less dramatic and qualitatively different from the quite precipitous change in British fortunes after the First World War. In the main it is not the 'fault' of the United States that its policies often have negative or destructive consequences for other countries. Indeed there is no perfect or optimal role for a hegemonic or near-hegemonic power. By definition, the concentration of military, diplomatic and economic power in one nation brings abuses, mistakes and sometimes tragedies – a fact which the growing field of hegemony theory now recognizes.[1] By many criteria, the United States has used its powers quite benignly. Until recently, many considered the country well suited to a leadership role. In stark contrast to most of the pre-war European powers and to post-war Russia, the U.S. was democratic, politically stable and apparently free from destructive irredentist and imperialist ambitions.

The era of congratulation and guarded respect is over, however, and without condemnation or prejudice it is now all too possible to question the American capacity to lead and to stabilize the international order. What has happened over the last twenty years to produce such a fundamental change in perceptions? We will deal first with international affairs and, in subsequent chapters, with American domestic politics.

Invidious comparisons between the 1960s and the 1980s

are common. Steady growth, low inflation, strong world leaders and improving East–West relations are contrasted with the economic dislocation, volatility and political confusion of the 1980s. Although such comparisons are often misleading – the 1960s may not be judged so attractive in a longer historical perspective – there is little doubt that the world is now perceived as a more uncertain place than twenty years ago. Three major changes can be identified, all of which have undermined the United States' capacity to lead.

Relative Economic Decline

In spite of an apparent improvement in the fortunes of the U.S. during the early–mid 1980s, the country is nowhere near as dominant in economic terms as it was even twenty years ago, let alone forty. This can be expressed in a number of ways. Although *per capita* G.N.P. in the United States has risen steadily, by some measures it is now lower than that of some other developed countries. In the case of Japan the relative improvement has been dramatic. If American G.N.P. *per capita* equals 100, in 1960 Japanese G.N.P. *per capita* was 16 and 82 in 1979. Germany has fared almost as well, the relevant figures being 46 in 1960 rising to 116 in 1979.[2] U.S. productivity has also declined in relation to most other industrial countries, with Japan, Germany and France improving rapidly in the 1960–80 period. Indeed only Britain performed more poorly than the U.S. during these years. The early 1980s demonstrated that the U.S. is far from being a burnt-out economic power. It remains the largest economy and in some ways the most resilient. But it is also quite vulnerable. Events in the outside world can and have had profound consequences for the economy. The most celebrated of these were the 1973–4 and 1979–80 oil shocks, both of which caused serious dislocation in America and other O.E.C.D. countries.[3] Such events would have been impossible in 1950 or 1960, when American indigenous oil supplies were plentiful and U.S. (and British) military clout was sufficient to guarantee subservience from commodity-producing countries.

The weakening of American economic power has been paralleled by (and is a cause of) a much less controlled and ordered international economic system. It is very much in the interest of dominant countries to proselytize the benefits of a more open international order – they do, after all, hold all the trump cards in terms of comparative economic advantage – and from 1945 to 1971 the U.S. led successive rounds of trade liberalization negotiations under the General Agreement on Tariffs and Trade (G.A.T.T.). At the same time American governments urged a move towards the free convertibility of currencies. So strong was the dollar during these years that the U.S. could quite happily live with balance of payments deficits and low reserves of gold and foreign currencies. No country was likely to refuse a currency that was the bench mark for the value of all currencies, that determined the price of gold (at $35 per ounce), and lubricated world trade. The mighty dollar was the foundation on which the more open global trading structure was built.

By the late 1960s, however, cracks in the edifice were appearing. Governments and investors were beginning to question just how high the U.S. trade deficits could get. Moreover commodity prices were rising everywhere as the prolonged economic boom swallowed up increasingly scarce natural resources. With these changes came a new and particularly virulent form of inflation, together with real pressure on the dollar. In 1971 Richard Nixon was forced to abandon the system of fixed exchange rates which had held the world monetary system together since the Second World War. Instead the dollar was to float freely in relation to the value of gold and other currencies. Few decisions in the post-war era have had such important consequences, for since then the value of the dollar has fluctuated wildly and international trade has acquired an endemic uncertainty and volatility. As the leading industrial nation, the U.S. remains vital to the health of rich and poor countries alike, but America is no longer unequivocally in charge. What happens to its currency, balance of payments, domestic interest rates and general level of economic activity is now as much determined by external events beyond any administration's influence as by domestic or controllable external events.

This new uncertainty has been compounded by the fact that the U.S. is now trading with the rest of the world to a much greater extent than ever before. Table 1 shows the quite dramatic increase in the share of gross national product accounted for by foreign trade since 1960. Some of this increase is a result of the higher cost of oil imports, but as the table shows very clearly, exports have been increasing almost as fast as imports. While these figures remain low compared with other industrial countries (for example 32.6 per cent of Japan's trade is accounted for by foreign trade, and 51 per cent of Britain's),[4] they are very high for a country long thought of as economically self-sufficient. Significantly, as the U.S. has become more interdependent with the rest of the world, so its share of world trade has dropped from 18.4 per cent in 1950 to 13.4 per cent in 1977.[5] At the same time the trade deficit has continued to increase steadily. In 1985 it was estimated that the U.S. would become a net debtor country by the end of the year.

TABLE 1

Imports and exports as a percentage of gross national product
U.S.A. 1960–81

Year	Imports	Exports	Total
1960–64 (average)	5.5	4.4	9.9
1969	6.0	5.8	11.8
1974	10.0	9.9	19.9
1978	9.7	10.2	19.9
1981	12.6	11.7	24.3

Source: O.E.C.D. Economic Surveys, *The United States*, various years.

So by every measure the U.S. is now weaker in relation to other economies. It is more vulnerable to external shocks, less able to fall back on the security of a strong fixed-value currency and, above all, less able to lead and dictate the terms of global economic relations. At the same time, American economic success remains vital for the rest of the world.

Open Markets and Information Overload

During the 1970s it was common to assert that the era of free trade was over and that a new protectionism was emerging. In April 1978, the *Wall Street Journal* bemoaned the fact that

after three decades of immense increase in world trade and living standards, exports and imports are causing tense pressures in nearly every nation and among the best of allies. The U.S. sets price floors against Japanese steel, Europe accuses the U.S. of undercutting its papermakers, the Japanese decry cheap textiles from South Korea, French farmers have smashed truckloads of Italian wine and A.F.L./C.I.O President George Meany rattles exporters world-wide by calling free trade – 'a joke'.[6]

Although such claims are still made, they are usually the province of those with a vested interest in trade restriction. More considered analyses conclude that trade is, if anything, becoming more, not less, open. Certainly the Tokyo round of G.A.T.T. negotiations in the late 1970s represented a relaxation rather than a tightening of barriers, for the leading industrial countries began seriously to discuss the thorny problem of non-tariff barriers – such things as subsidies, price supports and technical restrictions on imports – which were beginning to be recognized as long-established barriers to trade.[7]

After the advent of the Reagan and Thatcher administrations, the pressure to combat protectionism intensified further. Indeed it is not just trade in goods but also in money which is now more freely exchanged than ever before. Countries, corporations and individuals can move vast sums around the world in a way which would have been impossible in the 1950s or even the early 1960s. Of course the incentive to speculate is much greater now. Currencies do fluctuate significantly in value; interest rate levels are fiercely competitive; international banking has developed out of all recognition into a finely honed (but fragile) mechanism for playing the global money game – and not always successfully, as bad debts to Third World countries show. Talk of protectionism 1930s-style looks decidedly inappropriate in this context. All the pressures in the international banking scene are for more openness and more deregulation – no more so than in the U.S., as later chapters will show.[8]

None of this is to deny that protectionist sentiments exist – indeed they strengthened perceptibly in the mid 1980s as U.S. imports soared in response to a strong dollar. As Arthur Stein has observed, the 'hegemon's dilemma' during its period of relative decline is whether it should remain a prophet of free trade or batten down the hatches and protect what remains of a vulnerable domestic market.[9] So far, the U.S. has decided to bear the costs of openness: a huge balance of payments deficit and an unstable currency. How long this will continue, however, is impossible to predict.

Open international markets are generally recognized by economists as a good thing. But we have reason to believe that open markets in the 1980s are fraught with much greater danger than would have been the case in the 1950s or 1960s. One new problem has already been noted – the increasing vulnerability of the United States, the market leader. A second problem derives from the peculiar nature of information flow in the computerized media age. Information is the life blood of markets, but when this vital commodity is packaged and summarized in daily, weekly and monthly statistics and then flashed instantaneously around the world it has a great destabilizing effect on investment and economic planning generally. Herbert Stein, former chairman of the Council of Economic Advisors under President Nixon, was all too aware of this phenomenon in the American context:

I felt constantly harassed by the reporting of the economic statistics in the press and on TV, which seems to me always to be making a big deal out of each month's figures. Each month's figures, of course, seemed to be worse than the previous month's, and each month's figures were made to seem much more . . . record-setting and historical than they really deserved to be. There seemed to be very little possibility of getting a big picture out of the daily reporting . . . I felt that this was more than an irritation to me, that it did have some adverse effects on life in this country, that it kept the public in a constant state of anxiety and nervousness about the economy. The fact that our economy was producing the highest standard of living any community had ever enjoyed . . . was being lost in a kind of hypochondria about each month's statistics.[10]

By the 1980s the volume and frequency of summary economic statistics had increased enormously. Small wonder that interest-rate levels, currency values – indeed the very level of activity in an economy – respond so alarmingly to the publication of the latest money-supply, public-borrowing or inflation figures. Most alarming is the extrapolation of single statistics to predict trends over months or years. This undoubtably adds yet another element of uncertainty to an already uncertain world.

Again, this problem is most serious for the market leader, the United States. American deficits, inflation rates, money-supply figures – even housing starts – are the vital cues for public and private policies not only in the U.S. but just about everywhere else. The weaker the political leadership of the American public sector, and ultimately of the American economy, the less predictable and controllable these vital indicators become. As later chapters will catalogue, this leadership has been less than adequate over the last twenty years.

The Increasingly Limited Nature of U.S. Foreign and Military Power

Until the early 1960s it was broadly accepted that America had almost unlimited influence in world affairs. Except within strictly delineated spheres of Soviet and Chinese interest the U.S. was dominant to a degree unknown since the British exercised awesome naval power during the nineteenth century. One by one the old colonial European powers were aided, replaced or, in the case of British and French involvement in Suez, chastised by the Americans. First in Greece and then in the Middle East and South-east Asia, U.S. intervention was quickly acknowledged as essential by Britain and France. By 1960 American influence had become truly global, with U.S. dominance firmly established in the Americas, the Pacific, Japan and virtually the whole of Western Europe. Successive presidents characterized world politics in terms of a Manichean struggle of good versus evil. Consider Harry Truman's famous 1947 speech proclaiming the 'Truman Doctrine':

One way of life is based upon the will of the majority, and is distinguished by free institutions, representative government, free elections, guarantees of individual liberty, freedom of speech and religion, and freedom from political oppression. The second way of life is based upon the will of a minority forcibly imposed on the majority. It relies upon terror and oppression, a controlled press and radio, framed elections and the suppression of personal freedom. We [the U.S.] will not realize our objectives unless we are willing to help free people to maintain their institutions and their integrity against aggressive movements that seek to impose upon them totalitarian regimes . . . It is the policy of the U.S. to support free people who are resisting attempted subjugation by armed minorities or by outside pressures.[11]

Even more stirring was John Kennedy's inaugural address:

Let every nation know whether it wishes us well or ill, that we shall pay any price, bear any burden, meet any hardship, support any friend, oppose any foe, to assure the survival and the success of liberty.[12]

Although President Reagan talked in quite similar terms, his words were not received with the respect, relief or even the fear that his predecessors' speeches evoked. Instead, outside the U.S. at least, he often inspired derision, contempt or a grudging resentment at the continuing ability of the United States to exercise power.

Two major changes occurred between 1960 and the mid 1980s that transformed both the objective position of the U.S. and perceptions of that country's right to act as the world's policeman and moral example. First, Soviet power increased in relation to American. In 1947 the Soviet Union was dramatically weaker than the U.S.; even by 1960 the gap was wide. By 1984, however, although still unable to match American military power, the U.S.S.R. was much closer to a position of parity.[13] Perhaps more important is the distressing but by now obvious fact that East–West relations were not fated to progress in some predictable linear fashion. Following President Nixon's attempts at *détente* and the slow but steady advances in nuclear testing and arms limitations, it was assumed in the mid 1970s that progress would continue. It did not. Relations have deteriorated substantially so that now the two superpowers face each other almost evenly matched, and with no certainty of a withdrawal from constant verbal and occasionally rather more than verbal confrontation.

The second related change is the decline of both super-powers in relation to a host of Third World countries. Starting with Cuba in 1958 and reaching a climax in Vietnam some ten years later, the Americans slowly had to come to terms with the fact that they could not and would not 'pay any price' to 'assure the survival and the success of liberty'. Since then the U.S. has had to stand down, or has been openly humiliated, in Angola, the Lebanon and Iran. And in Central America military force has, in relation to parallel events in the 1950s and 1960s, been used quite sparingly. Part of the reason for this change derives from strictly domestic political events – of which more later. But even if there had been no pressures at home, the American policy of containing communism would have run into trouble. For one thing the super-powers (and others) have supplied other countries with increasing amounts of military equipment, creating what Mary Kaldor aptly termed the 'baroque arsenal'.[14] Competitive weapons markets have undoubtedly given numerous countries an independence undreamt of in the 1950s. And, of course, oil riches have enabled unstable, erstwhile impoverished states to build up impressive military resources. Perhaps more important than either of these factors is the gradual erosion of the solid ideological blocs which characterized the world in the immediate post-war years. Increasing numbers of poorer countries fail to fit into either the collectivist/socialist mould or the individualist/capitalist category which Harry Truman identified in 1947. Instead, many are non-aligned and eschew subservience to Russia and America while readily accepting their economic and military aid. This obviously complicates American foreign and defence policy enormously. Often, as in the Middle East today, it is not clear what policy is in the best interest of the United States. Certainly there are occasions when no matter what policy the country pursues it will arouse opprobrium abroad and criticism at home.

The United States is a country past the peak of its economic and military power. As with Britain after 1918 – or possibly even after 1880[15] – the rest of the world is highly ambivalent towards the declining *hegemon*. On the one hand, it yearns for the stability and order which dominant powers can enforce.[16] On the other hand, few would welcome a return to the immediate post-war years when the U.S. was all powerful. The great paradox for the Americans is that pressures exist both for greater intervention in world affairs and for less. Which is most in the interest of the U.S. or of other countries is by no means obvious. One thing, however, is certain: whatever the Americans do will continue to have serious consequences for the rest of the world. And what they do is likely to be profoundly influenced by a unique American ideology and a truly remarkable set of political institutions. Unfortunately, the last twenty-five years have also witnessed important changes in American political arrangements, most of which have served to complicate and often to undermine political authority. It is difficult to think of a single major political institution which is unaffected by some crisis or other. Leaders, commentators, investors, ordinary citizens all over the world study intently what appears to be a confused and fiercely independent Congress grappling with federal budgets, the size of which helps determine economic fortunes everywhere. Presidents responsible for wielding enormous military power and diplomatic pressure often seem more preoccupied with arcane party-political or electoral matters than with the future of East–West relations or peace in the Middle East. At any time it seems that American courts can overturn the seemingly well-considered policies of elected representatives. Before we proceed to a detailed analysis of how these political institutions have developed and changed in such apparently unfortunate ways, it is necessary to understand those beliefs and values which underpin American political life. As we shall see, these too have changed in a uniquely American fashion.

CHAPTER THREE

Ideology and Social Change

Foreign observers of the American scene are constantly struck by the apparent inability of American governments to get things done quickly and efficiently. In contrast to Japanese and British premiers or French presidents, U.S. presidents seem remarkably circumscribed by an often truculent national legislature and a fickle public. Congress itself is indecisive and fragmented, operating as it does on behalf of myriad constituencies and interests. American courts, state and local governments, even the Federal Reserve (the central bank), all wield power and influence independently of the chief executive. No doubt constitutional arrangements, in particular federalism and the separation of powers, help to account for such a fragmentation of decision-making. But institutional structures are only part of the picture. As important is the particular nature of the beliefs and values that underpin the political system. This chapter makes two important claims about the ways in which these beliefs and values operate. First, although they have helped make American politicians more accountable and responsive, they have rarely encouraged efficient government. Second, values and attitudes have changed significantly over the last twenty years so that today coherent and efficient policy-making is even more difficult to achieve – and this in a national and international context where good political leadership from the U.S. is essential. Let us start by describing what can be called the American ideology.

An American Ideology?

Marxist and pluralist scholars have argued long and hard over whether modern societies are characterized by a political culture, or what Marxists call a dominant ideology. The argument revolves around the central issue of whether societal beliefs and values are somehow imposed on the citizenry from above in order to ensure political obedience and economic subservience (the Marxist position), or whether beliefs emanate from below as a result of a complex mix of historical and cultural developments. To the Marxist, politics and political institutions are the instruments of the ruling classes; their function is to establish and maintain myths about society, therefore forestalling rebellion and a full realization of 'objective' economic and political conditions. To the pluralist, political culture can be independent of politics. Through democratic processes the exercise of political authority depends on public support and at least partly reflects mass public beliefs and values, which are acquired in society through socialization, from family, schools, neighbourhood, social class and so on.[1] It is easy to appreciate why, in many countries, academics disagree about whether public attitudes are imposed from above or emerge from below. Governments do, after all, often control channels of information and education, with the intent of instilling certain values in the population. It is not unusual for starkly competing ideologies to hold sway, as for example in Franco's Spain, suggesting that efforts to impose the 'official' ideology have been less than successful.

The United States, however, presents problems of a different kind. Almost every social group appears to subscribe to a particularly American set of beliefs, but there is little direct evidence that governments have imposed these on the population. There are two possible explanations for this unique American situation. First, American political culture may, for historical and other reasons, be peculiarly strong and resilient. Second, governments and those in control of the economy may have been remarkably subtle and sophisticated in imposing a highly successful dominant ideology. In spite of considerable efforts by Marxist scholars, the second explanation falls down when tested empirically. The U.S.A. is simply too heterogeneous a society, with too fragmented a system of government, to facilitate the sort of subtle indoctrination the theory suggests.[2] Realizing this, some Marxists have accepted that the absence of a feudal past and the conscious creation of a new, essentially bourgeois society discouraged the emergence of strong class antagonisms and facilitated a near-universal acceptance of the merits of hard work, equality of opportunity and freedom under the law. Antonio Gramsci, one of the most influential Marxist theoreticians, went so far as to call this 'Americanism', or 'a unique American ideology'.[3] Michael Harrington, a prominent American socialist, argues along similar lines:

Americanism, the official ideology of the society, became a kind of 'substitutive socialism'. The European ruling classes . . . were open in their contempt for the proletariat. But in the United States equality, and even classlessness, the creation of wealth for all, and political liberty were extolled in the public schools . . . 'The idea that everyone can be a capitalist,' Samson wrote in a perceptive insight, 'is an American concept of Capitalism. It is a socialist concept of Capitalism.'[4]

Significantly, pluralists also accept the unique nature of Americanism. Louis Hartz, the most celebrated exponent of the pluralist position, likens American society to a 'fragment' of European societies consisting mainly of people with liberal middle-class values.[5] More recently Samuel Huntington has pin-pointed the unique nature of Americanism, which is often referred to as American 'exceptionalism':

It is possible to speak of a body of political ideas that constitutes 'Americanism' in a sense in which one can never speak of 'Britishism', 'Frenchism', 'Germanism' or 'Japanesism'. Americanism in this sense is comparable to other ideologies or religions . . . To reject the central ideas of that doctrine is to be un-American. There is no British Creed or French Creed; the Académie Française worries about the purity of the French language, not about the purity of French political ideas. What indeed would be an 'un-French' political idea? But preoccupation with 'un-American' political ideas and behaviour has been a recurring theme in American life. 'It has been our fate as a nation,' Richard Hofstadter succinctly observed, 'not to have ideologies but to be one'.[6]

In one sense it is not necessary to choose between the Marxist and pluralist positions. Neither disputes the absence of deep, politically articulated class divisions in the U.S.; both accept that economic development has been greatly aided by Americanism. In strictly functional terms – the maintenance of political stability, economic growth – the American ideology has been remarkably successful. This is especially so given the great ethnic, regional, religious and linguistic diversity of the immigrant society. Ultimately, the difference between the two positions comes down to starkly contrasting and irreconcilable value perspectives. Marxists dislike the objective inequalities which capitalism has brought; they despise the shallow consumerism and psychological deception of a materialist capitalist society; they cannot understand the visceral appeal of a ruthless economic individualism.[7] Pluralists view these phenomena quite differently. Inequalities are unfortunate but inevitable in a high growth, enterprising economy; material wealth and high consumption are uplifting, not degrading, for most people; competition stimulates the best in the human spirit. Let us look in more detail at the nature of this ideology. It is common to identify four basic distinguishing features.

Equality

Few Americans believe in equality of condition or the achievement of equal wealth, income and access to basic amenities for all. Such a situation could be reached only through a strong central state imposing Draconian taxes and providing massive welfare benefits – anathema to most Americans. Instead, Americans emphasize equality of *esteem* and equality of *opportunity*. Nineteenth-century visitors to the U.S. – Tocqueville, Dickens, Bryce – noted the striking absence of deference to class and status. Compared with Europe, public manners in America were highly egalitarian. Few citizens had any sense of privilege or superiority based on birthright or inherited wealth. Such sentiments persist even today. An individual's worth is measured more in terms of what he or she has achieved rather than in terms of some fixed scale of values based on a rigid, class-determined system of social stratification. Of course, this equality of esteem is far from absolute. Deference does exist, and privilege based on class, race and ethnicity has played a prominent – and tragic – part in American history. Even so, few Americans would admit to *liking* privilege and deference. Compared with Europeans, they continue to be remarkably free of such notions. In effect, the U.S. has all the objective inequalities of wealth and income characteristic of capitalist societies,[8] but it lacks a popular acceptance that these inequalities are immovably rooted in class distinctions.

A widely held belief in equality of opportunity helps explain why this is so. Give citizens equal education opportunities and every individual should be able to achieve self-fulfilment. This myth 'that everyone can make it in America' is pervasive and provides a vital clue to the nature of American political culture. To most Americans, discrimination based on race, ethnicity, region, sex or religion is wrong because everyone should have an equal opportunity to reap the benefits of a free, energetic and successful society. This helps explain not only the existence of numerous civil-rights laws and affirmative-action programmes, but also the assumption on the part of politicians, broadcasters and other public figures that everyone either is, or at least should be, equal in America. The reality is, of course, very different. Total equality of opportunity is simply not achievable, and there is little evidence that the American educational and economic systems provide greater opportunities than those available in comparable countries. As we will discover later, the myth of equal opportunity plays a crucial part in American politics.

Economic individualism and antipathy to the state

It follows that, for most Americans, personal effort explains the success or failure of an individual's fortunes. Given that education is provided freely and universally, failure must result from laziness, stupidity or bad judgement. The U.S.A., so the myth goes, is an open, democratic and free society with an economic system which effectively sorts the wheat from the chaff. As Table 2 graphically shows, only in the U.K. are the public as attached to notions of self-reliance – even admitting that different survey questions make comparisons difficult. Table 2 also shows the antipathy to government spending in the U.S. Although this opposition waxes and

TABLE 2

Beliefs about the causes of poverty and opinions on governmental action in six countries, 1960s and 1970s (percentages)

	France	West Germany	Denmark	United Kingdom	Canada	United States
Cause of poverty						
Individual laziness	16	23	11	43	–	–
Social injustice	35	23	14	16	–	–
Bad luck	18	18	17	10	–	–
Inevitable	18	10	28	17	–	–
Lack of effort	–	–	–	–	30	40
Circumstances	–	–	–	–	34	27
Lack of effort and circumstances	–	–	–	–	30	27
Don't know	13	26	30	14	6	6
Poor don't want to work*	–	–	–	–	–	57
Poor don't have equal chance*	–	–	–	–	–	30
Level of government spending						
Too much	2	6	10	20	43	58
Too little	68	46	31	36	13	13
About right	23	40	48	35	26	25
Don't know	7	8	11	9	19	4

Source: Richard M. Coughlin, *Ideology, Public Opinion and Welfare Policy: Attitudes Towards Taxes and Spending in Industrialized Societies* (Berkeley: Institute for Contemporary Studies, 1980), adapted from Table 3.20.

*Responses to a separate survey.

wanes with changes in taxation and spending levels, it is always there and is much more firmly established than in other countries. The individual, not the state, is what matters. In fact, Americans have some difficulty conceptualizing what 'the state' is. So strong is society in relation to the state in the U.S., that most people think in terms of democratically elected governments consisting of aggregates of individuals rather than in terms of some abstract notion of the state. Predictably, as governments – and especially federal governments – have become larger and more remote, so they have provoked more criticism. To Americans, governments are not something above and beyond society; they are a part of society and constantly answerable to it. The institutions of the state have little moral authority in themselves, therefore. Federal civil servants, the presidency, Congress, even judges, are given this authority by the people. The American state does have some symbols of universal respect – notably the Constitution. But even the Constitution is a document formalizing the people's power, not the state's. As political scientists have repeatedly stressed, there is little sense in the U.S. of a 'public interest' that is above and beyond individual and group interests.[9] Apart from defence and foreign affairs questions, politicians are obliged, therefore, to emphasize broad societal or 'American' values when appealing to the people, rather than depending on citizens' sense of duty and obligation to the state.

Economic individualism and anti-statism are part of a broader distaste for all forms of collectivist economic thinking. Whether perpetrated by governments, political parties (of the left) or interest groups (trade unions), the subordination of the individual to collective action is distrusted and feared. At only 18 per cent in the U.S., union membership is the lowest of any major O.E.C.D. country. Socialist parties have always fared badly. America is the only Western democracy without representation by a socialist or social democratic party in its national legislature.[10] Radical alternatives to a free-enterprise economy are simply not on the policy agenda – although extensive regulation and government intervention are both accepted and a source of constant debate.

Liberty

By most standards the United States is a truly free society. Censorship is effectively absent; political and religious freedom is highly valued; arbitrary police power is largely kept in check by vigilant and fiercely independent courts. Above all, those freedoms associated with economic individualism – freedom of movement, inheritance, capital accumulation – are part of the very fabric of American society. Americans are rightly proud of the Bill of Rights and the Fourteenth Amendment – those parts of the Constitution devoted to protecting individual rights. But most citizens see these freedoms as more than merely constitutionally protected rights; they are those *natural* rights which served as the very rationale for the escape from Europe and the founding of a new society.

How is this high regard for liberty reconcilable with the blatant denials of freedom which litter American history? In part because the premium on freedom is part of the ideology, it has at times been as much myth as reality. Indeed the assertion of clearly 'un-American' values such as those embodied by communism and atheism has been almost impossible at certain times and places, as the hysterical anti-Communist or 'red-baiting' periods following the two World Wars demonstrate.[11] These anti-libertarian movements have never been centrally controlled or organized, however. They have generally come from below, or at worst have been led or encouraged by state and local political leaders.

In recent years evidence of an increasing tolerance towards un-American ideas has been mounting.[12] By many measures the United States has never been freer. And civil-rights protection is not just a matter of rhetoric. Affirmative-action programmes for women and racial and ethnic minorities sometimes actually work. Media freedom is extensive – probably greater than anywhere else in the world. The U.S. is now a genuinely open society where new ideas and alternative policies are freely debated, discussed and often adopted. Perhaps most importantly, U.S. citizens are able to band together to form groups designed to promote or defend some cause or interest, and they increasingly do so. As we shall discover later, there are also institutional and sociological reasons for this phenomenon, but no one questions the *right* to form and participate in interest groups. This is a basic liberty deeply rooted in American political culture.

Democracy

With over 526,000 positions subject to election, it is difficult not to view the United States as a democratic country. Very early in the country's history universal franchise for white males was established – although votes for women came much later (1920) and southern Blacks were not effectively enfranchised until the 1960s or even the 1970s. What is important to understand about American democracy is the very high value placed on what the *majority* want. It is taken for granted that a decision approved by a plurality is legitimate and just. So Americans use the referendum, recall and initiative[13] much more than in most comparable countries. At the state and local levels many judges and numerous executive branch positions are subject to popular election. Although turnout is low – a point we will return to later – elections remain the very life-blood of politics in the U.S. Very few key decisions are not subject to popular approval either directly or indirectly through elected officials or legislatures operating independently of executives. Compare this with Britain, for example, where the only direct popular checks on government occur via periodic Parliamentary and local elections.

Again it is necessary to distinguish between myth and reality when discussing democracy. A high incidence of elections and a widespread belief that the system is democratic does not mean to say that it actually is. Low income groups, minorities and, until recently, women have had little say in who gets what, how and when. By their very nature, complex modern societies with vast government bureaucracies cannot be truly democratic in the classical, direct sense. What is important about the U.S. is the *belief* that the system is democratic and that, if not quite unique, the U.S. is certainly unusual in this regard.[14]

Perhaps aware that remote political authority can never be properly accountable, Americans repeatedly display greater faith in state and local government than in the federal government in Washington. As a result Washington politicians have always had difficulty convincing the public of their veracity and good faith.

A final characteristic of American ideology is its uniqueness. No other country subscribes to a similar set of values and beliefs. Americans are also convinced of the superiority of their way of doing things. Exceptionalism, therefore, has always been expressed in moralistic terms. U.S. democracy, institutions and constitutional arrangements are believed to be inherently superior to those of other countries because they are the conscious creation of the people – not of some distant and arbitrary state.

So far, the discussion has implied that the American ideology is largely unchanging. Some readers may also infer that, because American politics are characterized by an absence of sharply conflicting ideologies, political parties and political mobilization generally have been free from contrasting ideological appeals. Neither is true. As will be discussed later, Americanism is constantly adapting to an ever changing economic, social and political structure. And there is ideological competition in the U.S. – even if it is of a highly attenuated variety. Let us deal with this second point first.

Historically the most difficult problem for American government has been building coalitions of sufficient strength to facilitate effective policy-making. Institutionally the system is uncommonly fragmented. The separation of powers ensures that each of the main branches of government – executive, legislative and judicial – has a near-independent power base. Congress, in particular, serves a constituency quite separate from the president's. In addition, federalism gives to the state and indirectly to local governments a remarkable degree of autonomy. For federal governments to act coherently and effectively, therefore, they must have the support of Congress, the Supreme Court and the governors' mansions – at least for part of the time. This assumes, of course, that governments need to act. In fact, for most of the nineteenth century and the first thirty years of the twentieth, governments were required to do very little. American capitalism flourished without great state intervention; the social role of government was kept to a minimum. Contemptuous of the corruption of the Old World, the U.S. required little in the way of defence expenditure. All this changed after 1917 with America's entry into the First World War, and even more so after 1929, when the country was plunged into economic depression. Between 1932 and about 1968 American politics underwent important changes which permitted an unprecedented degree of federal spending and intervention in the economy and society. Specifically, the Democrats built a coalition around the policy-objective of combating economic dislocation. By welding together the interests of industrial workers, minorities, poor southern farmers and increasing numbers of an insecure middle class, the Democratic Party became the champion of the underdog and the economically vulnerable in American society. At the same time the Republicans became associated with big business and the more affluent members of the middle class. As such they were relegated to minority status. Between 1932 and 1968 they won just two presidential elections – with the aid of a charismatic candidate, Dwight Eisenhower – and they lost every congressional election bar three (1946 and 1952 in the House, 1946 in the Senate).

The Democrats' New Deal coalition was not equivalent to the solid base of class support won by the British Labour Party in 1945. It was very much a coalition. Nor did the American ideology somehow disappear during these years. On the contrary, it profoundly influenced the social and economic reforms which the 1930s and 1940s brought. Social policy and welfare legislation were limited, with much discretion left to the states. Loan guarantees and price supports, not wholesale nationalization, were the hallmarks of industrial policy. An embattled capitalism was strengthened, not weakened, by federal government action. Union power, although greatly enhanced by radical legislation in the 1930s, was only to be weakened again by union-curbing laws in the late 1940s. The 1935 Wagner Act gave unions the right of recognition for collective bargaining purposes when they had the support of a majority of workers. It also created the National Labor Relations Board to help safeguard workers' interests. The 1947 Taft–Hartley Act outlawed secondary industrial action, imposed a 'cooling off' period in important strikes and allowed states to legislate against the closed or union shop. In fact, Taft–Hartley was probably less influential in causing union decline than rising affluence and a changing industrial structure after 1960, but it was an important symptom of a return to more traditional views about the proper role for unions in society.

Nonetheless, this was an unusual period in American history. The federal government grew enormously, particularly when American entry into the Second World War created a powerful defence establishment. This was the era of strong presidents – Roosevelt, Truman, Eisenhower, Kennedy. It was also, of course, the period of American economic and military hegemony. Small wonder that little criticism was directed at this seemingly un-American rise in state power.

As the last chapter demonstrated, however, such criticism was not far away, for during the 1960s and 1970s the U.S. was shown to be less than omnipotent. At the same time American domestic politics underwent extensive and often traumatic changes. What was the nature of these changes? And how did they interact with a constantly adapting American ideology? Three major changes can be identified.

The Declining Political Significance of Class, Region and Ethnicity – but Not of Race

Since 1960 the New Deal coalition has been in steady decline. No longer is the South solidly Democratic – indeed southerners normally vote Republican in presidential elections. With increasing affluence, more voters see themselves as middle class and are less likely to vote for the party identified with the workers and the disadvantaged. To put this shift in perspective, in 1960 19 per cent of American families had incomes over $25,000 (in 1980 dollars); by 1980 this figure had risen to 39 per cent. At the other end of the social scale, the percentage of families with an income of less than $10,000 fell from 28 per cent to 19 per cent. A more middle-class electorate has not necessarily produced a more Republican electorate. True, the Republicans have done well at the presidential level, but survey evidence shows not a permanent realignment favouring the Republicans but a more volatile electorate less inclined to voting along traditional class lines. Such a shift can help the Republicans to some extent, of course, but this change is not as important as the erosion of traditional allegiances. Americans are simply not as committed to a particular party as before.

Most Americans have a psychological commitment to one party or another, which political scientists call party identification. As Table 3 shows, fewer and fewer voters now identify with the Republicans or Democrats. Instead, they see themselves as independent, or willing to switch from one party to the other depending on the qualities of the candidates or on how candidates stand on particular issues. And among Democratic and Republican identifiers the strength of commitment to their party is now weaker.

TABLE 3

Changing patterns of party identification
1952–83

Party identification	1952	1956	1960	1964	1968	1972	1976	1980	1983
Democrat	47	44	46	51	45	40	40	41	40
Independent	22	24	23	23	30	35	36	32	35
Republican	27	29	27	24	24	23	23	28	25
Apolitical/ Don't know	4	3	4	2	1	2	1	*	*

Source: Center for Political Studies, University of Michigan.

* Apoliticals and Don't knows excluded from data.

A major reason for the demise of old-style party politics is the decline of homogeneous working-class neighbourhoods and communities, which provided the Democrats with a relatively solid base of support. Voting 'Democrat' meant voting for the party that was most likely to advance the interests of the 'working man' or the 'ordinary American'. Candidates and the issues of the day were important, of course, but usually not as important as the prevailing sense that the Democratic Party was the party of the voter's family, neighbourhood and community.[15] As far as local politicians were concerned, this allegiance extended to support for the 'party machine'. Machine politics have usually been identified with what is often called 'instrumentalism', or a politics where votes are exchanged for jobs or other benefits. But the classic machines of the nineteenth century, with their open patronage, bribery and corruption, had all but disappeared by the 1940s and 1950s. Machines of a sort remained – and in some cases, such as Mayor Daley's Chicago, little had changed from the earlier era – but civil-service reform and the rise of the welfare state had removed much of the machines' *raison d'être*. Local and county party organizations continued to dispense patronage on a limited scale. More important, however, was their role in helping to nominate state and national candidates for office. With virtually no national or regional party structure, presidential candidates depended heavily on local party organizations. In terms both of party identification and organizational 'connective tissue', therefore, the Democrats depended on class-homogeneous neighbourhoods and areas.

Republican support was never as dependent on social class as the Democrats, the main appeal of the Republicans, until their decline in the 1930s, being regional in nature (the North and the West). Nonetheless, the polarization of politics which the traumas of the New Deal brought confirmed in the minds of many voters that the Republicans were the party of business and the better off.

From the 1950s, the foundations upon which this political alignment was built began to crumble, slowly but surely. Older manufacturing industries, from steel to rubber, textiles, shipbuilding and automobiles, began to decline in relation to higher-technology industries and to the service sector. Americans moved in their millions, first to the suburbs and then away from the industrial North-east, to the South and West. The 'New South' of economic growth and high-tech industries emerged alongside the Old South of rural poverty and economic stagnation. Originally, southern defection from the Democratic Party had been in reaction to the integrationist policies of Democratic presidents (notably Kennedy and Johnson). State and local Democratic allegiance remained intact. However, residents of the New South – and also of the booming West and South-west – are products neither of the first industrial revolution nor of the rural provincialism of the traditional South. So the employees of new industries and services based in the South and West tend to shun trade unions. They live in suburban neighbourhoods often unclassifiable by class or ethnicity. They teach their children essentially bourgeois values, stressing the advantages of higher education, home ownership and material well-being. They vote for whichever candidate happens to appeal at the time, whether Democrat or Republican.

It is easy to exaggerate the sunbelt–snowbelt divide. Poverty and stagnation remain in many southern states, and many areas in the North and East, including virtually the whole state of Massachusetts, have made the transition from old to new industries remarkably well. Even so, the general pattern is one of a growing South and West and a relatively declining North and East, with such cities as Cleveland, Detroit, Akron, Buffalo and Newark showing an urban decay and blight as bad as any in the developed industrial world. Naturally, as the population and economies of the older industrial areas have declined, so their political significance has also waned.

The breakdown of traditional class and regional allegiances also applies to ethnicity. There was a time when most Italian, Polish and Irish Americans, as well as Jews, voted Democrat – either because they were among the poorer Americans or because, as with the Jews, they identified with the have-nots of society. Today the picture is much more complex. Upward mobility has made many of these ethnic-group members more like other Americans. As a result, their political allegiances and behaviour are not easily predicted. While it is true that Jews continue to identify more with the Democrats than Republicans, Blacks and Hispanics are in quite different categories. In spite of some progress – especially for the middle-class and employed – Blacks remain badly disadvantaged. Mobility has been slight and, almost alone among ethnic minorities, they retain an unbending commitment to Democratic candidates – although the motivation for this may be as much antipathy to Republican candidates as sympathy for Democrats. Whatever it may be, the figures are startling. In 1980 86 per cent of Blacks voted for Jimmy Carter, compared with 41 per cent of the population as a whole. In 1984, and against all the national trends, support among Blacks for the Democrats increased to 90 per cent. Yet Black Americans are by no means a homogeneous group. As Reynolds Farley has shown, great differences in incomes, education and life chances exist within the community. The greatest contrast is between Black families headed by women (41 per cent in 1982, up from 28 per cent in 1970) and single, employed Blacks and Black nuclear-family households.[16] The fact that political solidarity is so high among such a diverse group speaks volumes about the continuing alienation of most Afro-Americans from the mainstream of American life.

Hispanics are an even more heterogeneous group than Blacks. In fact it is misleading even to refer to them as 'a group', for the census classifies them by 'Spanish family name'. The term 'Hispanics', therefore, embraces Puerto-Ricans, Cubans, Mexicans, Central and South Americans. Like Blacks, their political allegiance is mainly Democratic – although in 1984 33 per cent voted for Ronald Reagan.

It is often assumed that the great period of immigration in America is past. Yet immigration remains at a very high level. During the decade of the 1970s more than four million legal immigrants arrived in the U.S. – mainly from Latin America, South Asia and Oceania. In addition, millions of illegal immigrants from Mexico and Central America periodically arrive in (and sometimes depart from) America's South-western states. In one crucial respect the new immigrants are different from the 'huddled masses' arriving from Southern and Eastern Europe during the 1880–1911 period, for, not only have they brought with them social and economic ideas that are highly compatible with the American ideology, they have also found themselves in an economic environment that, for the most part, prevents the emergence of alternatives to this ideology. Not for them employment in vast production-line factories, which encourage collective industrial and political action. Instead, employment opportunities are concentrated in small businesses and the service sector. The new immigrants may be poor and concentrated in the run-down neighbourhoods of Los Angeles, San Jose or Houston, but they present little in the way of a threat to mainstream American ideology.

Blacks apart, these social and economic changes signify a meeting of the objective and subjective in American ideology. Economic individualism, self-reliance and the freedom to mould one's own destiny 'should' result in a high rate of residential and occupational mobility and in economic success – or at least the *expectation* of future success. Since 1960 this is precisely what has happened for millions of American families. Such people have little interest in the old class-based politics. Higher taxes to finance expensive welfare and other social programmes seem to them unnecessary and unjustified. Indeed, true to an anti-statist, individualist tradition, comfortably off suburbanites are generally not aroused by a politics based on coherent programmes or platforms. Single issues – such as tax reductions – may inspire them, but not integrated programmes of social reform.

As a result, the business of political mobilization has become much more difficult. People are apparently less interested in politics than they used to be. Certainly turnout is down. During a period when education and income have increased and barriers to voter registration have all but vanished, turnout should, other things being equal, have increased. Instead, only 51.8 per cent of the population of voting age bothered to vote for Jimmy Carter, Ronald Reagan or John Anderson in 1980. And only 40.9 per cent turned out for the House of Representatives elections two years later. Compare this with the 62 per cent who voted in the 1964 presidential election and the 45 per cent turnout in the 1966 mid-term election. Political scientists have pondered long and hard over these figures, but no completely satisfactory explanation has emerged. It seems plausible, however, to infer that a more mobile, loosely knit society will be less interested in voting and politics generally than one based on well-defined class, ethnic, religious and regional divisions.

One thing is certain: coalition-building is very much more difficult when the citizenry's interest in politics is not based on traditional social cleavages. In an institutionally fragmented political system there is a desperate need for ideological appeals that go beyond the lowest common denominator of 'Americanism', to facilitate liaison between the president,

Congress, and state and local governments. Unfortunately, the American ideology usually discourages such linkages, for it is anti-statist, localist and individualist. Whether they like it or not, modern American governments are in the business of being statist, centralist and collectivist. The very nature of policy-making in areas such as social security, energy and defence demands an essentially centralist taxing, spending and bureaucratic apparatus. During the New Deal, the Second World War and much of the 1950s and 1960s, coalition-building in pursuit of such policies was possible. In today's much more loosely connected political culture, it is often impossible.[17]

The Rise of Single-Issue and Populist Politics

Paradoxically, while Americans turn out to vote less often than they used to, they are engaging in single-issue politics to a much greater degree than ever before. By some measures American politics has also become more populist.

Populism is quite compatible with American ideology. Indeed, mass democracy and an antipathy to central state power can be the hallmarks of populism. Throughout American history there have been surges of populist fervour inspired by the rebellion of the 'small man' against 'big interests' – governments, unions, monopolies, corporations – anything, in fact, that exercises centralized power over ordinary citizens. Manifestations of such sentiments in the late 1970s and early 1980s were tax revolts, disenchantment with federal-government institutions and politicians, and an often deep suspicion of big corporations, unions and, most recently, the media based in Washington and New York.

Significantly, populism has always been strong in the West and South – those regions whose political and economic importance has increased most in recent years.[18] As Table 4 shows, government comes in for particular opprobrium; very few Americans really believe that politicians and public officials have their best interests at heart. Moreover, all the signs indicate that public disillusionment is on the increase

TABLE 4

Public perceptions of efficiency of institutions
November 1981 (percentages)

Institution	Not efficient and well run	Efficient and well run	Don't know
Federal government	74	20	6
Local government	49	43	7
Large business corporations	33	56	10
Private voluntary organizations	23	60	17
Small business corporations	20	70	10

Source: *Public Opinion*, Vol. 5, No. 1 (February/March 1982) p.28.
©American Enterprise Institute.

(Table 5). Since 1966 the public has become openly cynical about government – although note also the improvement in public esteem since the election of Ronald Reagan.

The rise of populism since the mid 1960s has a number of related causes. As class, region and ethnicity have become less influential as social and political cues, so government has appeared more remote. As noted above, political machines, solid state party politics, and powerful trade unions have largely passed into history. All these played a role in political mobilization and served as mediating links between ordinary citizens and big government. Political-party machines, in particular, helped provide jobs and other benefits on a neighbourhood basis, in return for electoral loyalty. And although the more unsavoury elements of machine politics had been abandoned by the 1950s, strong local party organizations continued to thrive, especially in the older neighbourhoods in northern cities and in the South. Suburbanization, a changing occupational structure and the professionalization of government service (thus undermining patronage) had all taken their toll by the 1980s, however. Most local parties are now mobilized around particular

TABLE 5

Individual confidence in government items 1964–82 (percentages)

Question: How much of the time do you think you can trust the government in Washington to do what is right — just about always, most of the time, or only some of the time?

	1964	1966	1968	1970	1972	1974	1976	1978	1980	1982
None of the time*	0	3	0	0	1	1	1	4	4	2
Some of the time*	22	28	36	44	44	61	62	64	69	62
Most of the time	62	48	54	47	48	34	30	27	23	31
Always	14	17	7	7	5	3	3	3	2	2
Don't know	2	4	2	2	2	2	3	3	2	3
P.D.I.†	55	34	25	9	8	−26	−30	−39	−48	−31

Question: Would you say the government is pretty much run by a few big interests looking out for themselves or that it is run for the benefit of all people?

	1964	1966	1968	1970	1972	1974	1976	1978	1980	1982
Few big interests*	29	33	40	50	53	66	66	67	69	61
Benefit of all	64	53	51	41	38	25	24	24	21	29
Don't know	8	14	9	9	9	9	10	9	10	10
P.D.I.	35	20	12	−9	−16	−42	−42	−42	−48	−32

Question: Do you think that people in the government waste a lot of money we pay in taxes, waste some of it, or don't waste very much of it?

	1964	1966	1968	1970	1972	1974	1976	1978	1980	1982
A lot*	47	–	59	69	66	74	74	77	78	66
Some	44	–	34	26	30	22	20	19	17	29
Not much	7	–	4	4	2	1	3	2	2	2
Don't know	2	–	3	1	2	2	3	2	3	3
P.D.I.	4	–	–21	–39	–33	–50	–51	–57	–59	–35

Question: I don't think public officials care much what people like me think.

	1964	1966	1968	1970	1972	1974	1976	1978	1980	1982
Agree*	35	34	43	47	49	50	51	51	52	46
Disagree	62	57	55	50	49	46	44	45	44	49
Don't know	2	9	2	3	2	5	4	5	4	5
P.D.I.	26	22	12	2	0	–4	–7	–6	–8	–3

Source: As reproduced in Public Opinion, June/July 1983, p.17, from surveys by the University of Michigan, Institute for Social Research.

* Indicates cynical response.
† P.D.I. Percentage Difference Index: calculated by subtracting the percentage giving a cynical response from the percentage giving a trusting response.

candidates or around the salient issues of the day. As such
they are not so much permanent organizations, rooted in
essentially unchanging communities, as *ad hoc* electoral
coalitions, formed to promote the personality or cause that
has the resources to launch a campaign. Some members of
the public may become aroused by such campaigns. But these
electoral coalitions are not *community* organizations in the
way 'old-style' parties were. Interestingly, *national* party
organizations – and particularly the Republican – have been
strengthened over the last ten years. But these neither constitute a substitute for old-style parties, nor are they in any sense
the equivalent of European national parties.

The apparent failure of governments at all levels to solve
America's problems is clearly related to the rise in public
cynicism. From Vietnam, to energy supplies, rooting out corruption in government, provision of vital local services in
declining urban areas and balancing the national budgets –
in all these areas a widespread public perception of failure
prevailed, at least until the early 1980s. And this at a time
when government at every level was getting bigger. In 1959
government spending accounted for 26.9 per cent of G.N.P.
By 1975 it had risen to 35 per cent. Even after the onslaught
on domestic spending launched by the Reagan administration, the percentage of G.N.P. spent by the public sector
was still 35 per cent in 1984. In a culture infused with anti-
statism small wonder that this combination has resulted in
criticism and disillusionment with all that government represents.

Fortunately, the specific political consequences of the new
populism have not been riot and rebellion. Americans continue to believe in their constitutional structure; few want to
emigrate; regime change South-American style is inconceivable. Instead, the populist surge has changed the nature of
political discourse in the U.S. Few politicians now propose
tax increases without fear of electoral defeat. Efficiency in
government, not more government, is stressed. True to the
strong moralist element in populism – the little man is
basically honest, big institutions are inherently corrupt –
politicians and public figures must now not only appear
to be honest, they must actually show that they are. A host

of new laws requiring disclosure of personal finances and giving the public access to official files and records have been passed.

What all this amounts to is a shift to the right. The earlier populism of William Jennings Bryan, Teddy Roosevelt and La Follette was inspired by the exploitation and ruthlessness of the big corporations – the railroads and banks. Government intervention and regulation were prescribed as part of the remedy. Today government itself is seen as the problem. The solution, therefore, is less government, less regulation of the economy and society, with politicians and institutions more accountable to the citizenry. In this context, the resurgence of direct democracy (initiatives, recalls, referenda), the move towards more open, accountable government and the antipathy to grandiose programmes of social and institutional reform are understandable. Again, the immediate consequence of this shift in emphasis has been to make America a more difficult place to govern. At a time when governments need to act decisively and comprehensively in economic, energy and social policy, the ideological climate has changed in ways which make such actions much less easy to achieve.

In a recent article, Michael Barone and Grant Ujifusa observed that while Americans were becoming more alike economically, ethnically and regionally, they were becoming less alike culturally.[19] A sort of cultural fragmentation is under way, with increasing numbers of individuals making conscious choices about life-style and political and social preferences. This operates in two distinct ways, both of which have resulted in 'single-issue politics'. First, people are mobilizing not so much in terms of classes and regions, but rather in terms of categories and groups. Hence gender, sexual or religious preferences and even marital status have become increasingly important political cues. Much has been made recently of the 'gender gap', or Ronald Reagan's apparent problem in winning women's support. In spite of an apparent narrowing of the 'gap' in the 1984 presidential election, it remains the case that men and women are becoming distinct political categories, as are homosexuals, singles, Fundamentalist Christians and so on.

Second, politically active individuals now channel their

energies more towards discrete social and economic issues. Hence, since the 1960s the political agenda has become crowded with such questions as consumer protection, the environment, open government and abortion (for and against). What is significant about both varieties of single-issue politics is that they cut across not only traditional economic/class allegiances, but also each other. Pro-lifers may or may not be environmentalists. Nuclear freeze advocates may tend to the left or the right – as Ronald Reagan found to his embarrassment when he labelled all such people 'Jackasses' during his 1984 campaign.

Once again, the major consequence of single-issue politics has been to make the business of coalition-building even more confusing and problematical. How, after all, can politicians and parties provide coherent platforms and programmes for constituents who themselves are uncategorizable in traditional liberal/conservative terms? Of course liberals and conservatives do exist in America – indeed conservatism has been very much in the ascendancy in recent years. The problem is not so much that the new issues have completely replaced the old, as that new issues are being *added* to the old. As a result, public attitudes are much more complex – and confusing.

The Decline and Rise of American Exceptionalism

America has always been viewed as an exceptional country. The new society, free from a feudal past and built on notions of individualism, democracy and anti-statism, amid natural abundance, saw itself as unique. A strong moralist vein of thinking was involved here. Americans were free and served by a people's government; Europeans were steeped in ancient ideas of class and deference; they were exploited and abused by 'the state'. Until the Second World War, America's view of the rest of the world was one of distanced condescension, tempered by an occasional sortie into world affairs. After the war the moralism in American exceptionalism took on a quite different form. Instead of being removed from what was previously seen as the decadence of Europe, the U.S. became the economic and military saviour of the Old World. American economic and political institutions became the model to be copied or, sometimes, imposed on other countries.

This new variety of American exceptionalism was quite short-lived. Vietnam, a faltering economy, and Watergate convinced many non-Americans that U.S. power was not invincible and that America was just as capable of the imperialism and corruption associated with the Old World. Within the U.S. such sentiments also gained ground. The Ford and Carter administrations tried to teach Americans to come to terms with limited power. Problems, Jimmy Carter preached, could not always be solved. The U.S. was far from being omnipotent. In effect, the country was no longer exceptional. Daniel Bell caught the spirit of the times well:

. . . the belief in American exceptionalism has vanished with the end of the empire, the weakening of power, the loss of faith in the nation's future. There are clear signs that America is being displaced as the paramount country . . . Internal tensions have multiplied and there are deep structural crises, political and cultural, that may prove more intractable to solution than . . . domestic economic problems.[20]

Objectively, little has changed since Jimmy Carter's laments on the decline of his country. As the last chapter showed, the U.S. is now more vulnerable economically than before; U.S. influence and military might is strictly circumscribed. Above all, the rest of the world does not now accept the U.S. as moral leader and guardian angel. But under the guidance of the Reagan administration, American exceptionalism was revived. In a recent article, Wayne Shannon placed this phenomenon in the context of Ronald Reagan's speeches. Time and again the president made references to America's uniqueness. Consider the following:

If we look to the answer as to why, for so many years, we achieved so much, prospered as no other people on earth, it was because here in this land we unleashed the energy and individual genius of man to a greater extent than has ever been done before. Freedom and dignity of the individual have been more available and assured here than in any other place on earth . . . It is no coincidence that our present troubles parallel and are proportionate to the intervention and intrusion in our lives that result from unnecessary growth of government.

We are a nation that has a government – not the other way around. And this makes us special among the nations of the earth . . . It is time to check and reverse the growth of government, which shows signs of having grown beyond the consent of the governed.[21]

Even more extraordinary is a quote from a September 1981 speech:

An elderly, small-town gentleman and his wife [two American tourists in Europe] were listening to a tour guide go on about the wonders of the volcano, Mt. Etna. He spoke of the great heat it generated, the boiling lava, etc. Finally the old boy turned to his wife and said, 'We've got a volunteer fire department at home – put that thing out in fifteen minutes'.[22]

More recently, in his acceptance speech at the Republican National Convention President Reagan pleaded:

America is presented with the clearest political choice of half a century . . . The choices this year are not just between two different personalities, or between two political parties. They are between two different visions of the future, two fundamentally different ways of governing – their government of pessimism, fear and limits – or ours of hope, confidence and growth . . .

In the four years before we took office, country after country fell under the 'Soviet yoke'. Since January 20th 1981, not one inch of soil has fallen to the Communists . . . America is on the move again and expanding towards new eras of opportunity for everyone.[23]

Clearly Ronald Reagan has embodied – and encouraged – a new spirit of hope and confidence. Walter Dean Burnham has called him the 'high priest of America's civil religion',[24] and as such he tapped the deep-seated populism of the American people. Certainly, he has rekindled the belief that the U.S. really is different. It is a nation that can solve both its own and others' problems – whatever the obstacles. When Americans were asked in a recent survey whether the U.S. had a special role to play in the world compared with other countries, 84 per cent responded positively.[25] We have every reason to believe, however, that the new exceptionalism will aggravate, rather than solve, America's problems.

There are two dimensions to this claim. First, the rhetoric of economic growth and success is increasingly at odds with objective economic conditions. As a result, large numbers of middle-class Americans continue to expect the easy affluence and economic security that they have enjoyed for so long. In truth, the economy is probably as vulnerable and volatile as during the worst years of the 1970s. Millions of jobs may have been created during the early–mid 1980s, but only at the expense of a huge federal budget deficit. Eventually, something has to give and when it does, employment and growth are likely to be the victims. President Reagan's 'business as usual' optimism raised expectations precisely at the time when caution and realism were needed. As serious, years of inflation and dislocation combined with policies blatantly designed to favour the rich and penalize the poor have moved the U.S. further in the direction, if not of an unequal, two-class society, then certainly of a society with a large, affluent upper and middle class, and a smaller, despairing underclass. President Reagan's new brand of republicanism ignored these developments. By championing the strong and successful – and also by encouraging economic growth – the president is presenting his policies absolutely in the mainstream of American ideology. Meanwhile, the Democrats have been forced to operate in an ideological vacuum. The New Deal coalition, with its appeals to social justice and equality, has now passed into history. Socialism and social democracy are ideologically alien, leaving the Democrats effectively impotent and bereft of original ideas. Yet those ideas underpinning the surging confidence of the Republicans are ill-suited to dealing with the central problems of American society. Telling the people that they are great again and that the future holds nothing but hope and success does not solve American industry's productivity problem, the budget deficit, the volatility of the dollar and, above all, the harsh distributional questions of wealth and poverty which increasingly crowd the policy agenda.

Second, exceptional America is an imperial vision. As Ronald Reagan's speeches and actions – Grenada, Central America, the Korean Airline incident, the bombing of Libya – have demonstrated, his aim is to return the U.S. to its former position of strength and status in the world. A folksy, patriotic president rousing the nation into believing that America is once again great has often led to rash and foolish actions. The steady build-up of the U.S. military arsenal adds to the sense both of crisis and of strength, while denying myriad domestic programmes adequate funding. An enhanced military power in the context of declining world influence is a potentially dangerous combination. Should the reality of America's limited power be exposed – as it could be at any time – it could result in deep disillusionment at home and truly serious events abroad.

What all these changes add up to is a crisis of political mobilization and authority. America is becoming harder to govern at precisely the time when good government – that subtle combination of leadership and compromise, decisiveness and pragmatism – is most needed. Good government is communicated to the people only in part via ideas and values. Political institutions and processes are the immediate and direct link. How have these adapted to the social and ideological changes of the last twenty years?

CHAPTER FOUR

Congress: The People's
Not the Public Interest?

The Constitution of the United States assigned pride of place to the national legislature, Congress. Article I is devoted to Congress, which was given the crucial powers of taxing and spending, regulating commerce, raising armies and declaring war. In the context of the eighteenth century these, together with lesser but carefully specified powers such as establishing a post office and regulating the currency, added up to just about everything that a national government could do. During a time when governments at all levels did very little, no one argued that such functions as education or law enforcement should be national responsibilities. Indeed they were not even deemed state functions. Local governments were considered the appropriate bodies for running these essentially local services. With Congress elevated to the key policy role, what was left for the president and the courts? In strict constitutional terms, not very much.

Article II does make the president commander in chief of the army and navy and empowers him to enact treaties. But armies can only be mobilized and paid for by Congress, and only the legislature can declare war. Treaties have to be subject to the advice and consent of the Senate, as do all major executive appointments. This leaves the very vague requirement that the president 'shall take care that the laws be faithfully executed'. Again, Congress appears supreme, for it is the House and the Senate who actually make and pass the laws. Presidents were given the power to veto bills but even this was qualified, as a two-thirds majority in both houses could override the veto. Similarly, there is little in the Constitution which suggests that the courts, and in particular the Supreme Court, have great power – although quite early in American

history this authority was asserted when the Supreme Court
assumed the power of judicial review.[1]

The legislature's elevated status at the beginning of the new
republic was entirely understandable. Only too aware of the
danger of an overweening executive, the founding fathers put
their trust in the people's branch. Radical eighteenth-century
political thought was quite unambivalent on this question.
Democracy depended on a direct and intimate link between
voters and policy makers who could be held accountable for
their actions. Assemblies or legislatures were, therefore, the
collective voice of the people. Through majority decision-
making their actions would be both representative and, via
periodic elections designed to act as plebiscites on the members' performance, responsible. In line with this simple
scheme, the founding fathers decreed that members of the
House of Representatives should be subject to re-election very
frequently – every two years. The House was also to be responsible for taxation – the issue which in pre-revolutionary America had aroused so much controversy. Naturally House
members were popularly elected, although universal franchise was by no means established in late-eighteenth-century
America.[2]

Significantly, however, neither senators nor the president
were originally subject to popular election. Fearful both of
arbitrary executive power and of a democratic Congress pan-
dering to the whims of what was perceived as an ill-educated
and easily moved mass electorate, the founding fathers
checked the authority of the House with an upper chamber
appointed by the state legislatures on a territorial basis – two
senators for each state. The same reasoning applied to the
president, who was to be elected by an electoral college sup-
posedly consisting of wise and prudent men. As it turned out,
popular (but not direct) election of the president was quickly
established (by the Twelfth Amendment in 1804), although it
was not until the ratification of the Seventeenth Amendment
in 1913 that senators were subject to direct election.

The point of this historical diversion is to emphasize that
the present-day powers of Congress derive mainly from an
eighteenth-century Constitution. Congress is, above all, politically independent of the executive. Representatives are

elected every two years in 435 separate constituencies, and the 100 senators every six years in fifty separate constituencies. These electoral units bear no resemblance whatsoever to the national constituency responsible for electing the president and vice president. Without the sort of organic links prevalent in parliamentary systems where governments evolve from the legislature, there is very little, at least in formal terms, to bind Congress and president together. Congress also retains all of its formal powers. Not one dollar can be spent by the administration which is not appropriated by Congress; congressional approval of important executive appointments is mandatory; treaties must be submitted to the Senate; war cannot be declared by the president alone.

While in strictly constitutional terms little has changed, Congress today is a very different animal from that envisaged by the founders. It is also very different from the Congress of even twenty-five years ago. True, the American national legislature remains the 'people's branch'. As we will explore later, it is devoted to serving the individual constituency or the particular interest, but it tends to assert this power negatively rather than positively. The actual drawing up of programmes and policies was largely surrendered to the executive branch long ago. As is the case almost everywhere, it is the executive that tends to make the laws and implement them. Congress certainly has the capacity to make its own laws, and compared with, say, the British Parliament, it does quite often do so, but the main policy-formulation job is now firmly in the president's hands. What is the nature of this negative congressional power? And how has it changed over the last quarter century?

To outsiders, virtually all legislatures appear complicated institutions dominated by arcane rules and procedures. In part, this is because assemblies and parliaments are both multi-member and multi-functional institutions. Not only do they draft, amend and approve legislation, they also investigate and oversee executives and act as forums for the airing of alternative policies. In addition, as individual representatives, members protect and promote the interests of individual constituencies and constituents. Moreover, legislatures are collegial bodies; agreement has to be established among at least a majority of members before anything actually gets done. Faced with such formidable tasks, it is small wonder that rules play so important a part. Beneath official procedures, however, different legislatures perform each of these functions in very different ways. Almost alone among legislatures, the U.S. Congress has real power in each and every one of these capacities. Few dispute that the British Parliament is little more than a rubber stamp for government policies. Of course, it does have overseeing, investigative and other representational functions. But these are strictly circumscribed by the constitutional and political context of British politics.[3] In contrast, Congress can assert its many powers in ways which force the other branches of government – and particularly the executive – to take notice. As already established, the basic source of Congress's independence is its distinctive political constituency. Put simply, members of Congress tend to depend not on executive or party-political support for their electoral survival, but on their own performance, and in particular on what they can or cannot do for their constituents. This much has always been true. Over the last few years it has become even more true: members of Congress depend less and less on cues from party and president. Why has this happened and what are the consequences for policy making?

Members of Congress as Rational Actors

Easily the most extraordinary feature of the modern Congress is that members are performing their traditional function – representation – more directly and enthusiastically than ever before. They are not performing it more *efficiently*, although this is not for want of trying. Members now spend more time attempting to please constituents and nurturing their home base than they used to. They have to, for if they are seen as negligent or uncaring of the folks back home, they will surely be punished at the next election. Aware of this intimate elector/member link, political scientists have dubbed members of Congress rational actors: no matter what their ideological inclinations, party affiliation or relationship with the president, members will put their constituencies first. David

Mayhew, in an important book published in 1974, called this the 'Electoral Connection', and he identified three ways in which representatives and senators could win the support of voters.[4] First of all they could *advertise* themselves to constituents by seeking publicity or television exposure and generally making themselves known. It is now considered essential that members do this, not because local fame directly helps constituents' interests, but because voters assume that if you are not known you cannot possibly be prominent or important enough to be of any use. As Table 6 shows, House incumbents *are* well known to constituents — remarkably so, given the very low turnout in congressional elections. Note also that Senate challengers are almost as well known as incumbents. State-wide Senate elections require enormous resources on the part of challengers. Often they are established politicians already familiar to many voters. House challengers are usually starting their political careers.

TABLE 6

Percentage of voters recognizing the names of candidates 1978 congressional elections

	Incumbents	Challengers
House elections	93	44
Senate elections	96	86

Source: University of Michigan, Center for Political Studies.

Much of the 'down home' folksy style of American politicians is related to the need to advertise. Pressing flesh, kissing babies, attending receptions and generally being seen, and appearing to *enjoy* the business of being seen, are all part of the ritual. With the rise of television politics and the weakening of party ties, advertising has become more, not less, important in recent years. So too has Mayhew's second rational strategy for politicians, *credit claiming*. This is part of the 'pork-barrel politics'[5] long associated with American politics. In other words, members are expected to deliver the goods in terms of winning federal grants or contracts for the district, or of promoting or defending an interest strongly represented locally. A representative from the corn (maize) belt (Iowa, Nebraska, Northern Illinois and parts of neighbouring states) *has* to vote for corn-price supports. Obviously, there are only a limited number of policy areas where individual legislators can make any detectable difference. No one can banish inflation or unemployment, or ensure economic growth. Where politicians can make a difference is in what might be called *micro* policy areas – for example the federal grants for agriculture mentioned above, energy policy, the distribution of defence grants and the location of defence installations. Even in these policy areas, how can an individual make a *real* difference to whether, say, the cattle interests in the vast Twenty-first District of Texas, with its great ranches (and oil wealth), are satisfied with federal agricultural policy? To answer this question it is necessary to understand more about how Congress actually operates.

Congress is dominated by its work groups – 283 standing committees and subcommittees, including a number of other *ad hoc* and joint committees. It is the committees which actually make laws and, crucially, amend, modify and, more often than not, actually kill bills. Within committees members engage in what is the very essence of the American legislative process: bargaining, compromise, negotiation, wheeling and dealing. In such a complex institution, compromise is essential if anything at all is to be achieved. The American term for this is 'logrolling', or an exchange of favours – a sort of legislative quid pro quo. In this context, it is quite possible for an individual to achieve specific results. Consider the following: within the House of Representatives, the Banking, Finance and Urban Affairs Committee has responsibility not only for banking but for most housing subsidies. A conservative supporter of banking deregulation may well agree to support a vote for a low-income housing subsidy, in exchange for an inner-city liberal's support for deregulation. Multi-membership of committees and overlapping jurisdictions (one policy area is handled by several committees) increases the opportunities for logrolling. These complex coalition-building exercises greatly enhance the power of the individual.

Credit claiming is not just empty rhetoric on the part of

members, therefore. Representatives, in particular, can sometimes deliver the goods. Because their constituencies are
much larger and more complex, senators find it more difficult
to channel benefits directly to target constituents. Nonetheless, they try. Mayhew's final and most important strategy for
the rational member to pursue is *position taking*, or ensuring
that his or her stand on a particular issue is known to constituents and is, of course, approved by them. Hence in a Catholic
or Fundamentalist Christian district a member may find it
useful to identify with the pro-life (anti-abortion) lobby in
Congress. Members with large Jewish constituencies will
almost invariably support military aid for Israel. Senator
Charles Percy was not an enthusiastic supporter of Israel in
his capacity as chairman of the Foreign Relations Committee.
His subsequent defeat in the 1984 election was partly attributable to this stance. Conservative districts will expect their
members to take a strongly critical line on government spending. In all these cases, while the member cannot claim credit
for a particular policy, a display of sympathy for issues held
close to constituents' hearts can be highly beneficial in electoral terms. Note that the benefits involved in position taking
are likely to be collective or general rather than particular
and specific. Often, as with the abortion and foreign policy
questions, they have a high ideological content. It is not just
over nuts-and-bolts issues involving federal grants or defence
contracts that the coalition game is played, therefore.
Almost every policy area is affected by this intimate member/-
constituent link – even if the representative or senator cannot
come up with the benefits in strictly pork-barrel terms.

Critics of Mayhew's analysis claim that to view virtually all
of members' actions in terms of a calculating self-interest is
to oversimplify reality. Certainly, it is true that members
do have ideological biases independent of constituency
pressures. Motivations and ambitions beyond re-election are
quite common – especially among longer-serving senators
and representatives. The fact that both liberals and conservatives can serve a liberal or conservative constituency is proof
enough that the legislators are not always slaves to their constituents. Sometimes they are able to stamp their personalities
on a constituency. Paul Simon of Illinois, for example, first

served as representative in a highly conservative district and in 1984 unseated the aforementioned Charles Percy for a state Senate seat. His liberalism was overcome by his personal charisma. But it remains the case that, compared with legislators in other countries, members of Congress are tied to their constituents to a truly remarkable extent. Indeed since about 1970, these links have, if anything, strengthened, but they have done so in ways which make the job of members more difficult and the functioning of Congress more cumbersome. Let us deal first with the reasons for closer links between represented and representatives.

The Rise of Political Individualism

Three broad categories of explanation for these ties can be identified: sociological, political and technical. Most of the sociological reasons for change relate to the points raised in Chapter Three. Cues based on class, region and ethnicity have been getting weaker in American society, thus releasing members of Congress from traditional, mainly party-political pressures. Too much can be made of this point. Party voting has never been as strong in Congress as, for example, in the British Parliament. Even at the peak of party 'dominance' between 1890 and 1910, large numbers of congressmen voted against the party line. Recently, however, party ties have weakened even further. James Sundquist has characterized this in terms of the rise of political individualism.[6] There was a time when regional, state and local party organizations controlled the nominations, and to a great extent, the political fortunes of congressional candidates. Much as today local Labour Party organizations in Britain control nominations, so American political machines decided who would be the party's candidate for a House or Senate race. Today, party organization in the traditional sense of a tightly knit, hierarchical and disciplined institution scarcely exists. Instead, candidates win nomination through their own efforts and through control over what, in some ways, have become their own personal local and state parties – even if the label Democrat or Republican remains.

Both House and Senate are populated, therefore, with what

might be called 'new-style' members, who owe their political success to themselves rather than to others. James Sundquist has put this point well:

The new-style member contrasts with the old in political manners, political vocabulary, interests, and conception of the proper nature of the institution in which he [sic] serves. As a congressional candidate, he was self-chosen. Nobody handed him the nomination; he won it in open competition, usually by the vote of the party rank and file in a direct primary . . . He came to Congress with a sense of mission, even a mandate, to have an impact on the legislative process. He is impatient, for those who backed him expect legislative results. As an upstart as a candidate – self-selected, self-organized, self-propelled, self-reliant – he will be an upstart in the House or Senate, too. He has no habit of being deferential to the established and the powerful, and he will not be so in the Congress, either in committee or on the floor.[7]

Increasingly then, Congress is dominated by hard-working, highly motivated men and women who want to achieve results for their constituents, or possibly, for a cause (pro-life, a balanced budget, environmental protection, a nuclear freeze) that they share with their supporters and constituents. Yet party continues to mean something. Republicans are broadly more conservative than Democrats; and the coalition-building necessary for effective policy-making is still possible, as the first year of Ronald Reagan's 1981–5 administration showed. But at any time, members can go their own way. To repeat the point, party discipline in the British sense never existed in Congress. Yet it was possible in the 1950s or 1960s for a Sam Rayburn (the Speaker of the House almost continuously from 1940 to 1960) or a Lyndon Johnson (Senate Majority Leader 1955–60) to rally the party faithful around a particular bill or amendment. Leaders could not carry out the equivalent of removing the party whip from members, which in Britain can effectively destroy an M.P.'s career, but leaders could determine promotions and committee assignments. Access to power, therefore, largely depended on party cues. Crucially, party leaders *knew* their fellow members quite well. They were familiar with the context of their election, including who supported them and why, and so exercised an indirect but important influence over their political fortunes.

Within state delegations in Congress this influence could be anything but indirect. In Texas and most of the southern states with powerful Democratic Party organizations, junior representatives and even senators knew their place and showed a prudent deference towards their seniors. Today, equivalent attempts to build party machines almost always fail. And when attempted, they depend on the resources of one man, such as Senator Jesse Helms in North Carolina. In spite of enormous support from well-organized, conservative political-action committees, however, even Jesse Helms only just managed to win his 1984 senatorial race. North Carolina does not have a Republican party machine dispensing patronage and controlling nominations in the old style. Instead it has a party built around a personality. As such it is an essentially temporary arrangement. When faced with another appealing personality (former Governor James Hunt in 1984), voters can quickly switch allegiance.

The political reasons for the rise of the new-style member are hard to distinguish from the sociological. The causal lines run in many directions and interact with each other in complex ways. Nonetheless, we can quite easily identify the political changes, the most important of which are the rise of direct primaries and internal reforms within the House and the Senate. Direct primaries – intra-party elections to nominate the candidate to stand at the general election – have long been a part of the American political scene, but from about 1968 their use has increased markedly. The populist surge identified in Chapter Three was the main reason for the change. Within the Democratic Party, in particular, a deep disillusionment with machine politics and the sort of closed political process so well represented by the 1968 Democratic Convention led to a number of commissions and inquiries, all designed to open up the party to full participation by the mass membership, including women, Blacks, the poor and the young. The upshot was a convention in 1972 dominated not by the old-style party faithful, but by what Jeane Kirkpatrick came to call the 'New Presidential Elite'. Certainly women and minorities were well represented, but in this and subsequent conventions the typical delegate was more middle-class and better-educated than the earlier generations. Why? Precisely because the route to the convention had become more open, via the primary elections and more accessible party meetings or caucuses. Put simply, old-style parties recruit activists by punishing or rewarding them – with jobs, status, possibly even money. New-style parties recruit activists by appealing to their sense of duty or commitment to a cause or particular candidate. Such people, whose participation is essentially *voluntary*, need the confidence, information and time which only middle-class people have.[8]

These changes have received most attention in the context of nominations for the presidency. But at the congressional level exactly parallel changes have occurred. Old-style party nominating procedures, where a few party faithfuls decided on candidates, have been replaced by direct primaries. Campaigns are now much more personalized, with candidates depending on support generated by their own organizations rather than by permanently established parties. They have also become much more expensive. Ironically, it was the same populist surge that helped increase the cost of campaigns. Following Watergate, a general disenchantment with party finances led to the 1974 Federal Election Campaign Act, which put strict limits on party-political and corporate contributions to candidates. However, no limit was placed on candidates' own contributions, thus encouraging the wealthy and penalizing the less well off. In combination with the increased pressure to project a prominent and pleasing media image, the reforms have made it all but impossible for people of average income to stand for election to Congress. By 1978 it was estimated that a prospective House member needed a minimum of $200,000 to stand, and a Senate candidate $1 million.[9]

Once in Congress, members now operate in a quite different environment from that prevailing twenty or thirty years ago. As Norman Ornstein has noted, the Congress of the 1950s was 'a closed system. Incentives, rewards, and sanctions – all were internal to the Congressional process.'[10] Norms, folk-ways and formal rules dominated both chambers. Promotion and access to effective power were controlled by a relatively few senior (long-serving) members. The Speaker and Senate Majority Leader together with certain committees, notably the Ways and Means and Rules Committees in the House and the Democratic Steering Committee in the Senate, controlled nominations for chairmanships. Once in office, chairmen in turn had enormous power over the legislative agenda and the distribution of responsibilities to subcommittees. Reinforcing this formal structure of power was an unwritten code of informal behaviour. Junior members were suitably deferential to their seniors; no one rocked the boat; scandals were rarely advertised – although the material to fuel them was certainly there. 'Politics as usual' did go on, of course, with Congress as a major focus for lobbying and political activity generally. But it was structured, almost predictable political activity.

It was the changes outside Congress discussed above that inspired opposition to this system. Younger and new members elected by organizations owing more allegiance to them than to traditional parties expected and needed to exercise influence on the legislative process immediately, not in ten years. At the same time the new populism helped arouse misgivings about the closed, hierarchical and sometimes corrupt nature of the institution. From small beginnings in the early 1960s, reforms came thick and fast during the 1970s, first in the House and then in the Senate. Norman Ornstein has summarized them as follows.[11]

A decentralization of power

The dominance of committee chairmen has been removed. Starting with action by the House Democratic caucus between 1971 and 1973 and eventually spreading to the Republicans and the Senate, subcommittees and their chairs were given effective autonomy. The number of subcommittees also proliferated and no member could hold the chair of more than one subcommittee – thus guaranteeing a greater dispersal of power.

Resources for members have been greatly expanded

Even if British M.P.s had the formal power to act independently or to check the executive, they would have difficulty exercising it, because they do not have the resources to do so.

Members of Congress have always been more fortunate in this regard. Even in the 1960s each House member could employ up to ten staff. By the late 1970s this had increased to eighteen, while Senators boasted a staff of no less than thirty-six (and in practice it is often higher than this). Committee and subcommittee staff have also expanded rapidly, as have a host of research and other services available to members. So on arriving on Capitol Hill for the very first time, the new member can immediately start processing information, influencing legislation, contacting the federal bureaucracies, and can generally be seen to be working diligently on behalf of his or her constituents.

Congress has been opened up to public scrutiny

'Sunshine', or open-government, laws were a central part of the populist cry for more responsible and democratic government. Congress proved no exception. Since the early 1970s the crucial 'mark up' sessions, when committees actually construct bills line by line, have been open to the public. Conference Committee proceedings, where House and Senate versions of a bill have to be reconciled, also became subject to public scrutiny. Few secrets on who is supporting which part of a particular bill remain. Committee chairmen have also lost out with this reform, for they can no longer manipulate information in ways which may embarrass other committee members.

As important was the change from unrecorded to recorded votes on amendments – which can be as, or even more, crucial than final votes on bills. Now everyone knows, or can quickly find out, *exactly* how members stand on every detail of the legislative process. Political-action committees, public interest groups, the local and national press can and do publicize these facts. Many organizations even assign scores to members, which are quickly communicated to the relevant voters and constituents. The influential *Almanac of American Politics* publishes a summary of these scores every two years. Table 7 shows the scores for some of the leading Democratic contenders in the 1984 election. Naturally the folks back home are often aware of these records – especially when

TABLE 7

Group ratings, leading Democratic candidates for president and vice president, 1984

	generally liberal						generally conservative				
	A.D.A.	A.C.L.U	C.O.P.E.	C.F.A.	L.C.V.	L.W.V.	N.T.U.	N.S.I.	C.O.C.	A.C.A.	C.S.F.C.
Geraldine Ferraro											
1982	75	79	91	85	92	91	7	33	19	9	29
1981	85	–	88	93	93	–	19	–	11	17	33
1980	72	60	89	79	72	70	11	33	56	17	27
John Glenn											
1982	70	68	77	80	71	73	4	70	55	35	38
1981	80	–	76	57	56	–	13	–	44	25	33
1980	67	77	72	53	53	90	34	20	38	17	33
Gary Hart											
1982	95	96	79	90	66	83	9	30	40	15	32
1981	95	–	77	64	72	–	5	–	11	17	31
1980	61	83	47	53	73	75	48	30	39	36	36

	generally liberal							generally conservative	
	A.D.A.	C.O.P.E.	L.W.V.	N.F.U.	L.C.V.	C.F.A.	N.A.B	N.S.I.	A.C.A.
Walter Mondale									
1974	100	82	100	100	88	88	40	–	–
1973	95	90	100	100	–	92	–	–	4
1972	95	90	100	100	92	100	–	–	–

A.D.A.   Americans for Democratic Action: a liberal, libertarian pressure group.

A.C.L.U.   American Civil Liberties Union: very liberal on all 'conscience' and most economic issues.

C.O.P.E.   Committee on Political Education of the A.F.L./C.I.O. (American Federation of Labour/Congress of Industrial Organization): official committee of the labour unions; generally liberal.

C.F.A.   Consumer Federation of America: pro-consumer and pro-government spending.

L.C.V.   League of Conservation Voters: pro-environmental protection.

L.W.V.   League of Women Voters: liberal, pro-welfare, pro-women's rights.

N.T.U.   National Taxpayers' Union: against government spending at all levels.

N.S.I.   National Security Index of the American Security Council: generally conservative and very pro-defence.

C.O.C.   Chamber of Commerce: pro-business.

A.C.A.   Americans for Constitutional Action: very conservative at every level.

C.S.F.C.   The Committee for the Survival of a Free Congress: very conservative, especially on defence and conscience issues.

N.F.U.   National Farmers' Union: a liberal pro-farmers group supporting federal aid for agriculture.

N.A.B.   National Association of Business: generally conservative, pro-business.

Of the candidates listed, Walter Mondale appears the most liberal and John Glenn the least. Generally, Ferraro, Glenn and Hart are on the centre in the Democratic Party, while Mondale, when he was in the Senate, at least, was on the left. These scores are computed from key votes in the House and Senate. As the issues change from year to year, comparisons across periods can be misleading. No score is given when a member is absent for the key votes.

Source: Michael Barone and Grant Ujifusa, *The Almanac of American Politics* (Washington, DC: Barone and Co., various years).

issues close to their pocketbooks or affecting their dearest-held values are involved.

Ornstein also notes the ways in which the informal rules of the House and Senate have changed. Both institutions work faster, get through more business and are less courteous. Above all, Congress is less formal and rule-bound, and has become more accessible to lobbyists and constituents.

Finally, how have technological changes affected the relationship between member and constituent? In a word, profoundly. Television, in particular, has helped transform the landscape of electoral politics in the United States. Again, it is difficult to distinguish between cause and effect in this area. No one disputes the importance of television; the problem is establishing whether television has been the major cause of the new-style politics, or whether sociological and political changes have simply been reinforced by television. In his *Channels of Power*, Austin Ranney considers television to be the single most important development in post-war American politics.[12] Television has changed the nature of political discourse by reducing complex issues to relatively simple ones, emphasizing the sensational and prurient, and being constantly critical of public officials but never self-critical. As in the case of the presidency, television has helped politicians with the 'appropriate' media image, while penalizing the less charismatic. Candidates must appear to be *doers*; to be at once dynamic, moral, compassionate, concerned and confident. As Michael Robinson puts it:

. . . the increasingly greater reliance on the media for nomination, election, status in the Congress, and re-election is one sign of a new congressional character – one more dynamic, egocentric, immoderate, and, perhaps, intemperate. The evidence here is speculative and thin. But interviews and recent studies indicate that the media . . . have recruited, maintained, and promoted a new legislative temperament.[13]

Increasingly, the media have discovered that even U.S. representatives can make news. Jack Kemp of New York, for example, has become a media personality as a proponent of free-market supply-side economics. Scandals involving members attract national attention in a way that would have been unlikely a few years ago. Starting with Wilbur Mills in 1974 Congress has rarely been free of scandal since, 'Abscam' and the Charles Diggs affair being the most celebrated. In 1974 Wilbur Mills, respected chairman of the powerful House of Representatives Ways and Means Committee for twenty-seven years, was stopped by police while driving near the Potomac River Tidal Basin in Washington. Mills appeared drunk and his face was scratched and bleeding. When he stopped, Fanne Fox, an Argentinian strip-tease dancer, leapt from Mills's car into the water. Mills weathered the immediate storm well and was re-elected in November. However, he later appeared on stage in Boston with Fanne Fox and his health deteriorated rapidly. He resigned from Congress in December. 'Abscam' (a combination of Arab and Scam) involved an F.B.I. 'sting' on members of Congress. During 1980 agents masquerading as intermediaries offered to introduce members to rich Arabs wanting to invest in their districts and states and to arrange for gambling licences. Five members were actually videotaped receiving money and eventually six representatives and one senator were convicted by juries for corruption. Most resigned, but one representative, Michael 'Ozzie' Myers (Democrat, Pennsylvania), was actually expelled from the House on charges of dishonesty – the first such case in the history of the Republic. Representative Charles C. Diggs Jr (Democrat, Michigan) was censured by the House (also a very rare occurrence) in 1979 for misusing clerk-hire funds. He admitted spending $60,000 of this money on personal expenses, was later convicted and sentenced to jail.

A major policy consequence of the new media politician is a further shift towards the advertising and position-taking strategies when appealing to constituents. Credit-claiming requires a lot of careful, detailed work and even then success is hardly guaranteed. Moreover, with the advent of complex constituencies and the sort of cross-cutting issues discussed in Chapter Three, it is not always obvious what constituents' interests are. Sometimes interests within constituencies are simply irreconcilable. Take the case of water in California. In that state's agricultural areas members have traditionally voted for water and irrigation projects. Water is necessary for agricultural survival and agricultural interests were (and are) well organized. But with the advent of the environmentalists, the issue has become more complex. Now opposition to new water projects is considerable. This places some members in a no-win situation, and it takes a skilled political operator indeed, such as Richard Lehmann (Democrat) of the Eighteenth District, to satisfy everyone. Lehmann has kept together what are effectively two distinct parts of his constituency by being on the right committees and always holding back from complete commitment to either the farmers or the environmentalists. For Lehmann and most other members, the ground rules are both simple and demanding: be visible, appear active, avoid obscurity, don't tread on too many toes.

To summarize: members of Congress are now more closely tied to constituencies than before, but their re-election depends more on projecting the right image and appearing to be doing the right things, than on delivering the 'pork' in terms of contracts and specific benefits. 'Pork-barrel politics' remain very much alive, but for many members, more is needed. Being a media personality can be of enormous help. Within Congress, rank-and-file members are now both more powerful and less dependent on institutional norms and rules. Party and party leaders have been weakened, while committees, especially subcommittees, have been strengthened.

Policy-Making and the New Congress

As mentioned earlier, rational choice – understood as that branch of social science which considers all individuals to be rationally self-interested, seeking at all times to maximize benefits and minimize costs – has been applied to the motivations of representatives and senators. Rational-choice theorists have also speculated on how vote-hungry members will affect policy-making. Clearly if *all* the legislators are eager to bring home the pork and to engage in the logrolling and coalition-building necessary to do so, then there must be a tendency for public spending to spiral ever upwards and hence for governments to grow. No member will be satisfied until the size of the federal pie is increased and his or her state or district's share of the pie is given especially favourable treatment.[14] However, because the congressional market place is characterized by aggregates of self-interested individuals rather than by a corporate or collective spirit, the danger exists that the institution may be incapable of ordering priorities and making difficult re-distributional decisions. In other words, it cannot provide the sort of political leadership needed in modern America – especially in economic policy.[15] In the context of full employment, an expanding economy, and sound fiscal management by the federal government, such a situation might be tolerable. Indeed, between 1945 and the mid 1970s this was precisely what happened. Government spending slowly but steadily increased, with few obvious deleterious consequences for the economy. Congress did not order priorities as such; it was a reactive institution wielding negative powers in the face of executive initiatives and leadership.

From the time of the first oil crisis in 1973, however, things began to change. As Chapter Two outlined, economic volatility replaced stability. Odd and until then apparently impossible economic conditions emerged: low growth with high inflation; high unemployment with high inflation; and in the early–mid 1980s huge budget deficits combined with high interest rates and low inflation. At the same time the supply and price of essential commodities such as oil fluctuated wildly, and a deterioration in East–West relations increased demands for more defence spending. 'Business as usual' in Congress was clearly no longer appropriate. Because Congress had the power, its co-operation was essential to help presidents make the increasingly difficult decisions that the new situation demanded. The federal cake was getting smaller, not larger, so requiring Congress either to continue high spending levels but increase deficits, or to agree to cut expenditure and/or raise taxes and thus damage constituents' interests. What actually happened confirms in part the rational-choice hypothesis. Congress was often unable to act coherently, and the tendency towards increased spending was difficult to check. However, by 1984 it was clear that there *were* occasions when the House and the Senate could act decisively. And although spending has increased, priorities *have* been reordered, albeit not in ways which might have been predicted. Much of this discussion depends on the budget-making power of Congress, a process which underwent a thoroughgoing reform in both houses during the 1970s. Let us look in some detail at this process and how it responded to a changing political and economic environment.

Congress, Budgets and Presidents

Concern at the American national legislature's failure to make coherent economic policy is nothing new. Congress has always been a fragmented institution proceeding incrementally in an *ad hoc*, improvised manner. Disquiet at this way of doing things mounted steadily during the 1960s and early 1970s. By 1974 a combination of internal and external pressures led to the passage of the Budget and Impoundment Control Act – possibly the single most important piece of legislation affecting congressional economic policy-making this century. By creating new budget committees in each chamber designed to play a key role in a revamped budgetary process and by establishing a Congressional Budget Office (C.B.O.), the act intended to elevate Congress to a central place in the budget-making process. Historically, the pattern had been for presidents to present their annual budgets to Congress, whose appropriation committees then tinkered with the detail. No work group in either house considered the budget as a whole, let alone produced its own, alternative budget. The entire process was reactive, negative and incremental.

President Nixon had exploited this weakness by impounding funds (refusing to spend money appropriated by Congress) and generally acting in a contemptuous way towards congressional spending priorities. This, combined with mounting economic difficulties and the arrival of a new breed of assertive, independent legislators, led to the passage of the act. How has it worked in practice? In a word, erratically. The period since 1976, the first year of the new process, can be divided into four distinct phases. Between 1976 and 1979 the new system appeared to work in the technical sense, but little changed fundamentally. Congress certainly had more information at its disposal via the C.B.O., and a more coherent and purposeful atmosphere emerged in the budget-making area. A set of complex new procedures was adopted, and these were broadly adhered to. It is now sometimes forgotten, however, that 1977–9 were very good years for the American economy. Inflation declined, employment improved, economic growth was resumed. As a result, tax revenue was relatively buoyant, and although the Carter administration's plans for a balanced budget came to nought, the deficit in fiscal 1979 was 'only' $27.7 billion – small by the standards of the mid-1980s.

Between 1979 and 1981 both the economic situation and congressional budget procedures deteriorated badly. The new budget process depends on the co-operation of the major standing committees – particularly the Appropriations Committee and its subcommittees. If the relevant appropriations bills are not passed on time, the whole calendar can be upset. This was what happened in 1979 and 1980, as squabbling committee members failed to agree on priorities. As a result, the second budget resolution – which is meant to represent the final compromise on all spending plans – fell into disuse and Congress effectively reverted to the *ad hoc* practices of earlier years. Perhaps this is not surprising, for there is nothing in the new procedures which *requires* the authorizing, taxing and appropriating committees to co-operate with the budget committees by acting speedily and efficiently.

But this was by no means the end of the story, for during 1981, for the first (and so far the last) time, the post-1976 budget process did indeed work speedily and efficiently. The context was, of course, Ronald Reagan's first budget, when he proposed massive tax and spending cuts. The president had the advantage of the first Republican Senate since 1954, but the House, although somewhat more conservative than in the mid-1970s, continued to be dominated by the Democrats. According to Allen Schick, a Republican Senate was the major reason for the administration's eventual success.[16] Under the Democrats the Senate had always been the more liberal chamber, and while they retained their majority, major spending cuts were almost certainly impossible. In contrast, the Republicans were united, almost to a man, behind the idea of public expenditure reductions.

Victory in the House was less likely, and not only for partisan reasons. Representatives were more closely tied to constituents and were generally more fickle, less predictable. Why then did Reagan achieve so much in 1981? Four reasons can be identified. First, the president benefited from the 'honeymoon', or sympathy period which all presidents receive during their first few months in office. Second, Ronald Reagan proved to be a skilled political operator. As we will examine in more detail later, Reagan is the master of the 'soft sell of the hard message'. He relied not on the substance of argument, but on style and an almost subliminal art of persuasion. Allen Schick recounts the reaction of one southern Democrat when lobbied by Reagan as opposed to Carter.

I wasn't there [in the Oval Office] more than a couple of minutes, but I didn't feel rushed and I'm not quite sure how I was shown the door. A photographer shot the usual roll of pictures; the president gave me a firm, friendly handshake. He patted me on the back and told me how much he needed and appreciated my support. He said I should call if I need help on anything. And that was it.

The president raised no detailed question on the budget, and the congressman continued:

The last time I was in the Oval Office, Jimmy Carter was there, and I came out with other members to discuss the bill we were working on in committee. We had hardly got seated and Carter started lecturing us about problems he had with one of the sections in the bill. He knew the details better than most of us, but somehow that caused more resentment than if he had left the specifics to us.[17]

Third, the House, although still Democratic, had changed somewhat compared with just five or six years before. The conservative southern Democratic delegation – the so-called Boll-weevils – was, if anything, more conservative, and the moderate northern Republicans – the so-called Gypsy Moths – were reluctant to offend the new president. Some potential for a winning conservative coalition existed, therefore. Finally, in 1979 the economy suffered yet another oil shock and in 1980 and 1981 a truly serious recession set in.

FIGURE 1

Federal budget outlays, fiscal years 1950–82
(by category in constant 1982 dollars)

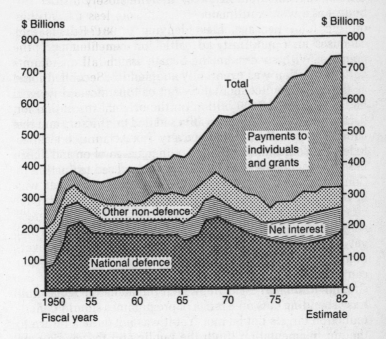

Source: U.S. Office of Management and Budget, *The Budget of the United States Government, Fiscal Year 1982* (Washington, DC: U.S. Government Printing Office, 1981) p.6.

Federal spending was accelerating less fast (see Figure 1) but tax revenue was in relative decline. Budget deficits were mounting fast. On Capitol Hill a strong sense that something had to be done prevailed. The actual mechanics of how the president achieved his spending cuts are important, for they involved the new budget procedures. 1981 started much as usual with individual committees voting for high levels of expenditure. Eventually the House Budget Committee proposed a budget of over $800 billion. Conservatives in the House led by Delbert L. Latta, the ranking Republican on the

House Budget Committee, and Phil Gramm, a Democratic committee member, proposed a substitute resolution which was eventually adopted via a device known as reconciliation. Crucially, reconciliation forces the House to consider the budget as a whole; ultimately it has to vote only a few times on the total package, thus denying to individuals and caucuses an opportunity to battle for every item or programme. With success in the Senate assured, the Gramm–Latta resolution was eventually adopted in a modified form as the Omnibus Reconciliation Act of 1981. Ronald Reagan had 'saved' over $100 billion on the original resolution for fiscal years 1982–4. Conservatives hailed this victory and the equally radical Economic Recovery Tax Act, which slashed federal income taxes for higher income earners and businesses, as evidence of a new coherence and determination in Congress.[18] They were wrong. By 1982 President Reagan was having almost as much difficulty with Congress as his predecessors. Indeed, during 1982 and every year since, Congress generally failed to respond to constant presidential pleas that yet more spending cuts were necessary to combat ever-increasing deficits. By 1985 Congress was forced into what can only be called a bizarre expedient: the adoption of the Gramm–Rudmann measure, which threatened to force arbitrary spending cuts on a range of programmes should deficit-reduction targets not be met. Yet it was not quite a return to the old fragmentation. Both the public and the media now look to Congress for leadership in budgetary matters, even if it is not forthcoming. The key budget-making committees now have vastly larger staffs and information flows than just ten years ago. Congress as a whole now spends much more time on budgeting. In sum, expectations are high, even if performance is low. Hence the new budget machinery has not solved the basic problem of Congress: political fragmentation. All it has done is make the mechanics of budgeting easier to expedite when the political conditions permit it. The budget of 1981 saw a rare coming together of those forces normally at loggerheads and divided. It was an exceptional period.

This section has concentrated on budgeting – easily the most important congressional function – to demonstrate both that Congress retains formidable power and that it rarely wields this power in a positive fashion by providing policy leadership. The analysis could equally well be applied to many other policy areas. President Carter encountered truly awesome difficulties when trying to create a national energy policy.[19] Within other substantive areas of domestic policy – urban, social, agricultural, health policy – Congress can hardly be called decisive. In some policy arenas, notably aspects of foreign affairs, Congress is much less influential. When dubbed ineffective (as opposed to obstructive or negative), as in these and other areas such as control over the courts and the Federal Reserve System,[20] Congress often takes corrective measures – only to be charged with being obstructive or negative! This is the 'Catch 22' of congressional power. Exercising influence in the American national legislature is inherently a negative, reactive business, and, as repeatedly suggested, recent electoral and procedural changes have done little to inhibit and much to enhance what might be called fragmented constellations of power.

Does this mean that the rational-choice critique is correct? Only in part, for within the rational-choice model there is at least the implication that *all* interests will be defended by members. The pattern of distribution that emerges simply reflects the relative power of individual senators and representatives. As such, the only changes over time should result from demographic and income trends, which shift power from some locales and regions to others. However, while it is true that the South and West have experienced population and income increases in relation to the North and East, the distributional changes in public spending seem unrelated to these trends. Consider the 1950–85 period. As a proportion of the total, defence spending has risen and fallen according to external events, presidential demands, and changes in what might be called the ideological climate. As Figure 1 on p. 75 shows, defence spending has increased steadily since the mid 1970s. Similarly, shifts in domestic spending follow an apparently unpredictable pattern, with some payments to individuals, such as social security and welfare benefits, continuing to increase, while others, together with grants to state and local governments, have declined relatively – again since the mid 1970s. Clearly factors other than constituency pressure have been at work. Ideology, party, and presidential leadership do play some role. When sharp cuts in federal expenditure were proposed, as during the 1981–5 Reagan administration, the response of Congress was not, as we have established, one of outright opposition. Many cuts were actually accepted and implemented, while others were fiercely resisted. Three broad generalizations can be made about these other influences on members of Congress.

Presidential leadership can be vital

It is common to identify two periods in recent American history when charismatic presidents presented radical programmes to a pliant Congress and achieved startling results: Roosevelt's New Deal and Johnson's Great Society. However these periods are always regarded as exceptions. In both instances, the U.S. faced national emergencies or crisis (the Great Depression and urban poverty and racial oppression) in the context of something approaching a national consensus on the need for action. The norm is a fragmented, difficult Congress and the absence of consensus. This is almost true, but not quite. As we will discover in the next chapter, presidents are uniquely placed to exploit public sympathy, to cajole, bully or manipulate legislators and generally lead campaigns in support of a particular policy or programme.

Whether they are successful or not depends on a number of factors – and not least on their own personal political resources. Jimmy Carter had little in the way of political insight, whereas Ronald Reagan clearly has a lot. Variations in congressional/presidential relations are important, therefore, and can affect the precise way in which Congress operates at particular times.

The national mood affects congressional behaviour

Quite independently of what is going on in individual constituencies, at any one time there is what might be called the 'national mood', or the prevailing ideological climate. In part this is moulded by presidents; but the media, the state of the economy and recent crisis events all play their part. Hence during the 1970s, laws opening up government to public scrutiny were much easier to pass than a decade earlier. Watergate and associated events ensured this. During the 1980s, a general concern that the federal government had become too big helped the Reagan administration to cut spending and to simplify, or remove, federal regulations. By the mid 1980s, concern had shifted to the budget deficit. A consensus on how exactly it should be reduced was absent, but there was little disagreement that it should, somehow, be cut. Very often the prevailing ideological climate reflects strictly moral concerns. Over the last twenty years the protection of civil rights, rights of accused and arrested persons, abortion, the treatment of homosexuals and drug users, and the use of school prayers in federally funded schools[21] have all figured large on the policy agenda at some time or other. Of course, constituency pressures on each of these issues exist – and indeed can be crucial in determining elections – but the moral fervour that such questions inspire is also a national phenomenon. Many senators and representatives are influenced by these trends and moods, which may or may not reflect constituency interests. Perhaps the most dramatic example of national mood affecting congressional inclinations is defence spending between 1970 and 1984. As we noted earlier, this has fluctuated greatly. Clearly this pattern does relate to the direct interests of constituents (defence installations and contracts). Other things being equal, this should have led to a consistently high level of defence spending. Instead, defence spending has varied in response to external events and changes in the ideological climate.

Congress is biased against policies which redistribute resources between income groups

Figure 1 on p. 75 graphically shows the rapid expansion of income-transfer programmes in recent years. Politicians and commentators often bemoan this trend, sometimes predicting that, with an ageing population, there must eventually be some serious cutback, at least in the rate of increase in such programmes. Often, the assumption is that governments have no control over welfare and social security spending. Both are assumed to be redistributive in the sense that certain social groups – the old, unemployed, disabled, and poor – are receiving benefits paid for by other social groups. In part this is true, but it is essential to make a distinction between strict welfare benefits, which are non-contributory and whose recipients pay little in the way of general taxation, and contributory benefits such as social security, whose recipients pay both social security and general taxes. As John Ferejohn has shown, although the elderly and disabled do benefit from both welfare and social security programmes, the old, at least, do pay for much of these benefits through what is a not very progressive tax system.[22] Recipients of welfare are also beneficiaries of genuinely redistributive policies, but the programmes involved (Aid for Families with Dependent Children, medicaid, food stamps) are both smaller and much more politically vulnerable than social security and medicare. Ferejohn is in little doubt that the way in which Congress operates is in part responsible for this pattern:

Because of the constitutional separation of the constituencies of elected office-holders and because of the absence of disciplined parties, coalitions have to be built separately in support of particular policies. These supporting coalitions must be formed in the context of a political institution that divides its workload among committees and subcommittees of specialists. Coalition-building is not assisted by the existence of unified political parties organized on class lines: both major parties appeal for support to all important social categories. In this setting, the three general methods that could be used to develop supporting coalitions in Congress – building a broad clientele through programme benefits, logrolling, and appealing to shared partisan or ideological values – do not offer much possibility of creating stable political support for effective redistributive programmes.[23]

In other words, institutional and ideological fragmentation ensures that genuinely redistributive policies are rarely adopted. It takes exceptional circumstances to overcome these obstacles, such as those that prevailed in the 1960s and early 1970s.[24] And when, as in the 1981–5 Reagan administration, pressures to cut government spending are great, it is the redistributive programmes which are hardest hit.

Figure 2 amply demonstrates this point. Those programmes characterized by the greatest degree of redistribution across

FIGURE 2

Relationship between fiscal year 1982 budget cuts and percentage of poor among 1974 recipients

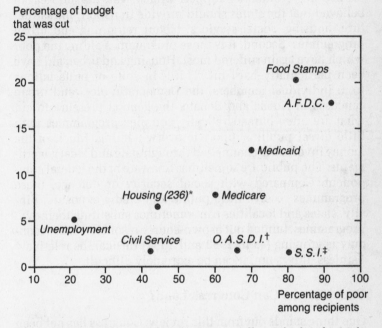

Source: John Ferejohn, 'Redistribution', in Allen Schick (ed.), *Making Economic Policy in Congress* (Washington, DC: American Enterprise Institute, 1983) Figure 5.1.

* Housing subsidies for 'moderate' income groups.
† Old Age, Survivors and Disability Insurance – the main pension programmes.
‡ Supplementary Security Income – welfare payments for the old.

income groups (food stamps, A.F.D.C. and medicaid) suffered most, while the less redistributive programmes suffered least.[25] In essence Congress is a conservative institution.

For those who continue to see members solely as rational

actors delivering the goods, one of the most curious features
of recent cuts has been the considerable decline in aid to state
and local governments. This category is, in large part, the very
stuff of pork-barrel politics, yet it is the most vulnerable –
even more vulnerable than welfare. Why is this? Four reasons
can be identified. First, under Reagan aid to states and localities had no presidential support whatsoever. Ronald Reagan
believed that the *states* should provide transport, infrastructure, housing, social services, labour retraining and urban
programmes. Second, it is those programmes aiding the poor
which have again suffered most. Housing and urban aid have
been particularly hard hit. Third, in spite of protestations
from individual members, the Democratic bloc, and urban
caucuses in House and Senate, the general pressure to cut
what are often bureaucratically complex programmes with
little *direct* public support is overwhelming. Much of the
money involved is channelled through state and local governments. The public are sometimes unaware of the federal com-
ponent. Compared with social security or defence, these
programmes receive little public and media exposure. Finally, states and localities can sometimes substitute their own
programmes, funded out of own-source resources. If the economy is growing (as in 1983 and 1984) this can be relatively
painless. If it is not, it can be extremely difficult.

Conclusions: Can Congress Lead?

One thing stands out from this review: Congress has not been
able to order priorities easily and provide political leadership. It would be overstating the case to say that assemblies
can never do these things. With ideological and party
cohesion, leadership may be possible. Without either, it is
much less likely. As we have seen, Congress can act with a
collective will, but it has to be bullied, cajoled or shocked into
doing so by external events or by skilled and manipulative
presidents. Recent internal reforms and changes in the electoral environment of congressional politics have almost certainly made it more difficult for presidents to win support
in Congress for radical change. With its apparently dramatic
fiscal events, 1981 was by no means equivalent to the 1933–6

or the Great Society periods, when the very foundations of modern domestic and economic policy were laid. Congress may still be able to respond to crisis events (the oil crisis, the deficit) with some degree of coherence; presidents may still manage to persuade members of the House and Senate that urgent action is needed in particular areas of policy such as tax reform; but there is never any guarantee that Congress will respond. And if it does so, it may not be for long. Members of Congress may not be the vote-hungry automatons that the rational-choice proponents would have us believe, but they are certainly not beholden to party or executive leaders as are so many legislators in the modern world. In effect, they act independently of any discernible hierarchy of political authority in the American system.

How, in the context of this review, has Congress responded to the three major changes affecting American society outlined in Chapter One? America's status as a declining hegemon in an increasingly interdependent world has affected (and been affected by) Congress in a number of ways. Most obviously, the national legislature is deeply involved in foreign economic policy, both directly and indirectly. Indirectly, budgets and deficits influence interest and exchange rates and foreign confidence in the U.S. generally. Directly, Congress plays a major role in trade policy. Indeed, some of the fiercest political battles in recent years over the level and extent of protectionist measures on everything from footwear to automobiles have either been conducted in Congress or have involved legislative/executive clashes. As Stephen Krasner has noted, Congress is the major conduit through which societal interests are expressed in the U.S. So it is hardly surprising that congressional trade and monetary policy should reflect the complex and conflicting interests in society. Protectionist sentiment has usually emanated from Congress, with the president championing free trade.[26] It would be wrong, however, to assume that Congress is always protectionist. Precisely because it is fragmented, coherent policy of any variety is hard to achieve. Broadly speaking, free-trade principles and policies have survived the traumas and upsets of the last twenty years. But this is in spite of rather than because of congressional leadership.

The same applies to general questions of foreign and defence policy. Few look to Congress for guidance when the collegial nature of the institution contrasts so sharply with the unitary nature of the executive. Presidents take decisions, Congress deliberates. As America's role in the world has become more complex and difficult, therefore, the burden placed on what is in any case a body ill-suited to foreign policy-making has increased.

As was noted earlier, the capacity of Congress to come to terms with big government – the second major change identified in Chapter One – is strictly limited. The history of budgeting over the last few years is evidence enough of this. If the national mood is anti-federal government – as it has been since the early 1970s – then members of Congress are obliged to project similar sentiments. This has led to all sorts of contradictions and absurdities, as senators and representatives preach the evils of big government while authorizing ever larger budget deficits and legislating new measures in almost every area of social life. Social fragmentation – the third change discussed in Chapter One – has fed anti-statist ideology by making it increasingly difficult to build coalitions around policies designed to redistribute resources across social groups, regions or localities. Put another way, Congress is increasingly the champion of aggregates of individual and group interests, and less a champion of sectional or class interests. Even more rarely does it project anything resembling the public interest. Indeed, most American political scientists reject the concept of the public interest altogether, preferring instead to interpret policy in terms of aggregated group interests. Of course, a faithful representation of group and constituent interests has some value in itself. Yet although Americans have little to fear from a remote, overpowering state, even this function is performed in a highly imperfect manner.

In a society where both constituents and government policies are highly complex, the individual member cannot hope to speak for all of the people all of the time. As we have seen, some interests are served more faithfully than others. As an essentially conservative institution – and can it ever be anything else when power is so fragmented? – Congress is biased against redistributive policies. It is no accident that the federal government spends less on social security, health, employment, welfare or housing benefits than any other major O.E.C.D. country. The constituents who benefit most from pork-barrel politics and logrolling, therefore, tend to be the well-organized, advantaged members of society. It seems highly doubtful that these benefits are worth more than the costs resulting from the failure of Congress to act in the collective public interest.

It would be wrong to end this discussion on a wholly pessimistic note. Congress has, on occasion, performed one vital public-interest function very effectively. Unlike most national legislatures it has the power to check abuses of executive power. As the next chapter will catalogue, there have been times in American history when presidents have acted irresponsibly. Congress is the major bulwark against such abuses. It has the power to investigate, publicize and condemn. The values represented by congressional diligence are not distinct from those of American society, however. Since Watergate, the emphasis has been on open government, executive abuses of power and honesty in public life. During the early 1950s congressional defence of the public interest dwelt on the need to root out putative Communist 'subversives' from the federal government. Put another way, Congress lacks a set of public values which are essentially independent of society's passions and prejudices. Congress in no sense represents the 'American State', therefore. As we shall discover later, virtually no U.S. political institution embodies a hierarchy of values which are above society, and of all political bodies, Congress is probably the most infused with societal influence.

This accepted, there have been periods in American history when the federal government, including Congress, has acted decisively in an attempt to solve major economic and social problems, the New Deal and Great Society being the most notable examples. On both occasions, however, Congress acted under the guidance and leadership of strong, charismatic presidents. How recent presidents have responded to a changing domestic and international environment is the theme of Chapter Five.

CHAPTER FIVE

The Most Powerful Office on Earth: Why Presidents Fail – but Sometimes Succeed

Non-Americans – and many Americans – are sometimes confused by the apparent paradoxes associated with presidential power. As the chapter title suggests, the office is often identified as one of great status and power – yet we are also constantly being told what presidents cannot do. They are variously constrained by public opinion, Congress, their own officials or the courts. The historical record itself presents a paradoxical picture of some incumbents achieving much, with others achieving remarkably little. Even in very recent years, the office has been graced by a John Kennedy and disgraced by a Richard Nixon, reduced in stature by a Jimmy Carter only to be elevated by a Ronald Reagan. Much of this contrast derives from the personalities of the incumbents, or results from unpredictable external events. And presidents cannot, of course, be all powerful – whatever their qualities. The U.S. is simply too complex, democratic and sophisticated a country for this to be possible.

Nonetheless, the paradox remains. A brief diversion into the constitutional status of the office provides some answers – although not that many, as the Constitution says remarkably little about the presidency. Article II is very short (just four sections, compared with ten devoted to Congress). Very few powers are actually enumerated. The president is assigned the role of commander in chief; is given the power to make treaties and executive appointments (but only with the advice and consent of the Senate); is instructed to recommend 'necessary and expedient' measures to Congress; and is required to 'take care that the laws be faithfully executed'. Apart from some additional minor powers, this is all that the

Constitution says – reflecting, perhaps, the conflicts among the founding fathers over the proper role for the president. Generally, Alexander Hamilton favoured a strong executive while James Madison preferred a fine balance of power between Congress and president.[1] Whatever the differences, few at the time could have doubted that the president would be at the very apex of the constitutional system. Indeed, originally he was once-removed from the electorate, being subject to election by an electoral college appointed by the state legislatures. Popular election of the president might have exposed the office to 'capture' by a particular interest or faction. A college of wise and able men would, it was hoped, be free of such pressures. As might have been predicted, the college itself soon became factionalized and the popular election of the president was instituted very early in the nation's history (Twelfth Amendment, 1804). In fact, the electoral college remains, but today the voters elect the members directly. They in turn have no choice but to carry out the people's choice of president.[2]

Constitutionally, the presidency is virtually the only centralizing, truly national institution in the whole structure (although the Supreme Court also eventually came occasionally to play this role). The founders may not, then, have expected presidents to be the main initiators of legislation – a role originally assigned to Congress, but they surely intended that he be head of state, national leader and manager of national and international crises. He remains all of these, of course, but is now also much more. Presidents have become party leaders. Indeed, they are virtually the only party leaders in the U.S., given the looseness of party organization and absence of anything remotely resembling an official opposition. Americans also expect the president to be the 'voice of the people', or a symbol of national unity and purpose.[3] Politically the U.S. is by no means a young country (the Constitution is the world's most enduring), but culturally it is. Without a monarchy or a long-standing national culture based on a distinctive language or religion, or distinctive customs and traditions, political institutions and leaders assume an important symbolic status. Presidents, above all, are regarded in this light. As we will discover later, some presidents have exploited this resource to some effect.

Presidents are also world leaders responsible for enforcing numerous treaties and for maintaining economic and diplomatic links with every leading nation. It is the president, not Congress or the secretary of state, who is normally held accountable for these relationships. As commander in chief, the president is directly accountable for the strategy (and even the tactics) of a vast military machine dispersed throughout the globe on land, in the air and at sea. Finally, presidents have gone far beyond the constitutional mandate to recommend 'necessary and expedient' measures to Congress; although Congress does pass important laws on its own initiative, it is presidents who are expected to produce programmes, budgets and new policies. In spite of all the efforts by Congress to play a leading innovative role, it still sounds odd to talk of a 'congressional budget' or a 'congressional foreign policy'.

With such an awesome array of powers, an analysis of the *paradox* of presidential power may seem inappropriate. But in the case of every one of these responsibilities, what presidents can actually do is limited – sometimes seriously – by Congress, the public, the courts, opinion, external events, or the incumbent's own political skills and aptitudes. The analysis of the precise nature of presidential power is greatly complicated by the constantly changing nature of these constraints. Even so, one variable stands out above all as the prime determinant of a president's quality – his personality and aptitude for the job. This is more than adequately demonstrated by the sudden shifts in public and expert perceptions of the presidency. In the early 1970s there was talk of the 'imperial presidency', as first Lyndon Johnson and then Richard Nixon exploited and abused the office at home and abroad with apparent impunity. Later, following the Ford and Carter years, it was common to talk of the limitations of presidential power. Yet just four years after Jimmy Carter's ignominious electoral defeat, Ronald Reagan had re-established the status of the office. Of course, events external to the incumbent's personal qualities help mould impressions of presidential performance. But personality and personal skills so often transcend these events that they must be given pride of place in any analysis of presidential power.

With this in mind, the remainder of this chapter will be divided into three parts. The first will examine the ways in which presidents are selected and ask the crucial question of whether the nomination process pre-selects certain, possibly inappropriate personality types. The second will examine the ways in which different presidents have actually managed the office and will make specific references to the *capacity* of the presidency for effective policy-making. The third section will assess the performance of recent presidents in the context of the three changes in American society outlined in Chapter One.

How Not to Select Presidents: Mysteries of the Presidential Nomination Process

In most countries chief executives are chosen by senior, often elected party members. More often than not the process is short, secret and effective – at least in the sense that those responsible for the selection are happy with the result. This peer-group review usually ensures the choice of moderate, experienced and politically astute men and women. German chancellors, Japanese and British prime ministers are often all of these. Candidates for the American presidency are, uniquely among larger democratic countries, selected indirectly by the public at large. Candidates are rarely exposed to careful peer-group review, and inexperienced, politically naive and immoderate men are sometimes nominated as candidates – even if such people are rarely elected president. Moreover, the selection process drags on for a good nine months, diverting the public and incumbent presidents alike from every-day affairs of state. The costs of running (financial and in terms of work effort) are such that 'unemployed, elderly millionaires' have a singular advantage. Having a suitable media image is also an essential qualification.

As a result, commentators have complained that the sort of men nominated may be better at practising the fine art of surviving the nomination process than at the very different job of being president.[4] How has this situation come about?

And are all the charges justified? It must, first, be stressed that the presidential nomination process has always been lengthy. Primaries and caucuses (party meetings) have long preceded the conventions (traditionally held over the summer), while the general election is fixed for November. Recently, however, the campaign has lengthened as the number of primaries has increased. The New Hampshire primary is held in February and the last group of five primaries is scheduled for June. Both the increase in the number of primaries and the relative absence of peer-group review result from one simple development – the decline of party organization in America. As was pointed out in Chapter Three, U.S. parties have never been strong, but in recent years they have declined further. Unlike most European parties, the Democrats and Republicans originally gained influence not so much by appealing to class, ethnic, religious or regional interests, as by promising first an extension of democracy, and later specific rewards and benefits (especially jobs) to party supporters.[5] Hence the *rationale* for involvement in presidential nominations used to be a hope that by supporting the eventual winner, jobs and other benefits would follow. Party regulars or 'bosses' could only influence the outcome of races by controlling delegates at the national convention. It was very much in their interest to keep the system open and flexible for as long as possible. In this way delegate votes could be switched to eventual winners should this be necessary. Candidates, in turn, worked hard to please these political kingmakers, both before the convention and, through patronage, afterwards, if they were elected. The whole pre-convention focus of candidates was, therefore, the party faithful rather than the public at large. A Roosevelt in 1932 or a Harry Truman in 1948 had little choice but to pursue just such a strategy. Naturally, candidates with established party ties who had already earned their apprenticeship, preferably in public office, had an enormous advantage. Peer-group review was intact; media-based public appeals were unnecessary – at least until after the convention, when the campaign proper got under way. Finally, personal financial resources, although helpful, were not essential. Instead, candidates could rely on party contributions received in the main from 'fat cat' contributors – the big corporations, the wealthy and the labour unions.

TABLE 8

Proportion of delegates selected in primaries, 1968–84

Year	Primaries	Number of delegate votes	Per cent
Democrats			
1968	17	984	38
1972	23	1862	61
1976	29	2183	73
1980	35	2378	72
1984	25	2431	62
Republicans			
1968	16	456	34
1972	22	710	53
1976	28	1553	68
1980	34	1516	76
1984	30	1551	71

Source: *Congressional Quarterly, Weekly Report*, various issues, 1976, 1980 and 1984.

The welfare state, civil-service reform (or the professionalization of government service) and the decline of tightly knit neighbourhood communities helped destroy this system by removing the need for patronage and the bribery and corruption that went with it. Local, county and state party organizations declined accordingly (there never were any national organizations worth the name in America). Candidates found it expedient to appeal directly to the public via primary elections, or by creating their own party organizations whose *raison d'être* was to elect them rather than to win favours and jobs. The shift away from control was accelerated by a number of other developments. After 1968 the use of primary elections spread rapidly, reaching a peak of over thirty for both parties in 1980 (Table 8). With so many delegates bound to particular candidates via the primaries, knowing the eventual winner before the convention became the rule. Indeed, there has not been more than one ballot in a Republican convention since 1948 and in a Democratic convention since 1952 (it used to be commonplace for several ballots to occur as delegates traded votes and favours). Knowing this, candidates have a huge incentive to enter the race at the very beginning, hoping to win early primaries and so establish a bandwagon effect, which ensures victory in subsequent contests. Television and television advertising have also helped cement the direct candidate/public link. Knocking on doors, leafleting and attracting people to meetings remain important, but all are poor substitutes for the intimacy and immediacy that television can create.[6] Finally, the parties themselves introduced a number of reforms in the late 1960s and 1970s that almost certainly aggravated the decline of old-style party organization. The motivation of the parties (and especially the Democrats) was clear. Disenchantment with the politics of the quick deal, closed meetings and manipulative 'bosses' had grown perceptibly during the 1960s, culminating in the notorious 1968 Chicago Democratic Convention, when Mayor Daley's cops ensured, in no uncertain terms, the exclusion of those radicals and war protestors who felt the proceedings were being fixed by the party élite.[7] There followed a flood of recommendations, commissions and inquiries, which eventually led to the democratization of party procedures at just about every level. Primaries spread to most states and delegate selection became subject to formal and informal quotas in order to ensure the representation of women, Blacks and the young. Caucus meetings were opened up and were subject to numerous procedural rules, most of which were designed to guarantee full and fair participation by all. The upshot was a 1972 Democratic convention very different in composition from its predecessors (Table 9), which nominated a very different sort of candidate, the ultra-liberal George McGovern. McGovern's resounding defeat at the hands of Richard Nixon in the subsequent election led to a further reappraisal. The critique went as follows. Democratization had encouraged participation by the sort of people who always tend to participate voluntarily – idealistic, young, well-educated men and women committed not so much to

TABLE 9

Composition of Democratic Delegates
National Conventions 1968–84

	Women	Blacks	Youth
1968	13	6	4
1972	38	15	21
1976	34	9	15
1980	50	15	11
1984	50	18	8

Source: CBS News/New York Times, surveys of Convention Delegates, 1968–84.

TABLE 10

Self-identified ideology of National Convention delegates, registered voters and mass public, 1972–80 (percentages)

Self-identified ideology	Delegates						Registered Voters		Mass Public
	1972		1976		1980		1980		1980
	D	R	D	R	D	R	D	R	
Liberal	79	10	40	3	46	2	21	13	19
Moderate	13	35	47	45	42	36	44	40	49
Conservative	8	57	8	48	6	58	26	41	31

Source: William Crotty and John S. Jackson III, Presidential Primaries and Nominations (Washington, DC: Congressional Quarterly Press, 1985) Table 5.5.

the party as to causes and candidates. Such people's political views were much more radical than those of registered Democratic voters generally (Table 10). Consequently, they were likely to nominate candidates with little hope of winning. In the light of Carter's nomination in 1976, the charges do seem exaggerated, but disquiet was sufficient to induce a further wave of reform in the early 1980s. Following acceptance of the recommendations of the Hunt Commission, the number of primaries was reduced from thirty-five to twenty-five (see Table 8 on p. 91) and party and public officials were assigned one seventh of all the delegates at the convention so as to reinstitute an element of peer-group review. However, as Howard Reiter has perceptively noted, these intra-party changes are almost certainly less important than the wider societal changes which continue to erode old-style party organization.[8] In 1984 Mondale was elected on the first ballot, having been very nearly beaten in the primaries by an archetypal outsider, Gary Hart. Television is more, not less, important than before. Direct candidate/public links have not been eroded by a partial return to caucuses, many of which are open to a wide cross section of Democrats.

Within the Republican Party the changes have been less dramatic, both towards democratization in the 1960s and 1970s and away from it more recently. Nonetheless, important changes have occurred, so that Republican candidates are now just as beholden to the electorate for nomination as are the Democrats.

To return to our original theme, these developments have changed the nature of presidential campaigns and the quality of candidates. Politicians can now use the campaign to bypass traditional party organizations by establishing their own media-based organizations. John Kennedy was the first to do this, at least in part, in 1960, followed by Barry Goldwater in 1964. George McGovern in 1972 and Jimmy Carter in 1976 had virtually no established base in the Democratic Party. In Jimmy Carter's case, brilliant use of a personal campaign organization and of television ensured the nomination and eventually the election of a man who had no experience whatsoever of Washington politics. We should be wary, however, of inferring that these changes have been entirely negative. We cannot easily judge the presidential qualities of those candidates not elected. Who is to say, for example, that George McGovern would have been less competent than Thomas Dewey (the Republican nominee in 1944 and 1948)? And although the quality of presidents probably did decline between 1968 and 1980, the sample is small, and there remains the case of Ronald Reagan who, although not a great president, is surely on a par with Dwight Eisenhower. Compared with his predecessors, Jimmy Carter and Gerald Ford, he looks really quite impressive. It may be that the particular historical circumstances of the late 1960s and early 1970s (Vietnam, followed by Watergate and the oil crisis) led both to the condemnation of Johnson, Nixon and Ford as failures, and to the election of Jimmy Carter, an unusually bland and self-critical president. By 1980 there was at least a partial return to 'business as usual', with the election of Ronald Reagan.

In other words, the demise of party organization and the rise of media-oriented candidates dependent on the mass public for success has not *necessarily* led to the nomination of inexperienced second-raters. Under some circumstances it can lead to such an outcome. Perhaps more seriously, the transformation of the nomination process has reduced the pool of talent from which candidates are drawn. Successful runners now *have* to be good on television; they *must* have the time and the will to withstand the punishing regimen of a five-month primary season. In effect, they have to have an unusual mix of resources (money, time, energy, contacts) in order to run. Undoubtedly, having a great deal of money is an advantage. Without the backing of old-style parties, funded in part by the big corporations and unions (a practice now effectively outlawed by the 1974 Federal Election Campaign Act), having sizeable personal resources helps a great deal. Of recent candidates, many have been millionaires (Jimmy Carter, Nelson Rockefeller, Ronald Reagan, Edward Kennedy). If, as in the case of Carter, the candidate is an outsider, personal wealth can be an essential requirement for the original 'launch' of the campaign. Matching federal funds are now available to help finance campaigns (primary and post-primary), and the law puts strict limits on how much campaigns can receive from individuals and organizations. However, following the celebrated 1976 Supreme Court decision *Buckley* v. *Valeo*, no limit exists on what candidates can contribute to their own campaigns. In sum, the 1974 Act and *Buckley* further reduced the importance of parties by helping to undermine the brokerage role that parties traditionally played between candidates and big contributors.[9] Again, we have no reason to suppose that richer candidates, or those (like Gary Hart) who relied on a large number of small contributors, would make inferior presidents to candidates relying on party-generated funding. To repeat the point, the problem is more one of reducing the number of eligible candidates than encouraging the candidacy of low quality men.

The new system may even have some advantages. Today it is possible for almost complete outsiders with no hope of nomination, but with some geographical, ideological or group base of support, to use the nomination process to advertise their cause, or to oblige the frontrunners to heed their presence. In 1984, for example, Jesse Jackson did just this, on behalf of America's Black community. By doing so, he elevated himself to the position of undisputed leader of the community and helped shift debate within the Democratic Party towards more concern for Blacks and their problems. It may also be that too much is made of the importance of peer-group review. Instead, the present system imposes a sort of 'national public review'. Candidates are carefully scrutinized and constantly exposed to analysis and criticism. Certain candidate flaws such as venality and moral indiscretion, which in earlier days went unnoticed, are today quickly revealed. Even a spouse's indiscretions can seriously damage candidates (a vice-presidential candidate in the case of Geraldine Ferraro in 1984). Whatever else, it is now highly unlikely that the United States will end up with a crook, lecher or alcoholic as president. Moreover, there was a time when dark horses or men with no government experience whatsoever could get nominated by party bosses dissatisfied with more traditional party candidates. Hence in 1924 John Davies won the Democratic nomination, and in 1940 and 1952 Wendell Wilkie and Dwight Eisenhower won the Republican nominations. None of these men were politicians; none had direct experience of politics. Today such candidacies are almost certainly impossible. Ex-governors and senators, not ex-businessmen and military leaders, are the norm.[10]

Finally, it is easy to exaggerate the historical importance of party contacts as cues for staffing the government. Of course, presidents did use the party as a guide for numerous federal appointments, and to some extent they still do so. But other networks exist which can be just as useful to presidents when filling the most senior posts. As we will argue later, too much can be made of the examples of Richard Nixon and Jimmy Carter, both of whom drew on very parochial networks when appointing their personal staffs. Neither Ford nor Reagan did so, however, so we should be wary of inferring that with the decline of party presidents simply do not know enough talented people to fill the key posts.

To conclude, clearly the nomination process is less than ideal. Spending one quarter of every presidency on re-election is excessive and can be damaging to public policy. Few first-term incumbents can resist the temptation of shaping policy to meet their electoral needs. Similarly, presidential hopefuls are now obliged to spend an inordinate amount of time and money in their attempts to win nomination. This does pre-select certain categories of people. But the charge that it pre-selects particular personality types is not sustainable. As we will discuss later, all of the last five presidents have been very different indeed from one another. In fact they are just as varied a bunch as the previous five or previous ten. Finally, the prominent public-relations orientation of candidates does little for America's reputation abroad. When, at the time of his 1984 nomination in Dallas, Ronald Reagan sat before a giant video screen viewing himself and being in turn shown nationally on TV, the media-based election came close to self-parody. Reagan's reputation abroad was hardly enhanced by this and similar events – a fact which reinforces our general conclusion that the nomination process rarely helps and often hinders the serious business of being president.

The President: Chief Executive, Managing Director, Party Boss, Commander in Chief, Voice of the People, Head of State, World Leader

Because the president is all of the above and more, the office is frequently labelled the most difficult job on earth. In this section we will examine how different presidents have managed these awesome responsibilities. On coming to power, the president's first task is to staff the White House and the key posts in the rest of the federal government. In many respects, how presidents handle the institutions and forces external to the executive – Congress, the public, world leaders – depends on the quality of these appointments and on how they use their cabinet and staff. It is appropriate, therefore, that we should start this section with a discussion of presidential/executive branch relations.

Presidents and the executive branch

There was a time when presidents could manage the White House with just a handful of staff and run the rest of the executive branch through a few loyal cabinet officers. However, with the advent of what is an almost indescribably complex federal government (see Figure 3), controlling the executive branch has become a truly demanding job. Consider the figures: the Executive Office of the President (E.O.P.), which was created by Franklin Roosevelt in 1939, employs around 2,000 people, 500 of whom actually work in the White House. In addition some 2.7 million civilians are employed by the U.S. government, spread through numerous departments, agencies and commissions (see Figure 3). The E.O.P. is directly under the control of the president and includes the National Security Council (N.S.C.), created in 1947 and responsible for foreign-policy/defence questions, the Council of Economic Advisers, created in 1946, and the Office of Management of Budget (O.M.B.) (originally the Bureau of the Budget, created in 1921 to help formulate the federal budget). In recent years the N.S.C. and O.M.B. have taken on an importance far outstripping the other units in the E.O.P. National security has, of course, become a vital question since the Second World War and some presidents have used the council as a major policy-making forum, especially during emergencies. But how, exactly, the N.S.C. is used depends almost entirely on presidential preference. Certainly some national security advisers have become key policy-makers. Henry Kissinger and Zbigniew Brzezinski effectively eclipsed the secretaries of state during the Nixon and Carter administrations. (Other members of the N.S.C. include the defence secretary, the secretary of state and the

FIGURE 3

The government of the United States

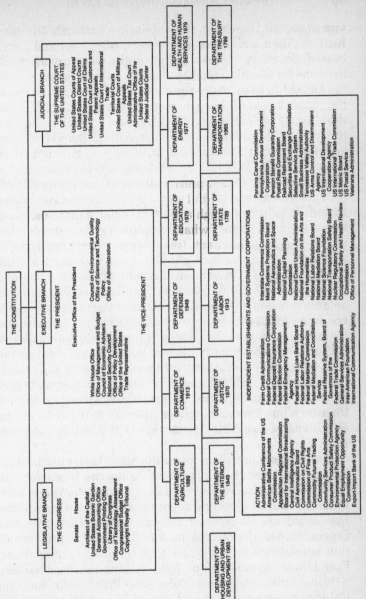

THE CONSTITUTION

LEGISLATIVE BRANCH

THE CONGRESS

Senate   House

Architect of the Capital
United States Botanic Garden
General Accounting Office
Government Printing Office
Library of Congress
Office of Technology Assessment
Congressional Budget Office
Copyright Royalty Tribunal

EXECUTIVE BRANCH

THE PRESIDENT

Executive Office of the President

White House Office
Office of Management and Budget
Council of Economic Advisers
National Security Council
Office of Policy Development
Office of the United States
Trade Representative

Council on Environmental Quality
Office of Science and Technology
Policy
Office of Administration

THE VICE-PRESIDENT

JUDICIAL BRANCH

**THE SUPREME COURT
OF THE UNITED STATES**

United States Courts of Appeal
United States District Courts
United States Court of Claims
United States Court of Customs and
Patent Appeals
United States Court of International
Trade
Territorial Courts
United States Tax Court
United States Court of Military
Appeals
Administrative Office of the
United States Courts
Federal Judicial Center

DEPARTMENT OF
HOUSING AND URBAN
DEVELOPMENT 1965

DEPARTMENT OF
THE INTERIOR
1849

DEPARTMENT OF
AGRICULTURE
1889

DEPARTMENT OF
JUSTICE
1870

DEPARTMENT OF
COMMERCE 1913

DEPARTMENT OF
LABOR
1913

DEPARTMENT OF
DEFENSE
1949

DEPARTMENT OF
EDUCATION
1979

DEPARTMENT OF
STATE
1789

DEPARTMENT OF
ENERGY
1977

DEPARTMENT OF
TRANSPORTATION
1965

DEPARTMENT OF
HEALTH AND HUMAN
SERVICES 1979

DEPARTMENT OF
THE TREASURY
1789

INDEPENDENT ESTABLISHMENTS AND GOVERNMENT CORPORATIONS

ACTION
Administrative Conference of the US
American Battle Monuments
Commission
Appalachian Regional Commission
Board for International Broadcasting
Central Intelligence Agency
Civil Aeronautics Board
Commission on Civil Rights
Commission of Fine Arts
Commodity Futures Trading
Commission
Community Services Administration
Consumer Product Safety Commission
Environmental Protection Agency
Equal Employment Opportunity
Commission
Export-Import Bank of the US

Farm Credit Administration
Federal Communications Commission
Federal Deposit Insurance Corporation
Federal Election Commission
Federal Emergency Management
Agency
Federal Home Loan Bank Board
Federal Labor Relations Authority
Federal Maritime Commission
Federal Mediation and Conciliation
Service
Federal Reserve System, Board of
Governors of the
Federal Trade Commission
General Services Administration
Inter-American Foundation
International Communication Agency

Interstate Commerce Commission
Merit Systems Protection Board
National Aeronautics and Space
Administration
National Capital Planning
Commission
National Credit Union Administration
National Foundation on the Arts and
the Humanities
National Labor Relations Board
National Mediation Board
National Science Foundation
National Transportation Safety Board
Nuclear Regulatory Commission
Occupational Safety and Health Review
Commission
Office of Personnel Management

Panama Canal Commission
Pennsylvania Avenue Development
Corporation
Pension Benefit Guaranty Corporation
Postal Rate Commission
Railroad Retirement Board
Securities and Exchange Commission
Selective Service System
Small Business Administration
Tennessee Valley Authority
US Arms Control and Disarmament
Agency
US International Development
Cooperation Agency
US International Trade Commission
US Metric Board
US Postal Service
Veterans Administration

Source: U.S. Government Manual 1981–2 (Washington, DC: U.S. Government Printing Office, 1981).

vice president.) However, Ronald Reagan's security advisers, Richard Allen and Robert McFarlane, were less prominent. Indeed, Secretary of State George Shultz has received much more media attention than McFarlane.

The O.M.B.'s rise to prominence is explained by the growing importance of budget matters generally, and, most recently, by the elevation of expenditure control to the very top of any president's list of priorities. Ronald Reagan appointed David Stockman, a brilliant young conservative congressman, O.M.B. director and gave him the specific brief of cutting public spending. In addition to these central institutional posts, presidents also appoint immediate aides, including a chief of staff, an assistant chief, a press secretary and a personal counsel. More controversy has surrounded these first-line advisers than any other presidential appointees. The reason is simple: immediate aides are the president's eyes and ears on a day-to-day basis. They can act as gatekeepers, intimate friends, official spokesmen and architects of grand strategy. Yet many of these appointees are not subject to Senate confirmation (the budget director and national security adviser being the main exceptions), and because they are in daily contact with the president in the Oval Office, they are frequently the objects of envy and resentment. Certainly, cabinet members can grow to resent the president's aides, for departmental secretaries are responsible for their own bureaucracies, whose interests may not be at one with those of the White House. We will develop this point later.

Almost every president this century has been criticized for being over-dependent on his staff or unwise in appointing particular people. Perhaps the most notorious cases have involved strong individual appointees accused of manipulating presidents or screening them from public criticism. Colonel House, Harry Hopkins and Sherman Adams were all thus condemned in, respectively, the Wilson, Roosevelt and Eisenhower administrations. More recently, Richard Nixon's personal aides, and in particular John Erlichmann and Bob Haldeman, were eventually shown to be a central part of the Watergate conspiracy, and served not so much as gatekeepers as a sort of presidential 'Berlin Wall' (so-called, with Press

Secretary Ron Zeigler, because of their German names). The Nixon experience highlights the obvious fact that different presidents adopt different management styles. As Richard Tanner Johnson has shown it is possible to contrast Roosevelt's subtle playing off of one aide against another (what Johnson calls 'Roosevelt's Feuding Fraternity') with Eisenhower's 'Organized Absenteeism', where the delegation of responsibility was taken to unusual extremes.[11]

Unfortunately, it is impossible to say which management style is the most appropriate or effective. Clearly Roosevelt was a more successful president than Nixon, but Roosevelt's management technique applied when both White House staff and federal bureaucracy were tiny by today's standards. What can be said with some confidence is that open styles are better than closed, and that presidents must know when to delegate and when not to. Of the most recent incumbents, Jimmy Carter failed on the second count. He was obsessed with detail and the need to grasp all the technicalities of a question. Ronald Reagan, by way of contrast, has delegated a great deal but remains open to new ideas. His first-term chief of staff, James Baker, was widely recognized as a shrewd political operator – moderate but firm, sensitive to the needs of Congress and the cabinet departments, while able to retain the president's confidence. His second-term chief of staff, Donald Regan, was less subtle, and soon earned a reputation as master gatekeeper to the president's inner sanctum. What all this amounts to is simply that presidents must have good management skills. In any context, a chief executive depends on immediate subordinates. For this reason, the quality of the White House staff will remain a key indicator of the quality of the presidents.

Arguably, British prime ministers do not need personal staffs because they are the 'first among equals', rather than unequivocally chief executives. The Cabinet, in other words, becomes the central policy-making forum, and cabinet ministers assume the role of advisers and aides.[12] By comparison, American presidents govern in splendid isolation. Constitutionally, they alone are responsible for the executive branch. They do have a cabinet, of course, but rarely does it perform anything resembling a collective policy-making role.

Anticipating serious management problems, every incoming president now promises to use his cabinet more extensively – and indeed Ronald Reagan has actually convened his cabinet more frequently than his predecessors. But strict limits on cabinet government exist. Why should a president share power with cabinet secretaries? They do, after all, have resources of their own. The Departments of Defense, State, Agriculture, Health and Human Services, Housing and Urban Development, Education, Commerce and the Treasury are huge bureaucracies, each with its own constituencies and distinctive interests. More often than not the E.O.P., and particularly the O.M.B. and the budget director, are in direct conflict with these departments. Presidents are well advised, therefore, to keep their distance, and to consult cabinet secretaries on a one-to-one basis. Indeed, few secretaries achieve national prominence, and the turnover of incumbents is high. In recent years John Foster Dulles, Eisenhower's secretary of state, stands out as a notable exception because the president was happy to delegate so many crucial foreign-policy decisions to him. Generally, Ronald Reagan has given his secretaries a relatively free rein. James Watt, his original interior secretary, achieved not so much prominence as notoriety in his pursuit of free-market, anti-conservation policies on natural resources and the use of federal land. Caspar Weinberger, the defence secretary, exercised considerable independent power. But no one cabinet secretary could be said to be as influential as the president's personal aides.

As earlier chapters indicated, American government has become increasingly fragmented and pluralistic. In such a context, a concentration of power in the White House has been a natural response of presidents. In this respect, Ronald Reagan has been no exception.

American presidents do genuinely staff the government, because the U.S. has a political civil service. Formally, presidents are responsible for over 100,000 posts throughout the federal system. However, most of these jobs are non-strategic. Only about 3,000 are policy-making positions, and of these only one third are the top civil-service jobs. Hence presidents can rarely transform the values and operating procedures which dominate some departments. On coming to power in 1969, for example, Richard Nixon tried to shift the emphasis of the Department of Justice away from vigorous civil-rights enforcement and towards a policy of 'benign neglect'. He failed to a large extent, because many of the attorneys in the Civil Rights Division simply would not go along with Attorney General John Mitchell's directives.

Ronald Reagan has probably been more successful in changing departmental values, in part because the times have changed – there has been a general shift away from the liberal consensus of the 1960s and 1970s – and in part because he has used all his management resources to ensure loyalty and ideological purity on the part of his appointees. As Figure 3 on p. 99 indicates, presidents are not only responsible for the E.O.P. and the Cabinet Departments. Numerous independent establishments and government corporations exist, over which the chief executive has at least some control. This usually amounts to the power to appoint directors, chairpersons or commissioners, and as chief budget-maker, the president can also limit or increase funding. Many of the independent agencies are, however, just that. In other words, Congress has ensured that they operate 'in the public interest', independently of presidents. The Consumer Product Safety Commission or the Commission on Civil Rights cannot be abolished or silenced. They have a legislative mandate to protect consumers or enforce civil rights. What presidents can do is to attempt, through appointments or public appeals, to change the climate of enforcement. Ordering changes within those executive departments responsible for the implementation of regulations issued by the independent agencies is also possible. Ronald Reagan has attempted to do just this right across the board in his first and second administrations. His aim was 'deregulation', or an easing of what many Republicans thought were over-restrictive consumer, environmental-protection, safety and civil-rights laws. Again, although Reagan has achieved substantial deregulation through use of the appointment power and by simply not enforcing the law as vigorously as before, strict limits exist on how far he can go. Agencies such as the Environmental Protection Agency (E.P.A.) are staffed by zealous environmentalists. The president's original appointee as E.P.A. director, Anne Burford, was so hostile to the ethos of the agency that she was eventually obliged to resign, after being indicted for contempt of Congress.[13] Resort to the courts – a commonplace in American political life – also puts a brake on reform ambitions.

In effect, how well the American chief executive handles the vast bureaucracy which makes up the federal government depends on his personal and political resources. Whatever these are, one thing is certain: all presidents now attempt to build up what Hugh Heclo has called 'a presidential party', or a coalition of supporters organized directly from the White House which cuts across institutions, bureaucracies and established parties.[14] Naturally, this is particularly necessary when presidents deal with the independent, powerful and often capricious legislators on Capitol Hill.

Presidents and Congress

No relationship is more central to American government than that between the chief executive and the national legislature. It has generated millions of words in comment, criticism and scholarship. It intrigues, confuses and even alarms almost all who make a study of it. The reasons both for the centrality of the relationship and for its intrinsic fascination are simple: the two share enormous power but the line determining each institution's share is constantly shifting. Additionally, Congress provides no clear focus of leadership or authority. That it is powerful is undisputed, but as Chapter Four showed, it has an indefinable, dispersed and amorphous sort of power. How different presidents deal with Congress, or even how a particular president handles Congress, varies enormously over time, therefore. Indeed, our perceptions of which institution is on the ascendant or is subordinate shifts with startling frequency. Consider the fifteen years from 1970 to 1985. Between 1970 and 1973 the 'imperial presidency' was in full bloom. Richard Nixon had impounded (refused to spend) monies appropriated by Congress; he failed to inform the legislators of drastic military actions taken in Cambodia and Vietnam; his congressional liaison was kept to a minimum.

Between 1973 and 1980, Congress reasserted itself in the most extraordinary manner. In 1973 the War Powers Act was passed, which placed strict limits on a president's ability to wage war in the absence of congressional approval.[15] In 1974 Congress began the process of impeachment (a formal accusation of wrongdoing, which, if established, is followed by a conviction) against Richard Nixon. Only his resignation prevented proceedings developing into a full impeachment. That year also saw the enactment of the Budget and Impoundment Control Act which effectively outlawed impoundment and strengthened congressional power of the purse. Gerald Ford encountered formidable resistance to almost everything he proposed in Congress, although admittedly he did face a solidly Democratic Congress. Jimmy Carter had what should have been the advantage of a Democratic Congress, but it appeared to help very little. Most agree that presidential/congressional relations were at a low ebb during the Carter years. All these presidents faced a Congress intent on close scrutiny of executive appointments. Many nominees were rejected, most were subject to a gruelling cross examination by an aggressive Senate. Then came Ronald Reagan with his startling 1981 successes with Congress. As Chapter Four indicated, these were not continued through the rest of his first term, but few dispute that Reagan has proved superior to Carter, Ford and Nixon in his ability to manipulate and influence Capitol Hill – especially as the House has remained solidly Democratic throughout this period.

To make sense of this waxing and waning of presidential fortunes it is necessary to look at three quite distinct sets of variables: changes within Congress; a president's aptitudes and determination to handle Congress; and external events which can serve to aggravate existing tensions and problems. Congress is, of course, much more open and fragmented than ever before. Party is a less useful and predictable cue in guiding presidential actions. Congressional barons have fewer sanctions to impose on members, so presidents must be prepared to work harder to cultivate a larger and more diverse group of legislators. Norman Ornstein has summed up these changes well:

TABLE 11

Presidential vetoes of public bills, 1945–84

	Total vetoed	Regular vetoes	Pocket vetoes*	Congressional overrides	Percentage of regular vetoes overridden
Truman	83	54	29	11	20.4
Eisenhower	81	36	45	2	5.5
Kennedy	9	4	5	0	0
Johnson	13	6	7	0	0
Nixon	40	24	16	5	20.8
Ford	46	35	11	8	22.8
Carter	29	13	16	2	15.4
Reagan	39	17	22	4	23.5

Source: Congressional Quarterly, Guide to Congress (Washington, DC, second edition, 1976) p. 626; Congressional Quarterly Almanac, 1980, 1983; Congressional Quarterly, Weekly Report, 17 November 1984, p. 2557.

* A pocket veto applies when the president fails to sign a bill at the end of a legislative session.

When Congress was characterized by a closed system, presidents had to work out deals and coalitions with the committee barons, or, on occasion, find a broader group to persuade. The style that past presidents used was identified with that of the congressional leaders like Rayburn [Sam Rayburn, Speaker of the House almost continuously from 1940 to 1960].

The challenge for a president in an open congressional system is, likewise, the same as the challenge to the contemporary party leaders. It requires a combination of new sensitivities and traditional skills. To prevail these days, a president first must accept a cardinal premise: he will be required to know and to deal regularly with a much wider array of players in the process, members and staff. Such dealings require a congressional-liaison staff that works to know not just who the members are, but what they like and dislike, who needs to be sweet-talked and who can be bullied, who will be satisfied with a special White House tour for constituents or an invitation to a state dinner and who will insist on a substantive concession.[16]

Ornstein also stresses that presidents now have to spend

more of their own precious time on Congress if they are to be effective. They must *want* to succeed, therefore, as well as having the skills necessary to succeed.

In most respects, recent congressional changes have simply served to reinforce the need for those talents which have always been necessary for successful congressional liaison. Lyndon Johnson had such skills, as has Ronald Reagan. Both showed a respect for Congress and its members, while always keeping their major legislative priorities uppermost in their minds. When Reagan was elected in 1980, he immediately accorded Senate Majority Leader Howard Baker a high status – even though Baker had fought him for the nomination. Jimmy Carter, in spite of working hard to establish a good relationship with Congress, largely lacked the aptitude for the job. He was, possibly, too honest, insufficiently manipulative and reluctant to engage in the sometimes unsavoury business of flattering egos, feigning friendships and generally building a 'presidential party'.

The record of Johnson, Ford and Carter also demonstrates the importance of external events. Johnson's congressional liaison deteriorated badly as he became preoccupied with the Vietnam War – although this was at least partly self-induced.[17] Ford was a victim of the post-Watergate political environment and even though very recently a House Minority Leader, found it well-nigh impossible to win the co-operation of Congress. Jimmy Carter also faced hostility and, perhaps more importantly, consensus on the issues of the day was sadly lacking. Energy policy is almost custom-built for conflict. Too many winners and losers exist, whatever is done. Carter also presided over first an economic recovery but not a recovery of national morale, and then an economic recession and a deep crisis of national morale induced by the Iranian hostage crisis. Ronald Reagan, in contrast, came into office in the context of a near consensus on the need for tax and expenditure cuts. When in 1982 and 1983 support for these policies waned, the economy recovered. Of course, Ronald Reagan has been more than merely lucky. As we have said, his personal political skills have helped his every move. The point is simply that external events test these skills to the full – and some presidents have been luckier than others in that they have been exposed to less trying, more comfortable political environments.

Unfortunately, we cannot easily quantify success and failure in presidential/congressional relations. As already established, party is a poor guide to performance – although it is still almost certainly better for incumbents to face a Congress controlled by their own party. Successful vetoes also tell us but a limited amount. Table 11 on p. 106 implies that together with Nixon, Ford and Carter, Truman and even Reagan were less than adequate at handling Congress. Yet Truman was exposed to a truly hostile external environment, as well as, some of the time, a fiercely critical Republican Congress. And Ronald Reagan, in spite of having 23.5 per cent of his regular vetoes overridden, is generally accepted as adept at dealing with Congress – especially given Democratic control of the House.

With Congress now more assertive and independent, *all* presidents are more likely to want to veto bills, and Congress is more prone to override them. Similarly, we cannot say that because President A managed to get more of his bills through Congress he was more successful than President B. Much depends on the president's personal investment in legislation and, above all, on media and congressional *perception* of how good at liaison the president is, whatever his legislative successes and failures.

We can really only make one clear, unambiguous generalization. Recent changes in Congress, in political parties and, ultimately, in American society itself have made the job of president increasingly demanding. Truly exceptional political skills are now necessary to create and maintain a successful relationship with Congress.

Presidents and the public

In their dealings both with the executive and (especially) with Congress, presidents exploit the broader political stage to the full. Appeals direct to the public on television are now quite common and at every opportunity – press conferences, meetings with foreign leaders, addresses to Congress – the broadcasting networks are there to cover the event. In this sense,

TABLE 12

Presidential press conferences 1932–84

President	Number	Average per years in office
Roosevelt	998	83
Truman	322	40
Eisenhower	193	24
Kennedy	64	21
Johnson	126	25
Nixon	37	7
Ford	39	16
Carter	59	15
Reagan (1981–4)	26	6

Source: Milton C. Cummings and David Wise, *Democracy Under Pressure* (New York: Harcourt Brace Jovanovich, 1981) p. 380; Samuel Kernell, *Going Public* (Washington, DC: Congressional Quarterly Press, 1986) p. 69.

television has greatly increased the visibility of presidents. As Austin Ranney points out, it is easier for television to focus on one man rather than on the 535 members of Congress. Each network has four full-time presidential correspondents but only two congressional.[18] However, this constant exposure can be a mixed blessing. Any faults, hesitations or weaknesses in presentation are picked up and amplified. Perhaps aware of this, some presidents have avoided too many unstructured public confrontations – especially press conferences. As Table 12 shows, there has been a decline in this forum since the advent of television (generally agreed to be a significant factor since about 1960), with Richard Nixon and Ronald Reagan especially eschewing the device. Presidents are also ill-advised to criticize openly one of the other branches, especially Congress. There is no surer way of antagonizing members than using the office to bully, cajole or intimidate them into compliance. Johnson knew this, as does Ronald Reagan. Nixon and Carter were less aware of the need for subtlety and tact. This is not to say that confronting Congress is not a rational presidential strategy. Ronald Reagan has opted for confrontation rather than bargaining on numerous occasions, but his approach has been to plead for public support against the 'irrationality' of Congress. Consider the following plea in his campaign for tax reductions:

I ask you now to put aside any feelings of frustration or helplessness about our political institutions and join me in this dramatic but responsible plan to reduce the enormous burden of federal taxation on you and your family.

During recent months many of you have asked what can you do to help make America strong again. I urge you again to contact your senators and congressmen. Tell them of your support for this bipartisan proposal. Tell them you believe this is an unequalled opportunity to help return America to prosperity and make government again the servant of the people.[19]

In sum, the public can be a valuable political resource, but they can also be a president's undoing. Richard Nixon's painful attempts to deny his guilt at the time of Watergate did him no good whatsoever. During the Iranian hostage crisis, Jimmy Carter's increasing frustration came over very clearly on television and helped confirm his public image as a weak, vacillating president.

Television and direct appeals are not the only public resources available to presidents. A president's margin of victory in terms of the popular vote is also important. Table 13 shows, for example, that in 1936, 1972, 1964, 1932 and 1984 the victors received a significant popular mandate, and in 1932 and 1964 this was translated into dramatic legislative success. It is too early to judge Reagan's second term, and Nixon's post-1972 presidency was dominated by Watergate. The mandate hypothesis is more clearly supported by the experiences of the four presidents who received the lowest margins of popular victories. None had startling success, and in the case of Truman and Carter very little was achieved. Clearly we should be wary of inferring too much from these statistics. They take no account of external events nor of the political acumen of incumbents, whatever their victory margins. Kennedy remained popular throughout his short presidency, in spite of his narrow 1960 victory. Jimmy Carter's

TABLE 13

Margin of presidential victories, 1932–84
(Percentage of popular vote)

Year	Winner	Loser	Margin of victory
1936	Roosevelt	Landon	24.3
1972	Nixon	McGovern	23.2
1964	Johnson	Goldwater	22.6
1932	Roosevelt	Hoover	17.7
1984	Reagan	Mondale	17.0
1956	Eisenhower	Stevenson	15.4
1952	Eisenhower	Stevenson	10.7
1940	Roosevelt	Willkie	9.9
1980	Reagan	Carter	9.7
1944	Roosevelt	Dewey	7.5
1948	Truman	Dewey	4.5
1976	Carter	Ford	2.1
1968	Nixon	Humphrey	0.7
1960	Kennedy	Nixon	0.2
Average			11.8

Source: U.S. Department of Commerce, *Statistical Abstract of the U.S., 1982/83* (Washington, DC: U.S. Government Printing Office, 1982) p. 472, updated for 1984 by author.

popularity fluctuated wildly in response to international events. This brings us to the general question of popularity – undoubtedly in itself a major factor in determining how successful presidents are in handling Congress, the executive and overseas events. Unfortunately the single most dramatic way for presidents to increase their popularity is to be involved in a major crisis which they *appear* to handle well. This usually means an international incident (of which more in the next section), but it could be something like Ronald Reagan's sacking of the air traffic controllers in 1981. His resolution to break the striking union, P.A.T.C.O., was carried through without hesitation, and he experienced a surge of popularity as a result. Once the 'crisis' has passed, public opinion usually settles down. The point is that the American public *expect* their president to behave like a national and world leader. When, as is often the case, they have insufficient information on which to make a considered judgement, they react to simplistic messages, usually conveyed by television. If the president appears to be acting like a proper leader they react favourably. If he appears indecisive or not completely in control, they react negatively.

TABLE 14

Rally events and the movement of public support for the president

President/Event	Percentage change in approval
Truman	
Truman doctrine (March 1947)	+12
Berlin blockade (April 1948)	+3
Soviet A-bomb announced (September 1949)	−6
Korean invasion (June–July 1950)	+9
Inchon landing (September 1950)	−4
China crosses the Yalu river (November–December 1950)	−3
Korean peace talks begin (July 1951)	+4
Eisenhower	
Korean truce signed (July–August 1953)	+1
Sputnik I launched (October 1957)	+3
U.S. marines land in Lebanon (July 1958)	+6
U-2 shot down by Soviets (May 1960)	+3
Kennedy	
Bay of Pigs incident (April 1961)	+5
Berlin wall (August 1961)	+1
Test-ban treaty (August–September 1961)	+4
Berlin crisis (October 1961)	+2
Cuban missile crisis (October 1962)	+12
Johnson	
Gulf of Tonkin incident (August 1964)	−5

Start of North Vietnam bombing (February 1965)   −2
Invasion of Dominican Republic (April–May 1965)   +6
Pueblo incident (January 1968)   −7
Tet offensive/U.S. embassy invaded (January–February 1968)   −7
North Vietnam agrees to peace talks (April 1968)   +4
Bombing halt (November 1968)   +1

Nixon

'Vietnamization' speech (November 1969)   +11
Invasion of Cambodia (May 1970)   +1
China trip (February 1972)   +4
Haiphong Harbor mined (May 1972)   −3
'Peace is at hand' speech (October–November 1972)   +6
Christmas bombing (December 1972)   −8
Vietnam peace agreement (January 1973)   +16
Arab–Israeli cease fire (May 1974)   +3

Ford

Cambodia falls to Communists (April 1975)   −5
Mayaguez incident (June 1975)   −11
Egypt–Israel treaty (August 1975)   +1

Carter

Panama Canal treaty (August 1977)   +6
Neutron bomb deferred (March–April 1978)   −8
Middle East summit at Camp David (September 1978)   +3
Middle East treaty (March 1979)   +6
Embassy seized in Teheran (November 1979)   +6
Soviet invasion of Afghanistan (December 1979)   +2
Hostage rescue attempt fails (April 1980)   −4

Source: Richard Brody, 'International Crisis: A Rallying Point', *Public Opinion* (December/January 1984) Table 1, p. 43.

Presidents and the world

In no political arena does this general point apply more forcibly than in foreign policy. Information about the rest of the world is at best scant in the U.S. Americans are peculiarly ethnocentric; world events are viewed from American perspectives. The public have high expectations that their president can mould and manipulate overseas events rather than being a passive victim of them. Table 14 demonstrates most graphically how different presidents have benefited or been penalized by a range of foreign-policy incidents and decisions. Several features are worthy of note. Although events negative to the U.S. but not in any way related to the president's immediate actions can lower a president's popularity (as with the Soviet A-bomb announcement in 1949 and Cambodia's fall to the Communists in 1975), they can also raise it. Hence the Berlin crisis (1961) and the Soviet invasion of Afghanistan helped Kennedy and Carter. With a few exceptions, adventurist actions raise presidential popularity *even when they fail*. So the fiascos of the Bay of Pigs and the Iranian hostage rescue actually helped Kennedy's and, at least at first, Carter's public standing. Events negative to the U.S. and American adventurism have one characteristic in common: they raise the public's expectations that the president will respond, or continue to respond firmly and decisively. The public at large are waiting for action, for a sign that their president will display all the patriotism and moral fervour which Americans demand of their chief executive. Needless to say, when the crisis is resolved in America's favour (as with the Cuban missile crisis) the president's popularity soars. Longer-term foreign-policy issues often evoke a more thinking response from the public. Presidents benefit when treaties are signed (the Vietnam peace agreement, the Camp David accords), and the pattern of presidents' adventurism being rewarded by the public was broken during the long and bitter Vietnam experience.

Nonetheless, given the crucial importance of public opinion for presidents' electoral fortunes and sense of self-esteem, this pattern must have a disturbing influence on foreign policy. Ronald Reagan's invasion of Grenada, widely regarded outside of the U.S. as illegal and gratuitous, raised the president's approval rating from 46 per cent to 53 per cent – and this just prior to a vital re-election campaign. Perhaps more serious is the way in which domestic pressures can shift a president's focus of attention away from the international arena. Vital world affairs are, in the strictest political sense, subordinated to domestic concerns. Ronald Reagan could eschew arms-limitation talks, knowing that the domestic repercussions would be slight. Indeed in his first administration, the president's generally negative attitude towards East–West relations almost certainly did him no long-term electoral damage.

This problem has become more serious as American political culture has become more populist, and as the standing of the U.S. in the world has declined. Fewer Western Europeans have faith in American ability to deal with world problems than ever before.[20] The spectacle of American presidents apparently more preoccupied with their domestic popularity than with solving such problems does little to enhance perceptions of America's strategic value. Most worrying is evidence that it is among European élites that the decline in confidence has been greatest.[21] It must be assumed that in poorer countries, and especially in those not directly dependent on the U.S., the estrangement is even greater. There was a time when presidential domestic popularity was matched by popularity overseas. Certainly Roosevelt was widely admired abroad, as was John Kennedy (whose domestic ratings remained high throughout his presidency). Ford, Carter and Reagan, in contrast, have inspired little confidence abroad.

We should be wary of making too much of mere popularity. Presidents remain commanders in chief, chief diplomats and heads of state. So extensive are their military and diplomatic resources that they can quickly transform a tarnished overseas image into one of glittering achievement. As with everything else that presidents do, much depends on their personal political skills. Look at Richard Nixon. On coming to power in 1969 he was widely regarded abroad as an irredeemable cold-war warrior. As a congressman, senator and as vice president he had been consistently and vehemently anti-Communist. Yet by 1973 he had visited the Soviet Union and China and was accepted in both countries as a man of great diplomatic and political vision. The yawning gap between Nixon's domestic standing and his reputation overseas (which remains to this day on foreign-policy questions) highlights the extent to which Nixon's foreign policy had become separated from U.S. domestic affairs during these years. But as American domestic politics have become more complex and pluralistic, so it has become increasingly difficult for presidents to 'escape' into the relatively insulated world of foreign policy. Eisenhower did just this, and Richard Nixon attempted to do it. Today domestic politics impinge so extensively on foreign affairs that this is simply not possible. Budgeting, for example, which is now the very essence of Washington politics, affects both. Ronald Reagan's position on military spending, foreign economic policy, the Lebanon, Central America and East–West relations is also part and parcel of domestic politics.

Presidents, Personality and the New America

Everything in the preceding sections points to the importance of presidents' personal resources – their aptitude for the job; their capacity to manipulate and persuade; to maintain a sense of judgement and perspective in the face of crisis and criticism. To some extent this has always been true, but the three changes identified in Chapter One have greatly increased the premium on personality. Put another way, as the role of government at home and abroad has been transformed, little in the way of fundamental institutional reform has occurred to help the president deal with a new U.S. world role, with big government and social fragmentation. In most political systems chief executives are aided by party, bureaucratic, class, regional or even religious or ethnic networks of power and influence. As we have seen, a loose coalition of class and regional interests held the Democratic Party together in a winning combination for most of the middle years of the twentieth century. But even this coalition has now passed into history, leaving little to replace it. Of course social fragmentation is a major cause of the political isolation of presidents, as well as being something they have to overcome. As suggested, parties in particular have grown weaker, thus largely removing what in most political systems are the major recruiting and training grounds for executive leaders. Without the connective tissue of strong political parties, liaison with Congress and management of the executive branch becomes more problematical. Yet the need for such liaison has grown more urgent as governments' domestic and international responsibilities have expanded.

The point is that whether presidents like it or not, they are the supreme conflict managers, not only in American society, but also globally. In a world where distributional questions become ever more difficult, an enormous burden is placed on the American chief executive. He cannot rely on cabinet colleagues, as in Britain, nor on a long-established *esprit de corps* among civil servants, which greatly aids French presidents. In the case of Jimmy Carter, his major supports within the executive branch were his wife and a small group of friends from his days as governor of Georgia. No chief executive in any other major country, East or West, is as institutionally isolated. In a recent article, Arnold Meltsner noted that 'There are no schools for presidents. No matter how experienced and intelligent a president might be, he will not be prepared entirely for the office.'[22] What Meltsner did not say, however, was that in most countries the equivalent of schools for presidents *do* exist, in the form of incumbency in cabinet office, lengthy peer-group review and party and other social networks of power.

Three broad conclusions emerge from this discussion. First, the American presidency is now, and is likely to be in the future, much less *efficient* as an institution than it used to be. Of course this begs the question of whether inefficient presidents must always be bad ones in the normative sense. Second, successive presidents, aware of the problems, have strived to concentrate power in the White House, by strengthening the White House bureaucracy, especially the Office of Management and Budget (O.M.B.), bypassing Congress by direct appeals to the people and by various other means. Presidents have thus been obliged to pursue a strategy of building up the power of the American central state. For anti-statist presidents such as Ronald Reagan this represents an obvious paradox. Third, personality is a crucial determinant of presidential performance. This in turn leads us to ask whether the last sixty years reveal a pattern of appropriate followed by inappropriate personality types. Let us deal with the third question first.

Presidential personality: the crucial variable?

Scholars of presidential personality are usually concerned either to classify incumbents by personality type or to judge whether recent changes in society and polity have encouraged the candidates of different, possibly inappropriate personality types. The most celebrated classification is that associated with James David Barber in his book *The Presidential Character*.[23] Barber's psychobiography of presidents produces a four-way taxonomy, one dimension measuring energy level in the job (active/passive) and the other measuring emotional attitude to satisfaction from the job (positive/negative). Barber favours the active/positives, who are self-confident individuals enjoying the experience of high achievement. Active/negatives, in contrast, are compulsive, driven men whose search for achievement is a long, lonely struggle. Franklin Roosevelt and John Kennedy are the archetypal active/positives, while Lyndon Johnson and Richard Nixon are clearly active/negatives. Such classifications raise two questions. Are the categories a good guide to presidential performance? And do they tell us anything useful about the relationship between candidates and the major changes in American society identified earlier?

According to Barber's analysis, Wilson, Hoover, Johnson and Nixon were all 'bad' presidents (i.e. active/negatives), while Roosevelt, Truman, Kennedy, Ford and Carter were all 'good' presidents (active/positives). Ronald Reagan, along with Taft and Harding, is classified as a passive/positive, or someone who invests little energy in the job but reaps great satisfaction from it. Clearly this is an unsatisfactory conclusion. Most historians mark Wilson high and Carter and Ford low.[24] As serious, the Barber scheme tells us virtually nothing about the relationship between personality and structural changes in American society. Earlier, we concluded that the new presidential nomination process does not pre-select certain personality types, although it does reduce the pool of talent from which candidates are drawn. What *is* true is that guiding America's greatly enhanced role in an interdependent world, taking those difficult distributional decisions which are now part and parcel of the federal government's job, and managing a society characterized by social fragmentation, all put enormous strains on the one man at the centre of events. In recent years the 'failed' presidencies of Johnson and Nixon (and to some extent of Ford and Carter) may be as much attributable to the 'times' as to the characters of the incumbents. Vietnam was the most divisive and damaging event since the Civil War. Anti-war and Black rebellion combined to make the United States close to ungovernable during these years. It was, perhaps, unfortunate that Johnson and Nixon happened to be presidents at the time. Ironically, both owed their incumbency to the pathology of the era – the assassination of John Kennedy and the split in the Democratic Party in 1968 induced by the war and the desegregation of the South. Ford and Carter were the unlucky heirs to a seriously tarnished institution. As such they started off at a considerable disadvantage.

Events during the presidency of Jimmy Carter emphasized a further dimension to the changed times. Unlike Johnson and Nixon, Carter handled crisis events rather well. Even so, the Iranian hostage crisis helped ensure his defeat in the 1980 election. He could neither be 'imperial' – for it was just this characteristic which undid Johnson and Nixon – nor could he appear to be weak and vacillating. In retrospect, few dispute that his options during the crisis were strictly limited. Any president would have suffered under the circumstances. We have here a good example of how events, not the man, were forging the institution's reputation. Ronald Reagan, who acquired the reputation of the 'Teflon' president, or the man on whom problems rarely stuck, has been lucky by comparison. The 1985 Beirut hostage crisis ended quite quickly, with the Israelis rather than the Americans making the concessions. Other horrors, from the shooting down of the Korean Airline's jet to events in Central America and Libya, have so far failed to realize their full potential for embarrassment, impasse, danger and confusion. None of this is to deny that Ronald Reagan is a very different man from Jimmy Carter. It is simply to emphasize that presidents now function in a much more difficult and volatile political environment. As such, there is a greater need than ever before for incumbents to display quite exceptional personality skills. Few dispute that most recent presidents, while not obviously inferior to the presidents of the pre-Roosevelt era, have also not been superior.

More power to the White House: the way out?

Whatever the personality of particular incumbents, it is clear that all presidents are subject to numerous structural or institutional constraints. Congress constitutes the greatest constraint but the courts, state and local governments and the president's own executive are others. Without well-developed party or other political or social networks, the national strategy for the modern president is to centralize as much power in the White House as is feasible, to bypass Congress if possible, and to use what is the greatest asset of most presidents – the general public – at every available opportunity.

Of recent presidents, Richard Nixon and Ronald Reagan went furthest in their attempts to strengthen and centralize the executive branch. According to Terry Moe, Ronald Reagan has been the most enthusiastic centralizer:

More than any other modern president, Ronald Reagan has moved with dedication and comprehensiveness to take hold of the administrative machinery of government. At the heart of the approach are the politicization of administrative arrangements and the centralization of policy-related concerns in the White House: developments in the institutional presidency with origins in past administrations, but now significantly accelerated and expanded.[25]

Above all, Reagan elevated the Office of Management and Budget to the status of executive gatekeeper and regulatory watchdog. He has also used his undoubted public popularity to bolster his position in struggles with Congress and the courts. Moreover, he has attempted to build a 'presidential party' in the more literal sense: the Republican National Committee (R.N.C.) has increasingly become the president's political tool during the Reagan administrations. From the appointment of Bill Brock as national chairman in the late 1970s, the R.N.C. has gone from strength to strength. In part this is because campaign-finance reforms have encouraged political action committees (P.A.C.s) to donate to national parties (and there are more Republican than Democratic

P.A.C.s), but it is also because the Republicans have benefited from the support of a strong incumbent president. While there are limits to national party growth, it is clear that the stronger they become, the more they will be used by presidents to overcome the particularism and independence of candidate-centred local and state parties.

What all this adds up to is what Theodore Lowi has called the 'personal presidency',[26] that is a presidency characterized by constant efforts to keep the policy initiative, to centralize power in the person of the president and to engage in constant plebiscitary appeals to the public to overcome the institutional impasse characteristic of the office. This, of course, is the catch. Like it or not, presidents need Congress and other institutions to get things done. No matter how much they bolster the White House staff, strengthen the O.M.B., exploit the newly invigorated national parties or make impassioned appeals to the public, without congressional approval or authority they cannot get far in solving America's problems.

Values and efficiency:
are efficient presidents good presidents?

So far our discussion of the presidency has been highly functional in character. The institution has been judged in terms of how well Congress is 'handled' or the public 'satisfied'. Critics – and especially those on the left – would argue that efficient presidents can also be bad presidents in the moral sense. So the fact that Ronald Reagan has sometimes been able to sway Congress has simply made it easier for him to expedite unacceptable defence, social and foreign policies. In contrast, Jimmy Carter, who is generally condemned as a failure in functional terms, made bold efforts to construct a national energy policy and to champion human rights abroad. Interestingly, this functional/normative dilemma has only become a perceived problem in very recent years. It was assumed that in the era of the modern presidency liberal presidents were active and effective, while conservatives tended to be passive and less effective. Franklin Roosevelt, Harry Truman and John Kennedy were in the former category, while Dwight Eisenhower was in the latter. Lyndon Johnson shattered the liberals' dreams through his conduct of the Vietnam War, while Nixon and Reagan have been anything but passive. Richard Nixon was absorbed with foreign affairs, although not as a conservative, while Ronald Reagan is a radical of the right.

In retrospect the tendency to join the objective and subjective when assessing presidents was quite unsurprising. Roosevelt did, after all, effectively create the modern presidency. Such was his stature and such was the ideological appeal of what he stood for – internationalism and New Deal liberalism – that his Democratic successors were bound to follow in the same tradition. Virtually the whole of the non-Communist world was agreed on these objectives. The welfare state and a 'free world' funded and led by the United States were accepted by democratic European governments of the left and the right. Only when this dominant policy paradigm began to break down in the late 1960s and early 1970s did we begin fundamentally to question the morality of American leadership – and indeed of American presidents.

Today, the problem is insoluble. Efficient and clever incumbents strengthened by a wide degree of support among the American people can pursue policies which are repugnant to many and anathema to some. And it is not just Republican presidents who attract opprobrium. As the Johnson experience showed only too graphically, Democrats are just as capable of producing controversial foreign policies as are Republicans. In the economic sphere, it is difficult to imagine a Democratic president producing a non-controversial foreign economic strategy. The complexities of economic interdependence are such that presidents of all political shades will be perceived to make mistakes.

In domestic affairs, it remains the case that Democrats are likely to be more sympathetic to America's disadvantaged than Republicans. But even here, the liberal critic would find it difficult to claim that this is always so. Welfare and urban programmes increased in size more rapidly during the Nixon and Ford administrations than during Jimmy Carter's tenure in office. As with foreign affairs, policy problems have become so complex that the simple equation 'Democratic means liberal' does not always hold true.

Can we claim that, other things being equal, an efficient president is preferable to an inefficient one? Probably. Men adept at wooing Congress or assuaging public opinion are likely also to be men of prudence and judgement. The trouble is that in both domestic and foreign arenas the mistakes that any president makes can be big ones. Hence incumbents successful at managing the system always have the potential for making even bigger mistakes.

Conclusions: Presidents and the Public Interest

Americans' reluctance to think collectively tends to reduce the notion of the public or national interest either to a mere aggregation of individual interests or to a crude projection of American ideology – God, free market and country. Only rarely in American history have political institutions and leaders successfully led, rather than reflected, these public sentiments. Because presidents are both the embodiment of the American state and at the very centre of political life, they, above all, have the greatest potential for providing the nation with a sense of public interest that goes beyond mere patriotism and individual interest. Franklin Roosevelt and to some extent John Kennedy managed – for some of the time at least – to instil a sense that the federal government had a major role to play in representing the interests of all Americans. Abroad, Roosevelt in particular became the embodiment of freedom, democracy and justice. Ronald Reagan, while popular at home, has failed to transcend his image in America and overseas as champion of the advantaged and scourge of the poor. With increasing social fragmentation and the current complexity of America's world role, this public-interest function of the presidency is becoming much harder to perform effectively. It always was difficult, of course, but now it is almost impossible.

It is this peculiarly American notion of the public philosophy which is at the very heart of the current presidential impasse. Americans have little sense of 'the state', which, by virtue of its neutrality and autonomy, is something above society. Federal civil servants are widely perceived either to be the agents of some societal group or other, or simply to be self-serving. As we have seen, Congress is deeply infused with societal interests, leaving only the judiciary and the president to play a public-interest function. Comment on the courts must be reserved for a later chapter, but from our discussion it is clear that presidents are under enormous pressures to be all things to all Americans. This they cannot be. The process by which they are selected is less than ideal; they increasingly lack the political and social networks to staff and run the government; Congress views them more as an adversary than an ally; myriad societal interests – not to mention foreign governments – often look to them alone for the resolution of conflicts. In response, presidents have sought to centralize power in the White House and have increasingly appealed directly to public passions in order to strengthen the office. This has more often led to failure than success. As we will discuss in Chapter Nine, prospects of constitutional and other reforms which might ease the burden of office are slight. We must resign ourselves, therefore, to the probably forlorn hope that the extraordinary American political system will somehow produce men or women who can at least come close to living up to the great expectations of the office.

CHAPTER SIX

Organized Interests: Champions of Democracy or Defenders of Privilege?

A major theme of this book is that because American society is very strong in relation to the central institutions of the state, it is inordinately difficult for governments to govern. 'Society', at least as far as politics is concerned, is made up neither of an amorphous mass, nor of discrete individuals. Even in elections the political impact of the public is expressed in group terms, hence the frequent reference to the 'ethnic', 'women's', 'southern', or 'yuppie' vote. But periodic elections are just one part – and in some respects quite a minor part – of American politics. As we have seen, Congress and president are constantly persuading, manipulating or reacting to organized interests. So pervasive are interest groups in the U.S. that it is common to argue that the real political power lies with them rather than with elected office-holders or bureaucrats. Scholars from virtually every school of thought have, at one time or another, come to this conclusion. Indeed, it is difficult to find interpretations that are at serious variance with this general view, and all agree that organized interests are much more active today than ever before. In the context of the three changes in American society mentioned in Chapter One, the prominent role of interest groups raises a number of questions. First, to what extent have groups contributed to the growth of big government? Second, has group activity reduced the efficiency with which political institutions make domestic and foreign policy decisions? Finally what have been the effects of social fragmentation on the ways in which interests operate, and in particular on the resulting pattern of costs and benefits for different social groups? A good way to approach these questions is to examine competing theories of interest group power. Before we do this, however, it is necessary to explain why it is that groups have apparently become so much more active politically over recent decades.

Groups and Politics in the Modern Era

Americans have always showed a tendency to band together and form groups and associations for political purposes. Even in the 1830s Tocqueville noted that 'in no country in the world has the principle of association been more successfully used or applied to a greater multitude of objects than in America.'[1] A major survey of political participation conducted in the early 1970s, found that 14 per cent of all Americans had actually helped form a group or organization to attempt to solve some local community problem.[2] As this statistic suggests, most group activity exists at the local or state level. Citizens form groups to protect the environment, support local schools, advance equal rights for women and minorities, defend their communities from development or 'social downgrading', and so on. The institutional structure of American federalism and localism (of which more in Chapter Eight) greatly aids group activity. Further encouragement is provided by the separation of powers. As we have seen, Congress is almost tailor-made for lobbying. The labyrinthine structure of the federal bureaucracy is also amenable to interest-group access, as are the complexities of the state and federal courts. But there is more to group resilience than mere institutional arrangements. The American premium on the idea of free association is also important. Firms are the most obvious, or even the archetypal, type of free associations, and the freedom to form companies and accumulate capital has always been central to American ideology. But this value extends to every other conceivable form of association, from tennis clubs to veterans' organizations. Perhaps predictably, the one form of association to struggle for legal recognition in the U.S. was trade unions. Not until 1935 did the unions win full legal acceptance.

Since the Roosevelt era, group activity in the U.S. has been transformed. It has become more nationalized, more pervasive, and has involved new interests and new lobbying tactics. In addition, the balance of influence between different groups has shifted quite substantially. The nationalization of interest groups has followed naturally from the general nationalization of politics in America. Cause and effect run in both directions here. Groups have organized at the national level in response to national legislation, but groups have also been a cause of many new federal laws and regulations. Take education. No area of public policy has by tradition been more firmly planted in local politics. Local school boards funded by local taxation and elected by the community were the very essence of American democracy. Higher education was funded primarily at the state level or privately. From the passage of the 1965 Elementary and Secondary Education Act to the end of the 1970s, however, law after law was passed by Congress designed to subsidize, improve and redesign state and local education programmes. Impetus for these reforms came not only from political leaders, but also from organized interests dissatisfied with the level of educational provision in cities, states and regions. By 1980, for the first time in the history of the republic, more than 50 per cent of the funding for elementary and secondary education came from state and federal, rather than local, sources. A similar pattern of nationalized political lobbying and bargaining can be identified in other policy areas. None of this is to deny that local and state politics are important; it is simply to point out that there are many fewer activities at these levels which are not in some way or other affected by national politics than there used to be.

A massive increase, by any standards, in the quantity and quality of 'policy information' has greatly aided the nationalization process. In Chapter Four we noted how group rating of members of Congress has become commonplace over the last ten years. In addition, statistical and other data on issues as diverse as environmental pollution, the frequency of abortions and regional wage rates are available as never before. Consultants ply a trade in political contacts, ensuring that particular lobbies meet the appropriate congressional or executive personnel. Formal access to government has been improved through the enactment of 'sunshine', or open-government, legislation. Interest groups have a *right* to information in a way which is virtually unknown in many other countries.

The present pervasiveness of group activity is compounded by the fact that over the last several decades many new interests have become active while few of the old have ceased to exist. There was a time when most of the lobbying in Washington was conducted by peak associations acting on behalf of the big three economic groupings – business, agriculture and labour. While these remain important, the balance of influence between them has changed, and numerous other groups have emerged or grown from small beginnings to become major participants in the lobbying game. Business is organized in peak associations such as the National Association of Manufacturers and the Business Round Table, as well as in trade associations and individual firms. We will discuss the relative influence of business later, but whatever its actual power, there can be no doubting that it engages in more *explicit* lobbying today than it used to. One reason for this is that it has to contend not just with the labour unions and governments, but also with occupational, consumer and environmental-protection organizations, which have grown in size and influence since about 1960. Armed with new, often far-reaching federal legislation, these interests target much of their efforts on the corporations or on those federal agencies responsible for regulating corporate behaviour.

Few dispute that since around 1970 union influence has been in decline. Even though the major Washington-based peak association, the American Federation of Labor/Congress of Industrial Organization (A.F.L./C.I.O.), together with its political branch, the Committee on Political Education (C.O.P.E.), remains active, only 18 per cent of the workforce are now unionized and the movement has suffered a number of defeats over labour-related matters. The Teamsters (two million truckers, warehousemen and others), the United Auto Workers (one-and-a-half million members) and the United Mine Workers (200,000 members) have all suffered loss of membership as industrial decline, deregulation and a shift of investment to the West and South, where union tradition is weak, have taken their toll. The 'new realism' of Ronald Reagan's America put many unions on the defensive. In the case of the air traffic controllers, the union, P.A.T.C.O., was broken by the federal government. In other cases, unions have accepted job security for minimal wage increases or even reductions. Others have been victims of the bankruptcy laws which allow companies to invoke 'Chapter Eleven', or to declare bankruptcy, sack all their employees and then re-employ a smaller non-union labour force in a reorganized company. Continental Airlines did just this in 1983 and reduced its workforce from 12,000 to 4,200 workers. The only union growth area in recent years has been the public sector. Educational unions and associations grew rapidly between 1960 and 1975 – although they have declined somewhat since then. The most rapidly growing union is the Association of Federal, State, County and Municipal Employees (A.F.S.C.M.E.), which had over a million members by 1980. Low-paid female and Black workers make up most of its members.

There was a time when the power of the agricultural lobby went almost unquestioned. Whether represented by product, region, state or peak association, the farm interests appeared virtually unassailable. Subsidies were high and taxes low. By the mid 1980s, however, the agricultural lobby had declined in influence. A falling agricultural population undermined the farm vote and pressures on public expenditure have led to some erosion of the specially protected status of agricultural subsidies.

We have already noted the rise of environmental, con-sumer, and occupational protection groups, to which should be added social group organizations (championing the cause of women, Blacks, the elderly and other ethnic, religious and sexual minorities), professional groups, intergovernmental interests and the foreign lobby. Although they often receive less publicity than some other groups, professional organiz-ations representing lawyers, physicians, surgeons, dentists and so on, have become major sources of policy intelligence and influence. This is not to deny the existence of a vested interest on the part of such groups. But the increased pro-fessionalism of virtually all white-collar occupations has added to their information resources and thus to their policy-making utility. A further novel development has been the growth of the foreign lobby, or those governments with an interest in American foreign policy. Almost every government has agents or lobbies in Washington, but some are particularly well organized. The Israeli lobby, for example, has an extensive network of contacts with members of Congress and the executive. Other active countries are Taiwan and South Korea. In addition, Americans of Jewish, Polish, Cuban, Irish and Greek origin are especially well organized in support of those issues affecting their mother country.

Assessing the influence of the foreign lobby is difficult. Generally, agents of foreign governments are more in the business of advertising their countries' interests than actually changing legislation. The Israeli lobby is a notable exception. Organized under the auspices of the American Israeli Public Affairs Committee (A.I.P.A.C.), Israeli interests are well defended, with A.I.P.A.C. targeting specific items of legislation such as foreign-aid bills as well as general foreign-policy questions relating to Israel.[3]

Finally, American governments themselves engage in extensive lobbying of each other. This can take the rather obvious form of congressional/executive interaction, but it also increasingly manifests itself in the form of the lower-level governments lobbying in Washington for federal aid. Hence the U.S. Conference of Majors, National Governors' Association, National League of Cities and others are in constant motion, providing advice, expertise and opinions, most of which are directed at increasing the size of federal aid programmes. Again, cause and effect are difficult to disentangle here. Intergovernmental lobbying both helped bring about new aid programmes and now feeds off such legislation. We will return to this point in Chapter Eight.

In addition to these permanent organizations, a number of *ad hoc* groups exist at any one time, depending on the salience of particular events or issues. American involvement in Vietnam, for example, spawned a number of anti-war organizations, which were not only highly active but, arguably, also highly effective. The anti-war movement highlights just how different the activities of groups can be. Generally, three distinct strategies can be identified, which are closely related to the established power of groups. First, they may operate almost totally outside the political system and hope to achieve results by raising the salience of an issue through direct action. Civil-rights groups in the South did just this during the 1950s and 1960s, as did the anti-war protestors. More recently, Puerto Rican nationalists and the most extreme anti-abortion activists have resorted to legal and illegal direct-action methods. Such tactics are sometimes the work of unrepresentative extremists, and are sometimes a futile cri de cœur. Often they are a prelude to, or are accompanied by, more conventional political activity. The anti-war movement, for example, embraced almost every conceivable strategy.

Second, groups may target key policy-makers from outside the main institutional structures, in the hope that policies will change within Congress, the courts or the administration. Mass mailing, for example, is an increasingly sophisticated means of advertising a cause or position. Computer listings of areas or individuals known to be sympathetic can give a member of Congress the impression of a national tide of anger against, say, abortion or busing schoolchildren to achieve racial balance. Richard Viguerie, the right-wing Christian activist, has formed a company specifically devoted to such tactics. Senators and congressmen can be swamped with 'personalized' letters pleading for legislative action against liberal causes and in favour of conservative ones. The effectiveness of such campaigns is extraordinarily difficult to measure. Mass mailings can backfire by espousing extremist causes. But given the strong electoral connection between member and constituent noted in Chapter Four, few members can afford totally to ignore a well-orchestrated mass mailing.

Mass mailings, telephone campaigns and television advertising are resorted to when support for a position within government is weak or uncertain. Society as a whole has to be mobilized, therefore, to put pressure on elected officials. Our third interest-group strategy is quite different, for it concentrates on intragovernmental contacts and pressures. Indeed, most of the activities of the groups discussed above are in this category. Professional lobbyists, consultants and public-relations experts may be employed (an estimated

15,000 full-time lobbyists are at work in Washington), but they cannot hope to be successful unless they can rely on the established support of officials or members of Congress. Business, labour, agriculture and so on have their champions on Capitol Hill and within the administration. Lobbying in this context often means providing information that is vital to the success of a particular bill or administrative ruling. On many technical issues, organized interests *have* to be consulted. Even over relatively simple questions, the political clout of some interests is such that consultation is automatic. Many defence, agricultural and public-works interests are not so much outsiders pressuring government into action as an integral part of the policy process.

One of the most interesting developments of the 1970s was the growth of Political Action Committees, or P.A.C.s. Concern at the increasing influence of the 'fat cat' contributors to election campaigns increased steadily during the 1960s and culminated in the passage of the Federal Election Campaign Act of 1971. As amended in 1974 and 1976, the act attempted to formalize and restrict interest-group contributions to candidates for federal office. Since 1974 groups contributing funds have to channel the money through P.A.C.s, and then only up to a limit of $5,000 for primary elections and a further $5,000 for general elections. Although this does not seem very much, in aggregate it can mount up to a great deal. Moreover, corporations, unions and others can solicit their own members or shareholders for funds. By the early 1980s few questioned the importance of P.A.C. contributions. Some 25 per cent (close to $100 million) of all campaign finance is now derived from this source. Around 3,500 P.A.C.s exist, with business P.A.C.s outnumbering the next-largest category, non-connected groups, by about two to one. But of the approximately 1,500 business P.A.C.s most are small. In terms of money contributions, trade-union P.A.C.s are almost as important, contributing $20 million to the 1982 mid-term elections, as compared with $27 million from business.[4]

In terms of money raised rather than specifically given to campaign organizations, unconnected, usually ideological P.A.C.s are even more significant. The National Conservative Political Action Committee, the National Congressional Club and the Fund for a Conservative Majority together raised $22 million in 1981–2. Much of this money went on overheads, and only around 2.5 per cent ended up as formal contributions.[5] The rest was spent on general campaigns, often highly negative in nature, to unseat selected liberal candidates. In 1980 the defeat of six liberal senators was in part attributed to such campaigns. As the law puts no limit on general spending (i.e. money which does not go directly to party organizations), P.A.C.s have been much criticized for indulging in expensive hate campaigns. P.A.C.s have also been criticized for being unaccountable and for having a strong right-wing bias. Certainly, right-wing groups dominate among unconnected P.A.C.s, and business P.A.C.s are more numerous and probably better organized than labour P.A.C.s. This accepted, in both 1982 and 1984 conservative efforts to remove or defeat liberals came to very little. And the liberals have fought back by forming their own P.A.C.s. Following a massive smear campaign against him, Senator Edward Kennedy formed his own P.A.C., the Fund for a Democratic Majority, in 1980. Ideology apart, the financial importance of P.A.C.s in congressional races cannot be questioned. Many candidates now rely on their contributions. If anything, labour and business are now more, not less, involved in congressional elections. Populist outrage with this intimate involvement of 'special interests' continues, therefore.

Competing Theories of Interest-Group Power

In order to understand the significance of interest groups in the United States it is necessary to go beyond simply observing and noting their activities. More useful is a comparison of those theories normally invoked by social scientists to explain interest-group power. A summary of these theories is given below, followed by an attempt to synthesize them in the light of the three major changes in American society which have been the theme of this book.

Pluralism: interest-group politics as the public interest

According to the pluralists, open competition between competing interests is the best way to achieve policies which approximate to the public interest. The reasoning goes something like this. American society is highly complex and consists of numerous competing and conflicting interests. Most of these are organized in the sense that they have formed groups to advance or defend their particular position. Hence business is organized by firm, by industry, and collectively through peak associations such as the Business Round Table or the National Association of Manufacturers. Because access to government is open, and because political institutions are themselves multi-layered and fragmented, the system does not necessarily favour one group over another. Put another way, pluralists view the state as essentially neutral. It is a kind of black box which sorts out preferences. On receiving inputs from groups, it processes competing demands and then produces outputs in the form of legislation, regulations, judicial decisions and executive orders. Crucially, these authoritative actions will be *compromises*. No one group is likely to get its way completely, because opposing interests will organize effectively. The public interest will be served, therefore – at least in the utilitarian sense that public policy will satisfy the largest number of interests possible.

Anticipating problems, David B. Truman,[6] one of the original proponents of this view, accepted that complete equality between groups was impossible because different interests have different resources (organization, wealth, size) and interests are sometimes complementary rather than competitive. Hence labour unions are not somehow 'equal' to employers, nor are consumers to producers. However, should the interests of workers or consumers be seriously threatened or damaged, they will, in an open polity, organize to win some redress. Truman points to the rapid growth of unions in America during the Great Depression, leading eventually to the legal acceptance of union rights (the 1935 Wagner Act), as evidence of this. Neither do most pluralists fall into the trap of denying that some groups or interests are at a serious disadvantage because their access to government is limited. In the early 1950s when Truman's major work was published, Blacks in the South were clearly excluded from politics, therefore pluralism in the South was very limited in nature.

As a description of how American politics works, pluralism has certain intuitive appeals. The most casual observer of the Washington scene could not help but notice the large number of interests engaged in frenetic lobbying of Congress, the executive and the Supreme Court. Similar activity characterizes state and local politics. Moreover, every policy position adopted by the president or Congress appears to inspire a counter position. At a more grandiose level, interest-group pluralism has a decidedly ideological appeal, because of its theoretical affinity to free-market economics. The analogy is clear. The polity is to interests what markets are to consumers and producers. Only a free and open polity can produce policies which approximate to the public interest, just as only free markets can produce prices which approximate to equilibrium. It is, perhaps, unsurprising that as a theory pluralism should have been so influential in a country so infused with free-market ideology. Pluralism also appeals to American political individualism. It implies voluntary membership of numerous groups, with no one group representing all aspects of an individual's life. Citizens' interests can be advanced, therefore, on a number of fronts, depending on individual preferences and life styles. This is very different from class-based theories, where membership of a social class is involuntary and the interests of members are represented by, say, a single trade union or working-class movement.

As with critics of the economic market place, critics of pluralism have been quick to point out that polities are not completely open and are not neutral arbiters. They have their own preferences and frequently discriminate against some interests. Similarly, not all interests in society can organize effectively, and many argue that some interests, in particular business, are highly privileged in relation to others.[7]

The radical critique: interest-group politics as the expression of economic power

This major critique of the pluralist position argues that, far from being a neutral arbiter between groups, the state has a special interest in promoting and defending some interests and not others. Finance and industrial capital – the banks and big corporations – are defended, while labour, consumers, minorities and the poor are exploited. Hence Congress, the president and the courts consistently favour the corporations. Only under very exceptional circumstances do other interests get their way. A number of variations on this theme exist, and literally millions of words have been written arguing the case for and against.[8] While this is not the place to summarize this debate, it is important to point out that the differences between the two schools are not just a matter of contrasting interpretations of a common body of empirical evidence. The radicals claim that it is necessary to go beyond observable facts and study what accounts for certain issues being discussed and others not. Hence what makes up the *policy agenda* is not simply a matter of interest-group action. Certain issues are kept off the agenda – consciously or unconsciously – because it is not in the interests of those in power to have them discussed.[9] For example, the nationalization of basic industries or ailing corporations is effectively not an issue in the U.S. This is not, so the argument goes, because interest-group politics have failed to raise the question. Rather, it is because power holders have successfully excluded discussion of the question by convincing all those interested that there is no alternative to the market. Naturally if this is done openly and directly then nationalization *is* an issue on the policy agenda. The conviction must, therefore, be imposed indirectly or even subliminally. All this suggests the manipulation of society through beliefs and values, or through the imposition of a 'dominant ideology'. As we pointed out in Chapter Three, formidable methodological problems exist when trying to demonstrate that the dominant ideology is somehow imposed on society. Who are the power holders? And how do they ensure the supremacy of such notions as self-reliance, individualism and market ideology?

Through the media, advertising and education? Possibly, but all three have a remarkable degree of organizational and political independence in the U.S.

Two further, slightly different aspects of the radical critique are worthy of mention. The first claims that disadvantaged groups are excluded by what might be called the structural conservatism of the political system. Such writers as E. E. Schattsneider and Grant McConnell have pointed out that it is inordinately difficult to get legislation or reforms through the American political system, but easy to prevent reforms at any one of a number of stages.[10] Our discussion of Congress appeared to confirm this tendency. Again, it is not some corporate or state conspiracy intent on upholding the *status quo* that accounts for this bias. It is simply that the constitutional structure, together with a fragmented and independent Congress, serves to support the *status quo*. Groups whose interests coincide with the existing order have a considerable advantage, therefore. Business, in particular, is identified as a beneficiary, while labour and the poor are penalized.

The second aspect of the radical critique is much more obvious. Put simply, groups representing small numbers of wealthy members fare better than groups representing large numbers of poorer members. Wealth gives groups resources for lobbying, access to law makers, status and recognition. Small membership brings coherence of purpose and unity, so business and the professions (lawyers, doctors) benefit, while labour unions and the poor are penalized. Even when unions are wealthy, they are at a disadvantage because, with a membership running into hundreds of thousands or even millions, they can rarely accurately reflect the interests of all their members. This argument also applies to the recently active civil-rights, consumers, women's and environmentalist groups. In all these cases, activists have to organize a large and varied constituency which is rarely united or agreed on a particular policy option. In most instances, participation in the cause is voluntary, and the influence of a group rises and falls with shifts in fashion. Business, by contrast, is permanently mobilized around very specific purposes. It also has the advantage of being able to claim that it alone is responsible for the efficient allocation of resources and the profitable generation of income and wealth.

Clearly, these radical critiques represent a number of different perspectives. Some (with the pluralists) see the state as neutral; others acknowledge that governments may have preferences independent of societal interests. Some talk in terms of the dominant ideology, while others concentrate on the institutional disadvantages which subordinate groups are subjected to. One common weakness exists with all these positions: none can adequately explain why it is that the fortunes of different groups *do* change over time – and not always in the favour of the big corporations or of the state. We will return to this point later.

The populist critique: big interests and government as partners against the public interest

The populist position overlaps substantially with the radical – so much so that in some instances it is difficult to know in which category to place some writers. However, there is a fundamental difference, which centres around the role of theory in explaining the influence of various groups. Very generally, populists eschew grandiose Marxist theories of historical change. Instead they see the growth of big government and big corporations as incompatible with the interests of ordinary people. Corruption and exploitation follow naturally when any organization becomes remote from the people, and remoteness is inevitable if decisions are taken, in secret, by the big interests in Washington. Labour unions are just as culpable as the corporations, for they too are remote from their members and privy to the secret world of power and influence in the national capital.

Unlike the radicals, whose only remedy is a transformation of the political and economic system, the populists see the solution readily at hand, in the form of American democracy. Indeed they view the emergence of giant corporations, unions, and an overweening federal government as an essentially un-American phenomenon. The answer is more accountability, more open politics, more democracy and less centralized government. Such sentiments are hardly new in

America. On the contrary, they have been populist rallying cries for many decades. During the 1970s, following Vietnam and Watergate, the populist critique received fresh impetus and produced a wave of legislation designed to curb the alleged evil-doings of both big business and big government. 'Sunshine laws' gave citizens freer access to government records and congressional committee proceedings. 'Sunset laws', enacted mainly at the state and local levels, imposed strict limits on the life of particular programmes and agencies. Annual review of the purpose and performance of government programmes would ensure constant control by the people.

A further difference between the populist and radical critiques is that the populists generally do not identify private enterprise as the villain in the piece. It is *big* business in league with government that is responsible for monopoly, exploitation and restrictive practices. Hence the consumer advocate, Ralph Nader, who pioneered automobile safety regulation in the 1960s and continues to work for consumer rights, is by no means a socialist. His critique is based on the 'betrayal' of corporations and government of Americans' democratic rights. A related theme is the allegation that Washington is dominated by impenetrable 'iron triangles', or closed policy systems comprising special interests, congressional sub-committees and government bureaux (the bureaux are those organizational units within departments responsible for day-to-day contact with government clients). The analysis goes like this. All three have an interest in maintaining and expanding existing spending patterns. Agriculture is a classic case. Subsidies are supported by members of Congress eager for the farm vote; within the Department of Agriculture officials in individual bureaux intent on self-preservation and career advancement also support subsidies; so, obviously, do the farmers. The system is impenetrable because no outside political authority can actually break it down. Congress cannot act as a whole; presidents cannot see to the minutiae of every programme. Consumers are generally incoherent and unorganized. Although agriculture and defence are usually identified as the major policy arenas susceptible to this development, critics have extended the model to a number of other arenas,[11] thus condemning virtually all of Washington politics as closed and 'fixed', rather than open and flexible.

Since the 1960s a number of changes have occurred in American politics which should lead us to doubt the validity of the iron-triangle model. Politics have become more open; spending on various programmes has fluctuated unpredictably; some interests have clearly benefited while others have lost out. All this suggests that such adjectives as 'iron' or 'closed' are highly inappropriate to describe interest-group politics in the 1980s. What is true, however, is that the big interests – particularly government and corporations – have become even bigger and in some respects more remote during the last thirty years, so fuelling populist sentiments.

Rational choice: groups as a threat to economic efficiency

In what can only be called a remarkable intellectual transformation, many erstwhile pluralists abandoned the core of their analysis during the 1970s and early 1980s and instead embraced a theory which viewed groups in anything but a benevolent light. The critique is based on the following assumption: a pluralist political system characterized by open government and institutional fragmentation encourages ever higher and/or more wasteful levels of public spending and regulation, as congressional committees, courts and executive agencies are obliged to satisfy the needs of ever more demanding groups. So governments, and especially the federal government, are not some kind of neutral arbiter efficiently sorting out societal preferences. They are the source of subsidies, grants, benefits and regulations, and the easiest way for them to satisfy conflicting demands is to give more to everybody. Such an outcome leads to inflation and fiscal crisis. Worse, as public expenditure and the regulation of society increases, so the only truly efficient sorter-out of preferences, the market, is undermined. Ergo, economic decline must follow. Hence both government and groups are responsible for inefficient resource allocation, and the more open the system the worse the situation becomes.[12] This analysis is, of course, related to the 'overload' thesis, which argues that governments are increasingly unable to accommodate the myriad demands of competing groups.[13] Both can be called rational-choice theories, because it is rational for interests to form groups, pressure government and squeeze as much as possible out of the public purse. As we discovered in our discussion of Congress and the presidency, the American system is highly amenable to such activity. In recent years more open government, independent members of Congress, the proliferation of congressional subcommittees and the increasing complexity of issues have given further impetus to group activity.

At first sight, the analysis seems convincing. As previously noted, Washington is simply alive with interest groups, as consultants, lobbyists and the media jostle to advance one position or another. Moreover, government did expand in size and scope rapidly and consistently between 1932 and 1980, and the fiscal health of the federal government has deteriorated badly over the last dozen years. One thing is certain: the Reagan administration is convinced that this analysis is valid. Almost its every move has been designed to limit group activity in Washington. Two main sets of policies were designed to achieve this objective. First and most obviously, the administration has attempted to reduce the size of government by cutting expenditure, removing regulations and abolishing some programmes altogether. Second, Reagan's New Federalism involved proposals for a dramatic devolution of powers and functions to state and local governments. By so doing, the president hoped to fragment and thus weaken interest groups. Clearly, being obliged to operate in fifty state policy arenas rather than in one federal arena puts groups at a disadvantage. As we will see in Chapter Eight, although the New Federalism came to very little, some devolution did occur in the 1980–84 period.

A major problem with the rational-choice analysis is its failure to explain why it is that some interests do very much better than others. Few dispute that trade unions, for example, are well organized, have good access and enjoy the support of some key politicians. Yet they have hardly enjoyed good fortune compared with, say, defence contractors, who, on the face of it, do no more lobbying. In sum, the rational-choice approach shares the pluralist emphasis on explicit participation in decision-making. Little distinction is drawn between different sorts of groups. Nor is there any place for the role of ideology and the possibility that the policy agenda may be biased against some interests and in favour of others. It seems odd, for example, to condemn local government, labour and poverty groups (often the major butt of the rational-choice critique) alongside business, defence and agricultural interests, when the latter account for a much higher proportion of public spending and tax-relief benefits than the former.

Interests and Interest-Group Theory: A Synthesis

From the point of view of interest-group theory, simply observing groups – including P.A.C.s – tends to confirm the pluralist thesis. Business is countered by labour, right-wing groups by liberal ones, and so on. The same conclusions follow from an analysis of lobbying generally in Washington. For every group working against an issue, another is striving to force public policy in the opposite direction. Complexity and fragmentation in decision-making tend to reinforce the pluralist position. Few clear-cut outcomes emerge from the administrative and political morass. All interests appear to derive some satisfaction from the resulting public policies. The rational-choice thesis also has great intuitive and some empirical appeal. Battles over the budget deficit during the early–mid 1980s seem almost a confirmation of the theory on their own. Ronald Reagan simply could not hold off the competing lobbies, each with its champions in Congress, the media and the administration. As a result, spending has continued at a high level. By 1985 the deficit problem had reached the stage where most members of Congress were accepting that some real cuts would have to be accepted. Even so, the assumption was that lobbying could ward off some of the more savage reductions, and even if it could not, most lobbies would emerge from the battle equally scarred. In December 1984 the *National Journal* noted that:

By the hundreds, representing almost every conceivable position and interest, they are organizing, drawing up battle plans and forming alliances: Washington lobbyists are preparing for next year's budget fight, and many of them are preparing for the worst.[14]

In one sense this is a classical pluralist statement, for there is little indication that some groups *start off* with enormous disadvantages in relation to others. If the cruder pluralist and rational-choice perspectives are rejected, what can be said about the nature of interest-group politics in the United States?

Observing Washington lobbying alone can be misleading

It is a natural tendency for students of interest-group politics to concentrate on the Washington scene. It is in the national capital, after all, that the most publicized politics occur – especially following the nationalization of politics noted earlier. Washington is, however, often the forum for 'last resort' politics. Many interests have recourse to explicit lobbying only when they have failed at the state and local levels, or because national legislation threatens their members. Sometimes, Washington politics simply reflects the distribution of power at the state level. Until the late 1970s, for example, energy, and particularly oil, interests had powerful established bases of support in the energy-rich states. Oil depletion allowances and other tax benefits for energy producers were essentially inviolate because of the commitment to energy interests by key members of Congress and the administration. These benefits did not result so much from explicit lobbying in Congress as from a policy consensus based on state and local power.

At a rather different level, most labour disputes in the United States are settled in state and local contexts. Labour law is essentially a state not a federal domain, and most unions are correspondingly organized on a state basis. Moreover the public sector is highly decentralized. States and localities may receive federal aid, but the vast majority of public employees have to bargain with state and local authorities.

Of course, federal laws affect trade unions and workers in general, and this inspires sometimes fierce lobbying. But the real stuff of labour politics in the United States goes on elsewhere, and only in dramatic cases (such as a violent dispute, or the 1981 air traffic controllers' strike, when President Reagan 'bust' P.A.T.C.O., the controllers' union) does it attract national attention. So we should not be misled into believing that because politics have been increasingly nationalized over the last thirty years, important distributional decisions are not still taken at the state and local level.

Those instances where policy comes from the top down, with little reference to the broader society, are different again. Some aspects of foreign policy do, for example, originate within the White House. During implementation, lobbying may occur, but the resulting policies are not merely the result of interest-group interaction. The terms of debate are first dictated from above, leaving only the detail of implementation to pluralist politics. In other words, Congress and the president have policy preferences independent of societal influences. Groups do not decide everything. Sometimes they are hardly involved in the decision-making process.

On class-based issues the distribution of public benefits changes little over time

At first glance the evidence supporting the view that interest-group politics have produced dramatic changes in who wins and who loses from public policy over time is formidable. Welfare, social security and other social-policy programmes have expanded very rapidly since the 1930s. Over half the federal budget goes on such items. Yet when examined carefully, the redistributive effect of all these measures is small. In order to calculate the net effect, it is of course necessary to look at both the spending and taxation sides of the equation. In an important book published in 1983, Benjamin Page does just this. On what might be called the class-based issues – income and wealth – very few people have benefited to the extent that inequalities have been reduced over time.[15] Put another way, those families at the top or bottom of the social heap twenty or thirty years ago are still there today. Of course some upward (and downward) mobility occurs, and of course some individuals have benefited more than others, but the *general* effect of public policy on the major social groups has been slight. The reasons for this are complex, and far from uncontroversial. Page shows that most personal and corporate taxes in the U.S. are regressive – the poor, proportionately, pay more than the rich.[16] Interest-group politics may account partly for this pattern. Following the radical critique, the political system may simply be biased against the disadvantaged. However, the public in general do not appear to disagree with the existing distributional pattern. As Page puts it:

We should be skeptical of the simplest versions of the interest-group theory, in which campaign contributions and lobbying by the wealthy and machinations by members of the tax committees bring about regressive tax policies and thwart the will of the people. Processes of group influence undoubtedly occur, and they certainly have a pro-rich bias. But the resulting policies do not appear to clash with the expressed preferences of the public. If interest-group arguments are to be sustained, therefore, they must encompass the facts of popular preferences about taxes, perhaps by showing that public opinion is manipulated.[17]

Showing exactly how the public are manipulated is extremely difficult, however.

Spending on social benefits also has little effect on the distribution of wealth and income. There are a number of reasons for this. First, the major benefit programmes (social security, medicare) are financed in part through regressive payroll taxes. Recipients effectively pay for the benefits earlier in their lives, even though they may be poor when they actually receive them. Welfare programmes (income-security payments, some housing, health and social-service benefits) can be redistributive, but they are much smaller than contributory, earnings-related programmes, and they very rarely raise the relative positions of recipients in the social pecking order. The poor are less poor than they would be, but still poor. Moreover, of all the money spent on welfare, the recipient population actually gets only a proportion of it. Much goes on what are often byzantine administrative arrangements. Finally, what about education, that public service so frequently identified as 'different' in the United States because it is well funded and universally available?[18] As with welfare, education spending can be redistributive. However, richer areas have a higher *per capita* spending than poorer ones and the value of free education in terms of improvements to life-long income and wealth prospects is low.[19]

None of this is to deny the existence – and the vitality – of Washington lobbying by trade unions, the poor, minorities and state and local governments eager for federal social-policy aid. All of this goes on and no doubt helps keep the level of social spending up. The point is that this activity does very little indeed to affect the fundamental position of America's disadvantaged. Put another way, open access, lobbying and all that is normally labelled pluralism is not neutral in its policy outcomes. Some interests are advantaged in relation to others. The corollary of this is that the major wealth producers in the United States – the business corporations – are especially privileged. Their tax burden is low, their access to decision-makers especially easy and, above all, unlike most other groups, they are permanently organized for purposes other than lobbying government. General Motors or IBM already has powerful organizational structures and clear operating rationales. Lobbying is a rational part of the business of maximizing profits and minimizing costs. Corporations do not depend on subscriptions and a fickle membership whose benefits from participation are often unclear or even non-existent. As Mancur Olson has pointed out, it is not always rational to join a trade union or a civil-rights, consumer-protection or environmental group, when the extra increment to that organization's efforts resulting from the individual's contribution is tiny. In contrast, the personal sacrifice to the individual (paying a subscription, joining a protest march) may be great.[20] Corporations have no such problems. Nobody *volunteers* to lobby or support a corporation; its direct or indirect participation in the political process is part and parcel of its operating procedures.

On non-class issues the distribution of public
benefits does change over time, but not in ways
which fundamentally threaten business interests

For those who subscribe to class-based theories of American politics, the events of the 1960s and 1970s present something of a problem, for during this period a number of new issues appeared on the policy agenda which, on the face of it, bore little or no relationship to traditional class alignments. The new social fragmentation combined with 'issue politics' to enable consumer, environmental-protection, women's and minority-rights interests to produce extensive and sometimes quite radical legislation and judicial decisions. How could the system not be pluralistic, and how could it be character-ized only by class-based relationships when such apparently radical changes were occurring? By the mid-1970s two further developments supported the pluralist cause. First, defence spending declined rapidly in relation to social spending, suggesting that interest-group politics had shifted resources from one major priority to another. Second, a new batch of 'conscience' issues such as abortion, capital punishment and religious instruction in public schools emerged, which had few obvious class implications.

All these changes demonstrate that rapid shifts in public policy can occur in the U.S. Moreover, the distributional consequences of these shifts are clearly important, even if it is not very easy to quantify them. As Graham Wilson has shown, environmental and consumer-protection legislation was sufficiently Draconian to spur business into leading a counter-attack.[21] The relative decline in defence spending also had far-reaching consequences – not only in economic terms, but also for American foreign policy. Advances in women's and minority rights also produce costs and benefits. There are, as Lester Thurow demonstrated in his influential book *The Zero Sum Society*, only so many resources to go around. When women or Blacks move up by finding skilled employment, white men must lose.[22] While accepting all of this, none of these issues is entirely class neutral. In his *Who Gets What from Government*, Benjamin Page points out that the costs of environmental and consumer protection fall unevenly on the poor.[23] But the calculation of net costs and benefits is complex. In some cases (the conscience issues for example), a 'who gains, who pays?' approach is simply inappropriate. Quite different value perspectives apply, which render class-based analyses unworkable. Similarly, it is not easy to express 'national defence' exclusively in class terms. In theory at least, everyone benefits from the defence effort. And in the sense that more defence spending means more jobs for lower-income groups in the armed forces and in industry, increased defence spending might actually help redistribute resources to disadvantaged groups.

Shifting patterns of public preferences as expressed through interest-group politics undoubtedly help explain why the policy agenda apparently changes so rapidly over time. In a secret or institutionally closed system such sudden changes are surely less likely. This accepted, some of the changes are obviously not attributable to pluralism. Defence spending, for example, is determined in part by external factors such as the perceived threat posed by foreign powers. Some policy initiatives may be imposed from above by the executive or the courts, rather than deriving from society. Above all, none of these shifting priorities has fundamentally challenged business interests. When threatened by the consumerists and environmentalists, business counter-attacked with reasonable success. And of course such regulations rarely fatally undermine profitability. As is often the case, old-style regulations have *increased* profitability through price fixing, oligopoly and restrictive practices.[24] If evidence is needed of the privileged position of business, data on corporate taxation provides it. As a percentage of total tax revenue, corporate taxes have been declining steadily since the Second World War.[25]

Pluralism, Efficiency and Equality

Pluralism is limited in the United States. Some social groups are greatly advantaged in the Washington lobbying game and others are permanently disadvantaged. It is hardly startling to discover that business is in the first category and the poor are in the latter. Who could possibly conclude otherwise? It is more difficult to assess the role of those interests whose appeal is to the public interest, or who represent large, amorphous social groups such as women or minorities. The last twenty years show that such appeals have been heard by decision-makers and have led to some real changes in public policy. A form of pluralism remains alive and well in the U.S., therefore, even if on class issues lobbying and interest-group politics are mainly confined to defending weak positions, or are more procedural than substantive in nature.

In other words, the social fragmentation that was the precondition for the growth of the 'new issue' groups has had important distributional consequences – but not of the sort that are easily expressed in class terms. For the rational-choice critics the distributional consequences of interest-group politics are almost irrelevant. What matters to them is how *efficiently* the system is working. As Arthur Okun put it in a pithy little book written a few years ago, the great trade-off today is 'efficiency versus equality'.[26] Rational-choice theorists consider that the pressure for more equality which is at the heart of most interest-group politics is essentially destructive. It leads to a non-rational pattern of public provision and/or to ever bigger government and ever higher expectations that governments can deliver. Only by reducing the size of government and high expectations will a more efficient society and economy be produced. Unfortunately, actually measuring efficiency is notoriously difficult. In simple quantitative terms, government is not in fact especially big in the U.S.A. With around 34 per cent of gross national product in the public sector, America is in the bottom third of the league table of O.E.C.D. countries. Moreover, expenditure has not increased rapidly over the last ten years, so by this measure the rapid increase in interest-group activity has had relatively little effect. Of course lobbying also results in laws and regulations that are not amenable to simple quantitative measurement. But again, little evidence exists to suppose that Americans are significantly more regulated than the Swedes, Germans or Japanese. What is true is that government is bigger and regulations are more extensive today, compared with forty years ago; interest groups have no doubt contributed to this development. Perhaps this accounts for the popularity of the rational-choice critique. Whether or not this larger state apparatus has led to a less efficient society and economy is very difficult to say.

'Efficiency' can be measured in another sense. Regardless of the level of public provision or its distributional consequences, it may be that the decision-making process is lengthy, complex and fragmented. Pluralism, with many groups winning access to multiple institutions, would seem to encourage such inefficiency. As the system has become more pluralistic and more complex over the last thirty years, this charge seems sustainable. Certainly outside observers bemoan the apparently byzantine way in which America conducts her world role. Trade policy is perceived less as a function of the state than as a function of conflicting societal pressures. Policy on exchange and interest rates is similarly clouded by institutional complexity and interest-group lobbying. Even mainstream foreign policy is confused by foreign-lobby interests and by apparent incompatibilities between and within the executive and legislative branches. By this measure at least, the claim that in the United States society is strong in relation to the state seems valid. Interest groups are not all-powerful, but by acting as veto or blocking groups with multiple access to multiple institutions, they do greatly complicate the business of making public policy in the United States.

CHAPTER SEVEN

Judicial Power: A Rootless Activism?

The U.S. has always been a litigious society. As long ago as the 1830s, Alexis de Tocqueville noted that 'scarcely any political question arises in the United States that is not resolved, sooner or later, into a judicial question'.[1] However, even Tocqueville would be surprised at how much further this tendency has gone since the nineteenth century. Americans take recourse to judicial action much more readily than most. More than half a million lawyers are currently at work, and billions of dollars are spent annually on litigation. In the public domain, the courts are now active in virtually every sphere of economic and social life. Since 1970, the future of a president, the precise meaning of federal campaign-finance laws, and the constitutionality of bans on abortion and capital punishment have been decided by the courts. When trying to explain the pervasiveness of the judiciary, two major factors stand out. First, the United States has a British common-law tradition, according to which society rather than the state is accepted as a crucial force in deciding disputes between citizens or between citizens and government. This shows itself in the adherence to a body of law established by precedent rather than imposed from above by statute, in jury trials, and in an adversarial court system where defending counsels are nominated not by the state but by the accused. Reinforcing this tradition is the individualism characteristic of American society. Recourse to the courts is more likely in a country where citizens see themselves as discrete economic actors rather than as members of broader-based social classes, regions or linguistic and regional groupings. Put another way, consumer/producer relations predominate in the United States. This applies not only to business and property, but also to services such as medicine and housing. It can even

apply within families, as numerous contested divorce settle-
ments and custody disputes testify.

The vast majority of the resulting civil cases, which make up
the bulk of litigation in the U.S., are initiated and concluded in
the fifty state court systems (which also deal with most criminal cases). Very few of these find their way through appeal to
the state high courts, and a tiny proportion of these are in turn
appealed to the U.S. Supreme Court. Nonetheless, many of the
Supreme Court's most important decisions do originate in the
state systems. Additionally, the Court (Court and Supreme
Court will subsequently be used interchangeably) has appellate jurisdiction over cases involving federal law which originate in the ninety U.S. district courts and reach the Supreme
Court via the twelve U.S. Courts of Appeal. So the Court is the
final court of appeal for the whole U.S. system. But the Court's
importance does not stem so much from this status as from its
power of judicial review. This is the second reason why the
courts are so prominent in the U.S. It is also easily the most
important reason for the political role of the courts. Although
not explicitly established in the Constitution, judicial review,
or the power to declare any law or action of Congress or the
president unconstitutional, was asserted by the Supreme
Court as early as 1803.[2] It also enables the Court to establish the
constitutionality of all state laws as well as the decisions of state
high courts. Armed with this weapon, the Court has at least
the theoretical power to veto literally any political decision. In
reality, its power is much more limited. In this chapter we shall
analyse these limits to judicial power and attempt to explain
why it is that the Supreme Court's influence has apparently
fluctuated so dramatically over the years. We will also discuss
how social fragmentation and the general politicization of
American society have created a much more complex and
demanding judicial policy-making environment. Indeed, it
may be that the Supreme Court *cannot* now play the role of constitutional arbiter without arousing fierce controversy.

The Court as Policy-Maker

As political actors, courts are quite different from legislatures
and executives. Judges are rarely elected. The nine U.S.

Supreme Court justices are appointed for life by the president, subject to the advice and consent of the Senate. So although the other branches are involved in selecting justices, their control is indirect. Once appointed, the justices are free from all those immediate political pressures which are a constant source of worry for elected officials. But the difference is much more fundamental than this. Politicians set out to please the public by identifying with certain ideas or specific policies that constituents support. Whether appealing to the public's baser instincts or to its more noble sentiments, politicians are very much in the business of selling themselves. Judges are not. Instead, their point of reference is something above mere interests and ideologies. The Constitution is not a partisan document but the revered, definitive guide to relationships between governments and between the state and the citizen in the United States. As such, judges must, as far as possible, appear to be above politics and interests. Now it is quite plainly the case that the Supreme Court cannot in fact be above politics. When deliberating on the constitutional status of slavery, the proper role of the federal government in regulating the economy, or the personal veracity of a president, it has been right in the thick of political controversy. Indeed, there has hardly been a time when it has not been a source of controversy. In one crucial sense, however, there must be a limit to the political role of the courts: their effectiveness depends on their authority rather than on the exercise of power. Courts lack bureaucracies, armies or police forces. Without these, they depend on the other branches to enforce their decisions. Should the Supreme Court step over the line and hand down decisions that are simply unacceptable to major sections of society supported by the other branches, it will lose its legitimacy and, ultimately, its special status. This effectively happened in 1857 in the famous *Dred Scott* case, when, by declaring the Missouri compromise extending slavery north of the Mason–Dixon line unconstitutional, the Court sanctioned the extension of slavery to the territories. Ultimately, Congress and the president could not accept this, and the decision helped precipitate the Civil War. It took the passage of the Thirteenth and Fourteenth Amendments abolishing slavery and providing all citizens 'equal protection of the laws' to overturn the Court after the war. Since then the Court has come close to similar confrontations, but has never been openly ignored in the way it was during the Civil War.

Legal scholars have searched long and hard for principles which might define the precise political role of the Court. However, the search is almost certainly in vain, for no matter what individual justices may write in their legal opinions, the limits to the political role of the Court are primarily determined by the prevailing political climate. In other words, expediency rather than adherence to the highest judicial principles often decides the Court's stance. For example, in 1946 the Court refused to uphold the plea by a Northwestern University political scientist that the Illinois state legislature had deliberately failed to draw up its congressional constituencies on a fair (i.e. equal) basis. For forty years the constituencies had remained unchanged and were therefore grossly malapportioned (re-apportionment is the American term for congressional constituency redistricting). The Court argued, however, that this was 'a political question', and that 'courts ought not to enter this political thicket'.[3] Less than twenty years later, the Court reversed itself, and in two landmark decisions, *Baker* v. *Carr* (1962) and *Reynolds* v. *Sims* (1964), held that mathematical equality in state and congressional districts was required. Similar examples of an issue being political at one point but not at another could be cited. Of course the political salience of issues does change over time, and the courts cannot be expected to discount this. But any claim that the Supreme Court can ever be 'above politics' is clearly unrealistic. Instead the justices are obliged to make decisions that sometimes have profound political consequences – while being ever aware that arousing fierce controversy will undermine their authority. As we shall see, the Court has found it increasingly difficult to walk this political tightrope in recent years.

The actual decision-making mechanisms of the Court both help and hinder this political balancing act. As with all higher courts, the Supreme Court decides which cases it hears on appeal. By granting *certiorari* the Court accepts a case or appeal from a lower court (*certiorari* literally means making the details of the case 'more certain'). In some instances, the constitutional issues raised by the case are so important and pressing that the Court has to review it. Such was the situation in the above mentioned *Dred Scott* case, as it was in 1971 when, very quickly, the Court decided that *The New York Times* was constitutionally entitled to publish the Pentagon Papers containing confidential details on the conduct of the Vietnam War.[4] More typically, the Court waits until the issue which the case raises is generally salient and in need of clarification. Obviously this is a subjective exercise. Four of the nine justices have to agree to grant *certiorari* and individual judges almost always have conflicting views on what should be heard and what not. Such an appellate process gives scope for considerable interest-group activity. During the 1940s and 1950s, for example, the National Association for the Advancement of Colored People (N.A.A.C.P.) filed numerous cases in federal district courts claiming that southern governments, school boards and individuals were denying Blacks protection under the Fourteenth Amendment. Eventually, the Court reviewed certain key cases, most notably in the area of school segregation. The American Civil Liberties Union conducted a similar campaign over criminal procedural rights in the 1960s, and most recently the pro-life anti-abortion campaign has been flooding the federal courts with suits challenging the Supreme Court's 1973 decision *Roe* v. *Wade*.

Once a case is granted *certiorari*, the justices hear written and oral arguments and then hold a closed conference to decide the case. During such sessions the position of the justices emerges, and one justice is assigned the task of writing the Opinion of the Court. When one of the nine justices is absent, in the event of a tie (4–4) the decision of the lower court stands. The Opinion of the Court is the decision that counts, but the paths to that decision may vary. Some justices will only *concur* in the decision, or will argue the case on different grounds even though they agree with the outcome. Others will disagree with the opinion and will formally state their reasons for doing so in a dissenting opinion. In some instances these dissenting opinions are highly significant and can form the basis for later majority opinions. For example, during the 1920s and 1930s Justices

Louis Brandeis and Oliver Wendell Holmes frequently dissented in civil-liberties cases. Later, during the 1960s their dissents were cited in cases extending rights to persons accused of engaging in subversive activities. Similarly, Hugo Black, a champion of individual freedom during the 1940s and 1950s, dissented from what he saw as the anti-libertarian decisions of the Court. But during the 1960s he was the architect of several famous decisions on criminal procedural rights in which his former dissents were translated into the majority opinion.

Clearly it is misleading to talk in terms of 'the Court', for its decisions are the product of the individual opinions of nine men and women. Some of the Court's political difficulties stem from this fact. Coherence and consistency, which are so important in the law, are difficult to achieve if individual justices seriously disagree among themselves. Nonetheless, we are used to naming courts after the incumbent chief justice, hence the 'Warren Court' or the 'Burger Court', implying some unity of purpose. Sometimes this exists – at least in terms of a particular position being supported by a majority of the justices. What principles do, in fact, guide the decisions of the justices? We can divide the answer into two parts. First, almost all justices exercise a degree of self-restraint, that is they assume that existing laws are constitutional. It takes an exceptional case or the accumulation of considerable pressure before they go so far as to declare a federal law unconstitutional – although there is a greater tendency to proclaim on the constitutionality of state and local ordinances (Table 15). In all instances justices will prefer to argue cases on procedural grounds or will modify law through statutory interpretations. This said, Table 15 shows that the propensity to use the power of judicial review has changed considerably through history. In part this reflects the increasing number of cases filed throughout the court system which require resolution. But it also reflects changes in judicial philosophy. The Court was more self-restrained or passive during the early nineteenth century than it is today. The second factor which guides judicial decision-making is, therefore, how individual justices see their role. Although it is common to characterize judicial philosophies in terms of a passive–active continuum,

this can be misleading. Activism can lead to conservative or
liberal outcomes, as can passivity. For example, before the

TABLE 15

*Provisions of federal and state laws and local ordinances
held unconstitutional by the Supreme Court,
1790–1979**

Period	Federal (number)	State and Local (number)
1790–99	0	0
1800–09	1	1
1810–19	0	7
1820–29	0	8
1830–39	0	3
1840–49	0	9
1850–59	1	7
1860–69	4	23
1870–79	8	37
1880–89	4	45
1890–99	5	36
1900–09	9	38
1910–19	5	118
1920–29	15	140
1930–39	13	91
1940–49	2	58
1950–59	4	69
1960–69	18	140
1970–79	16	177
Totals	105	1,007

Source: Adapted from Lawrence Baum, *The Supreme Court* (Washington, DC: Congressional Quarterly Press, 1981) Tables 5.3 and 5.4.

* Through 1977 Term.

Second World War the White, Taft and Hughes Courts (1910–
41) were active in defending corporate interests against the
federal government. Very conservative interpretations of the
interstate commerce clause and the due process provision
of the Fourteenth Amendment[5] led to decisions invalidating

federal attempts to regulate and later to control the corporate
and banking worlds. This was very different from the activism
of the Warren Court, which in its liberal interpretation of the
Fourteenth Amendment and the Bill of Rights greatly
advanced civil rights and liberties during the 1950s and
1960s. Very generally, those justices, often labelled positivists, whose main point of reference is the actual wording of
the Constitution will produce more controversial opinions
than those judges who attempt to act as arbiters between competing interests in society. Put another way, positivists
believe that, whatever changes are occurring in society or
whatever the prevailing political climate, the principles represented by the Constitution are timeless and inviolate. Of
course, they may be open to varying interpretation – after all,
what is free speech, or an unreasonable search and seizure?
But when applied, principles must be applied consistently
through time. Hence Justice Hugo Black, one of the most
prominent members of the Stone, Vinson and Warren Courts
(1941–69), adhered resolutely to libertarian values, even
when the Court was handing down clearly anti-libertarian
decisions on such matters as alleged Communist subversion.
Positivism of this sort will lead to an active and controversial
Court, which can be liberal (as with the later Warren Court)
or conservative (as with the pre-1941 Courts). Those justices
who see the Court's main job as balancing different interests
in society are less devoted to the letter of the Constitution.
For them, the vagueness of the document leaves sufficient
room for constant re-interpretation. As society and politics
change, so can the Court. Between 1941 and the mid 1950s,
just such a philosophy dominated the Court. Self-restraint
and accommodation of the prevailing balance of political
power were the defining features of successive Supreme
Court decisions. Under the intellectual, if not formal, leadership of the formidable Justice Felix Frankfurter, the Court
assiduously avoided conflict with the federal government on
economic policy, federalism, civil rights and civil liberties.
On economic questions this led to liberal decisions (the prevailing balance being in favour of government intervention).
On individual-rights questions this led to conservative outcomes, as the Court implicitly endorsed the internment of the

Japanese Americans and did nothing to prevent the harassment of supposed left-wing subversives.[6]

Courts are rarely wholly passive or active, however. Often the justices are split between competing philosophies. Moreover, since the 1960s it has become increasingly difficult for the Supreme Court to take a consistently passive or self-restrained position. There are two major reasons for this. First, the pressure on the Court to make decisions has increased. Americans are not only much more litigious than they used to be, what we have called the new populism has also led them to be increasingly prone to appeal to basic constitutional rights on a wide range of issues. This has resulted in an increase in the number of cases filed: from under 1,000 before the Second World War to about 2,000 in 1960 and around 4,000 in the mid-1980s. Few of these cases result in a written opinion; most are quickly dismissed. Even so, the range of subjects and issues involved is vast. Modern justices have to deal with everything from abortion to electronic bugging, consumer-safety regulations and the proper constitutional role of the president in relation to Congress. With such an agenda it is very difficult to remain consistently self-restrained. Second, as earlier chapters have outlined, American society has become increasingly fragmented over the last twenty years. Today's political issues often cut across more traditional allegiances. Consensus is correspondingly more difficult to achieve. This applies both to what are normally understood as questions of 'issue politics' (abortion, environmental and consumer protection, equal rights and so on), and to more fundamental questions affecting the separation of powers and the proper division of functions between state and federal governments. It is extraordinarily difficult for the Court to remain neutral or passive when feelings on these issues run so high, or when the issues involve fundamental conflicts of interest. For example, in the celebrated *U.S.* v. *Nixon* case in 1974, the Court was asked to deliberate on the constitutionality of the president's attempts to withhold the White House tapes from a federal court; the decision had to be either for or against the president. A compromise was not an option. In a very different context, *any* compromise on a question such as abortion or the publication of obscene articles is going to outrage (and indeed has outraged) large sections of the American public. We will return to these questions in more detail later.

A truly self-restrained Court is, therefore, an impossibility in the 1980s. And just as passivity is unattainable, so is a coherent policy of activism. This is all too obvious from the above examples. There are simply too many conflicting interests intent on seeking redress from the courts for the Supreme Court to be anything close to universally admired. However, even though something approaching total coherence is unattainable, scope continues to exist for decision-making which is constructive, logical and clear in the guidance it provides for the other branches and for lower courts. How has the Burger Court measured up to this task?

The Burger Years: A Court under Pressure

From the appointment of Warren Burger as chief justice in 1969 until about 1975 it was common among liberals to bemoan the passing of the liberal Warren Court and to condemn the new conservatism of Burger. Such a response was not at all surprising. Richard Nixon had been fortunate in making no less than four appointments to the Court in just three years. All were at least moderately conservative by reputation. The Warren Court had been unequivocally liberal in its later years. Few expected the Burger Court to continue in the same tradition. Yet during this period, the Court did little more than modify or clarify many of the Warren decisions. By the mid 1980s a clearer picture had emerged. In essence, the Burger Court has not been consistently more conservative than the Warren Court. It is simply different. It has certainly not been self-restrained. Indeed it has made some truly momentous decisions. We can divide its decisions into three broad categories, in each of which something approaching a pattern exists.

On the 'Warren issues' the Burger Court has generally retreated from a libertarian position

The Warren Court established its liberal reputation in three broad areas: civil rights, criminal procedural rights and reapportionment. In all three areas the Burger Court has ended what was a rapid extension of individual rights, although it has by no means directly reversed the Warren decisions. In the case of reapportionment the Court has modified the strict mathematical equality between the size of districts, which the Warren Court implicitly required in its famous *Baker* v. *Carr* (1962) and *Reynolds* v. *Sims* (1964) decisions. In *Mahan* v. *Howell* (1973) a deviation of 16.4 per cent was tolerated, and generally the Court has allowed considerably less than mathematical equality where political questions of community and convenience are deemed paramount. So, although 'one person, one vote' remains the major objective, this can be compromised on a pragmatic basis.

Much more important changes have occurred in the area of criminal procedural law. Warren was responsible for a number of rulings greatly extending the protection afforded arrested persons, which were real landmarks. In *Gideon* v. *Wainwright* (1963), the right to a counsel irrespective of ability to pay was established. *Mapp* v. *Ohio* (1961) greatly strengthened the exclusionary rule, or the extent to which police could use evidence discovered during 'search and seizure'. *Miranda* v. *Arizona* (1966) required the police to read suspects their rights (essentially the right to remain silent) before arrest. In the latter two instances (and a number of others), the Burger Court has qualified these rulings. The greatest controversy has surrounded the exclusionary rule, which conservatives have long condemned as a criminals' charter. Most anger has been inspired by the apparent need for the police almost always to obtain proper search warrants specifically designed to help discover evidence related to the alleged offence. Three questions are raised here. Under what circumstances must a warrant be issued? Must the police believe the warrant to be correct? And once in a property, can evidence unrelated to the alleged crime be used in connection with prosecutions for other crimes? The Court has widened police power to stop and search suspects and to search automobiles without a warrant.[7] It has decided that even if a warrant is defective (not properly drawn up), the evidence resulting from its use is admissible provided that the police *believed at the time* the warrant was correct.[8] In 1984 the

Court decided that the exclusionary rule could not apply to a prison cell.[9] Perhaps most significant was another 1984 ruling, which allowed the use of evidence that 'ultimately or inevitably would have been discovered by legal means'. The case actually involved the discovery of a body following an illegal interrogation of a suspect.[10] It would, of course, have been patently absurd not to allow this evidence to be used. But the ruling was sufficiently general to widen the police power significantly.

Finally, the *Miranda* ruling has been weakened by a decision that an arrest can be made without the suspect's rights being read, in 'the interests of public safety'. Again, the actual circumstances surrounding this case (the arrest of a suspect wearing an empty shoulder holster where the policeman asked him first where the gun was and then advised him of his rights) seem entirely to justify the ruling. Libertarians retorted that it would establish a much broader precedent for arrests with little protection for suspects unaware of their right to remain silent.

What of civil rights, the area for which the Warren Court's activism was most widely known? In a recent article, Paul Brest noted that:

The Warren Court really had it pretty easy. By 1953, when the new chief justice assumed office, the overt racism of the Deep South was no longer an American dilemma, but was widely perceived as a national moral disaster. *Brown* v. *Board of Education* was a decision whose time was long overdue . . . It was the egregious nature of discrimination in the 1950s and 1960s that made life so easy for the Warren Court. The underlying claim in almost every case was that someone . . . was currently and intentionally discriminating against Blacks for no other reason than that they were Black.[11]

Brest goes on to point out that the Burger Court has had to deal with much more complex questions, including having to distinguish between legally sanctioned, or *de jure*, segregation and 'naturally evolving', or *de facto*, segregation. Affirmative action, or attempts to correct a general pattern of past discrimination rather than simply providing redress for specific acts of overt discrimination, has also figured prominently on the Court's agenda. In broad terms, the Burger Court has consistently condemned de jure segregation, but has held in most instances that de facto segregation is permissible. It is not, however, quite as simple as this. In *Swann* v. *Charlotte Mecklenberg* (1971) the Court sanctioned busing within a district which had a long-established history of segregation. In *Keys* v. *Denver School District No. 1* (1971) no legally mandated segregation existed, but the schoolboard had been *conscious* of race when building schools and deciding catchment areas. As Justice Brennan put it in this case, 'the differentiating factor between de jure segregation and so-called de facto segregation . . . is *purpose* or *intent* to segregate.'[12] In this and subsequent decisions, the Court has reiterated its commitment to finding only de jure segregation unconstitutional, while striving hard to end segregation in schools. Although liberals have condemned this policy as a retreat from Warren's radicalism, it can hardly be construed as such, because Warren never had to confront the complexities of de jure versus de facto segregation. The same analysis could be applied to the later Burger Court, with the qualification that sympathy with the idea of an extension of civil rights has waned. Hence in the celebrated 1978 case *Regents of the University of California* v. *Bakke*, the Court found that a quota of sixteen places out of one hundred reserved for Blacks and other minorities at the University of California at Davis Medical School was a violation of a qualified white applicant's rights under the equal protection clause of the Fourteenth Amendment. The Court was at pains to emphasize that this condemnation of reverse or positive discrimination applied only to the specific circumstances of the case. Since then, in *Steel Workers Union* v. *Weber* (1979) the Court has ruled that *voluntary* quotas in employment, which advance broad objectives beyond mere racial balance, are permissible. However, in 1984 the Court appeared to go one step further in the direction of restricting reverse discrimination policies. The case involved the Memphis, Tennessee, Fire Department, which laid off white firemen with seniority in order to implement an affirmative-action programme. The Court unequivocally rejected the programme, declaring that discrimination applied only when individuals were 'actual victims' rather than merely members of minorities or disadvantaged groups.[13] While there is no doubt that the Court has failed to continue the almost evangelical devotion to civil rights of the Warren Court, it has not reversed any of the landmark civil-rights decisions of the 1960s. As stressed earlier, it has had to deal with a much more complex set of issues, as indeed it has in other policy areas.

On 'conscience issues' the Court has been active but inconsistent

Few decisions of the U.S. Supreme Court have aroused more hostility than the 1973 Roe v. Wade opinion on abortion. Abortion had been a controversial issue for some time before the decision – in part because a number of states (notably California and New York) had legalized the practice, and in part because a few had actually legislated to ban it. Dozens of suits were being filed for and against, and eventually the Court had to deliberate. Its 1973 decision followed an extraordinary process of bargaining among the justices with Justice Blackmun proposing one formula and Justice Marshall another.[14] What was eventually agreed was a compromise which prohibited states from banning abortion in the first trimester (three months) of pregnancy but which prohibited abortion in the third trimester. Abortion in the second would be permitted on medical grounds. Roe v. Wade has been criticized because of the apparent arbitrariness of the three-trimester division. Justice Blackmun had argued that the state (government) has no interest in the foetus until it is 'viable'. But what is viable is obviously a matter of medical and moral controversy. Later, in 1977, the Court handed down a further decision which clarified little. In Maher v. Roe the Court declared that the states did not have to provide medical help for women requiring abortions. The inconsistency here is that if aid is often provided for childbirth and other medical matters, why not for abortion? Poor women, the critics argued, would be the victims of this decision.

Since 1973, the political salience of the abortion question has increased enormously as the 'pro-life' lobby has mobilized opinion in opposition to Roe v. Wade. Blaming the Court for this wave of populist sentiment is unfair, of course. Any decision liberalizing abortion would have provoked a reaction. But the Court's inconsistency over state spending has also angered the liberals. In this sense, the abortion issue is a good example of how the Court *cannot* win when society is deeply divided over an issue. A decision to allow the states to decide would have been almost as controversial, with poor people's advocates and women's rights groups protesting loudly. In fact in other 'conscience issue' areas such as capital punishment and obscenity, the Court has left matters to state and local governments, but the controversies have raged on.

In *Furman* v. *Georgia* (1972) the Court held that *as presently administered* the death penalty was a 'cruel and unusual' punishment. Inconsistencies in the application of the law rather than the penalty itself rendered existing laws unconstitutional. In 1976 the Court's emphasis changed, as it sanctioned the particular rules governing capital punishment in three states. Since then the death penalty has been applied in several states – at first sparingly and only following prolonged legal battles – but in recent years much more frequently. So, although discretion has been left to the states, the Supreme Court remains involved. Capital convictions are still sometimes overturned as cruel and unusual punishments, even though the Court's stance in this area has slowly grown more conservative and less pragmatic over the years.

What might be called a confused pragmatism applies in other conscience areas, including obscenity and religious instruction in schools.[15] Put simply, the Court cannot be pragmatic and popular on issues involving moral absolutes. Opponents of abortion or capital punishment see no middle way (and in practical terms there often is no middle way). Even though most Americans may broadly agree with the Court's rulings, as is the case with both these questions, vociferous minorities ensure that the issues remain highly political. Dozens of suits continue to be filed in these and other conscience areas, and the Court has declared its intimate involvement in all of them. The Burger Court has not washed its hands of these questions in the way that an earlier Court effectively did over Communist subversion in the 1940s and 1950s. As a result, further potentially momentous decisions on abortion, capital punishment, obscenity and the state's role in religion can be expected.

On questions affecting fundamental political powers the Court has been active and controversial

When, in 1974, the Court ordered President Richard Nixon to release the White House tapes to a lower federal court, almost everybody hailed the decision as proper and necessary. Activism of this sort, which effectively prevented a major constitutional crisis, was certainly justified. Since then, however, the Burger Court has extended its activism to three other political areas. In all three fierce controversy has resulted. Perhaps the most celebrated case is *Buckley* v. *Valeo*, which struck down certain key features of the 1974 Campaign Finance Act. Some restrictions on contributions to election campaigns were upheld but, crucially, limits imposed on individual candidates' own contributions were invalidated. Few dispute that a major consequence of this decision has been a further weakening of political parties and a strengthening of personalized campaigns launched by wealthy candidates.

More arcane, but no less important, was the striking down of the legislative veto in 1983. This decision (*Immigration and Nationalization Service* v. *Chadha*) was extraordinary in its potential scope. No less than 200 statutory provisions controlling the regulatory agencies were implicitly invalidated. The legislative veto is a procedural device attached to statutes delegating discretionary regulating powers to agencies. When formulating these powers, agencies are required to submit them within a specified time period to Congress for approval. For example, in 1981 the Federal Trade Commission (F.T.C.) issued a regulation requiring used-car dealers to place stickers on cars showing defects and the condition of the warranty. This regulation was subject to a legislative veto which Congress subsequently applied. Congress's motives in employing the device were simply to extend control and accountability to areas where detailed statute law would be inappropriate. Indeed, it is a good example of how an overworked legislature has tried to come to terms with the size and scope of government. Unable to legislate every detail of the law, some discretion has to be left to the executive. The veto is not subject to presidential veto but instead can be sanctioned by a simple (one house) or concurrent (House and Senate) resolution. It was this provision which offended the Court and led to the conclusion that the veto was an unconstitutional incursion by Congress into the executive power. However, if the Court is to declare on every such ambiguity in the present-day relationship between president and Congress, this would soon lead to a dangerous political inflexibility. As Michael Horan has noted,

A rigidity is attributed to the separation of powers [by the *Chadha* case] which Madison and the post-New Deal Court warned against. Repetitive citations to what the Chief Justice calls 'explicit and unambiguous provision of the Constitution' (which they clearly are not) are more patronizing than edifying. A future generation of jurists may yet appraise *Chadha* in the same way as the present generation looks upon such rulings as *Schechter* [one of the cases striking down a New Deal law in the 1930s] as reactionary rather than progressive.[16]

Finally, and again reminiscent of the 1930s Courts, the Burger Court has re-entered the political jungle of federal–state economic relations. In *Garcia* v. *San Antonio Metropolitan Transit Authority* in early 1985, the Court ruled (by five to four) that a federal-government law could help regulate the wages of San Antonio, Texas, bus workers. There is nothing remarkable in this, of course. However, writing the Opinion of the Court, Justice Henry Blackmun did not invoke the commerce clause or any provision of the Constitution as such. Instead he said that what the states could or could not do depended not on any constitutionally protected right but on what 'inhered principally in the workings of the national government itself'.[17] In other words, federal–state relations were essentially politically, rather than constitutionally, defined. Given the great fiscal and political power of the federal government, this decision is tantamount to providing Congress and president with a virtual *carte blanche* to order the states to do almost anything. Of course, in economic affairs the federal government has long been dominant, but no Court has enshrined this *de facto* supremacy in what

amounts to a constitutional abandonment of federalism. It
remains to be seen whether the *San Antonio* case will pro-
voke a crisis in federal–state relations or not. One thing is
sure: this decision by a Court dominated by justices
appointed by Republican presidents flies in the face of the
Reagan administration's efforts to devolve power to the states.
What all this adds up to is a Court characterized by what has
been called a 'rootless activism'. It is quite wrong simply to
label the Court 'conservative', for while it has eschewed the
consistent libertarianism of the Warren years, it has sometimes handed down liberal decisions. More importantly, it
has spread its brief to encompass areas and issues far broader
than those dealt with by Warren. Legal scholars have been
quick to condemn the resulting pattern of cases as bad jurisprudence. In some instances – and especially in cases dealing
with the division of powers among the different branches of
government – the Court has been unnecessarily active and
even pedantic. But in other areas, notably civil rights and
the conscience issues, whatever the Court decides will arouse
controversy. This is a serious matter, for when courts attract
public opprobrium, their authority and ultimately their legitimacy are threatened. As Table 16 shows, public satisfaction
with the courts has deteriorated substantially during the
Burger years. Admittedly, this question was directed at the
court system as a whole rather than at the Supreme Court as
such. Other federal courts are profoundly influenced by the
highest authority, however, and we have little reason to
believe that recent Supreme Court decisions have reassured
the public. It is more likely that there is a general sense that
the courts are increasingly failing to set clear moral examples
for society, and that the Supreme Court has done little to
reverse this trend. To state this is not somehow to identify
with the Christian right-wingers or with those convinced that
the judiciary is undermining 'traditional American values'.
During the 1960s, the Court's criminal-law decisions were
deeply unpopular. Most were coherent and consistent, however, and they did, at least, please libertarians. Today the
Court pleases almost nobody. The Burger Court's rootless
activism raises the question of how the courts can be controlled, and whether, given the complexity of modern policy-

making, the other branches can mobilize to curtail the power
of the judiciary.

Judicial Power: How Far Can the Courts Go?

As previously suggested, the greatest single constraint on
judicial power is lack of enforcement powers. When the other
branches and most of the public oppose the Supreme Court,
as in 1857 and 1937, there is little, ultimately, the Court can
do about it. In the *Dred Scott* case, a constitutional amendment was necessary after the war to cancel the Court's
opinion. On very few occasions is the amendment power
used, however. The most significant other examples are the

TABLE 16

*Public perceptions of permissiveness of the courts as a
source of the country's problems (percentages)*

Major Cause of Our Problems	1973	1974	1975	1977	1979	1982
Lack of good leadership	49	57	54	34	52	44
Permissiveness in the courts	39	47	51	50	51	53
Permissiveness of parents	43	40	43	47	42	43
Selfishness, people not thinking of others	51	47	46	52	50	50
Wrongdoing in government	51	64	56	47	51	50
Radical attempts to force change	19	21	26	19	19	20
Growing conservatism	6	7	6	5	7	10
Too much emphasis on money and materialism	46	40	36	42	41	41
Too much technology	6	8	8	9	9	7
A letdown in moral values	50	53	53	57	56	57
Too much commitment to other nations in the world	48	54	52	38	49	51
Too little interest in other nations in the world	6	5	5	6	7	9

Source: Roper Report, Roper Organization, various months and
years.

Sixteenth Amendment (1913), which sanctioned a graduated federal income tax and overturned an 1895 Court ruling, and the Twenty-sixth Amendment (1971), which overturned the Court's 1970 ruling that the vote could not be extended to eighteen-year-olds. Less dramatic means of control are available to the president and Congress, including control over appointments and over the size and jurisdiction of the Court.

The appointment power is potentially a formidable weapon in the hands of presidents. How it works out in practice, however, depends on a number of factors, including luck. Presidents have the power to appoint all federal judges, not just Supreme Court justices, and through appointments can attempt to fill the federal judiciary with men and women who think as they do. Easily the most obvious cue available to presidents is party, and close to 100 per cent of recent appointees have been supporters of the incumbent president's party. As we know, however, each party embraces a wide cross-section of the political spectrum. A southern Democrat is often a very different animal from a northern Democrat. Even among Republicans, the spread is wide. Presidents can attempt to overcome this by appointing judges who are known to be sympathetic to their policies, whatever their party associations. Ronald Reagan, for example, has made very serious efforts to move the federal judiciary to the right. As Table 17 shows, he has been much more reluctant than Jimmy Carter (and even Nixon and Ford) to appoint Blacks to U.S. federal district courts. Blacks are rarely conservative in judicial philosophy. Jane Wilcox of the Justice Department has commented that '. . . in the last four years we were very successful as far as putting on the bench judges we believe were qualified as well as being believers in judicial restraint [was concerned].'[18] 'Judicial restraint' is, of course, a coded phrase for conservative decision-making. Lower-court appointments are important because it is at this level that most cases are resolved. The federal appeal courts, in particular, help set the agenda for the Supreme Court.

By 1986 Ronald Reagan had made only one appointment to the Supreme Court, Sandra Day O'Connor. She was the first woman to be nominated and turned out to be consistently conservative. With five of the nine justices over seventy-five

TABLE 17

Presidential appointments to the federal courts by ethnicity and sex, 1964–84 (percentages)

	Johnson	Nixon	Ford	Carter	Reagan
U.S. court of appeals					
Women	2.5	0.0	0.0	19.6	9.1
Blacks	5.0	0.0	0.0	16.1	3.0
Hispanics	*	*	*	3.6	3.0
U.S. district court					
Women	1.6	0.6	1.9	14.1	9.2
Blacks	3.3	2.8	5.8	14.1	0.8
Hispanics	2.5	1.1	1.9	6.8	5.4

Source: *Congressional Quarterly Weekly Reports*, 8 December 1984, p. 3,075.

* Data not available.

years old in 1985 it is possible that Reagan will be given the opportunity to make further appointments during his second term. Senatorial review of nominations can be a constraint, as the ignominious rejection of two of Richard Nixon's nominees, Harold Carswell and Clement Haynsworth, showed. But the criteria employed by the Senate are not political. As with the American Bar Association, which assesses all federal nominations, quality is the first criterion. Carswell and Haynsworth were incompetent and, in the case of Carswell, racist. Since then a number of conservative but higher-quality jurists have been appointed to the Court. Presidential preferences are more likely to be limited by the complete absence of control they can exercise once justices are appointed. Earl Warren, a Republican appointee of President Eisenhower, eventually became synonymous with an unambiguously liberal Court. In more recent years, another Republican appointee, Justice John Paul Stevens, has turned out to be one of the more liberal members of the Court, and Henry Blackmun, although having been conservative in many cases, has also written some of the Court's most active, even radical, decisions. What is almost certainly more important than any of these points is the increasing complexity of the Court's agenda. As we have seen, the Court cannot stay completely out of politics when the issues are as complex as they are today. No president can predict the precise nature of these issues and how they are likely to change over time. No matter who is appointed to the Court, some unpredictability and controversy will remain.

Congress's power over the Court is, theoretically at least, much greater than the president's. Article III defines the original jurisdiction of the Court and then goes on, 'In all other cases before mentioned, the Supreme Court shall have appellate jurisdiction, both as to law and fact, with such exceptions, and under such regulations, as the Congress shall make'. Armed with this provision, legislative opponents of the Court's decisions have repeatedly introduced jurisdiction-stripping bills into Congress. In recent years these have increased, as right-wing opponents of Court rulings on abortion, school prayers and busing have grown more vocal. During 1981 and 1982, for example, no less than thirty such bills were initiated.[19] So far, none has been successful – mainly because most members of Congress are loath to assert what is a formidable constitutional power. Indeed, some dispute that Congress has such a power – especially when it comes to curbing the Court's role in protecting rights. Most experts agree, however, that Congress could act in this area (it actually did so in the post-Civil War period), just as it could with respect to the size of the Court. So Roosevelt's famous 1937 Court-packing plan, when he proposed that Congress increase the size of the Court to fifteen, appointing one new justice for every incumbent member over the age of seventy, was almost certainly constitutional. It was highly unpopular, however, but not because Congress agreed with the Court's inflexible contempt for New Deal legislation. Rather, Congress feared that a delicate constitutional balance between the three branches would be upset in the name of political expediency.

Finally, the judicial system itself constrains the Supreme Court, for not only does the Court lack a bureaucracy and a police force, it also has limited control over other 'inferior' courts. Very often the district courts are ordered by the Supreme Court to implement decisions. In the civil-rights area, for example, what began in 1954 as an apparently unambiguous injunction to desegregate schools 'with all deliberate speed' was at first virtually ignored by southern district courts and later transformed into very specific instructions as to how desegregation should occur.[20] More recently district courts have had to grapple with the detailed implementation of desegregation in housing, and with instructions on school prayers and criminal procedural rights. In all these areas, the lower courts sometimes cannot (or will not) carry out the spirit of the Supreme Court's decisions. As a result, the meaning of the original opinion is blurred and further clarification is necessary, following yet more lengthy litigation.

Conclusions: A Dangerous Court or a Court Confused?

The Court has been labelled dangerous by a variety of interests and individuals in the post-war period. From southern bumper stickers urging the impeachment of Earl Warren, to Jesse Helms's 1984 threat that 'There is more than one way for Congress to provide a check on arrogant Supreme Court justices who routinely distort the Constitution',[21] the radical right has been almost continuously outraged. But liberals too have been worried by what they see as the gradual erosion of those individual rights established during the Warren era. As already argued, any degree of activism on the part of the modern Court will arouse controversy. Put simply, although the U.S. does have a written constitution and a Bill of Rights, the interpretation of the basic document is open to enormous variation. The most fundamental institutional relationships – those between Congress and president, state and federal government – are ambiguous. Political and economic power rather than arcane judicial definition has been the final arbiter through history, even though the courts have sometimes reinforced or weakened the position of one institution or another. The equally important relationship between state and citizen is also open to widely varying constitutional interpretation. Having done little to protect the individual against the state in the century and a half before 1955, the Court has slowly but surely extended individual rights since then. But even here much ambiguity remains, and we have yet to witness a period equivalent to the two post-World War 'red scares', when the Court complied with a Congress, president and public opinion united against individual rights. The true test of the Court's defence of freedom is when it stands alone against other forces in society, including public opinion. When, as during the 1980s, opinion and institution are divided, the Court's role becomes both crucial and difficult. This applies in every sphere of public policy, from the most basic questions of the separation of powers to the thorny conscience issues such as abortion and capital punishment. Add to this the fact that there are simply more issues on the policy agenda today and it is easy to see why the Court is sometimes accused of being muddled or confused.

What of the incumbent justices? A priori we should not expect them to be activist. Most were appointed by conservative presidents – or at least those who believed in judicial restraint. Neither should we expect them to be exceptional jurists and intellectuals. Such men (and women) have been rare in American history, and Richard Nixon (responsible for four of the nine 1986 incumbents) was not known for favouring great intellectuals. In reality, the intellectual quality of the mid 1980s Court is not high, but the Court is activist. As has been argued, a major reason for this is the peculiar nature of late-twentieth-century American society, which puts an almost impossible burden on the Supreme Court. It has become the final arbiter between irreconcilable interests; the institution held responsible for compromising on what, for many, are moral absolutes. As successor to the remarkable Warren Court, it has had to refine and clarify the enormously difficult problems that the extension of individual rights have raised. Small wonder that it is accused of muddled thinking. In effect, the Court is a victim of the rapid politicization and nationalization of American society. Government now does very much more than it used to, and in a litigious society this has greatly increased the adjudicatory role of the courts. Social fragmentation and issue politics have made this role even more burdensome. As a result, the Court, rather than being above politics, is very much at the centre of political debate and controversy.

CHAPTER EIGHT

Federalism and Localism:
Power to the People?

To the outsider, American federalism presents itself as something of a paradox. On the one hand, the fifty states, each with its own legal and political systems, appear to preserve a remarkable degree of separate identity. Across a wide range of criminal and civil laws every state is unique. Capital punishment exists in most states, but in thirteen it does not; in some divorce is easy to obtain – in others not. Off-track betting is now legal in several states but casino gambling is permitted in only two (Nevada and New Jersey). As much variety exists in fiscal matters. No state income tax is levied in Connecticut, even though in all of the adjacent states – many of which are very similar in other respects – state income taxes are mandatory. Sales tax variations are also wide ranging from 0 per cent (Nevada) to 7 per cent (New York). Add to this complexity very considerable *local* variations within and between states, and the system appears to be characterized by an unusual degree of political, social and economic decentralization.

On the other hand, even the most casual observer cannot fail to be struck by the remarkable homogeneity of many aspects of American life. An interstate highway (motorway) in San Diego California is identical to one in Maine or Florida. The same retail outlets, restaurants, and modern residential architecture prevail throughout the nation. The way Americans work and play – notwithstanding limitations imposed by climate – is broadly similar in every state. Claims by Americans that the pace of life is slow in the South, business-like in the Mid-west and 'zany' in California are simply not convincing when compared with the regional cultural differences in much smaller countries such as Spain, Italy or even the British Isles. Indeed, for the tourist or business traveller exposed to identical hotels, airports, highways, resorts, fast food and car-rental companies, any sense of state or local uniqueness is hard to identify. Uniformity seems to have been reinforced, moreover, by an ever more intrusive federal government. Since the 1930s federal legislation has played an increasing role in subsidizing, controlling or regulating virtually every aspect of what used to be strictly state and local government. In order to make sense of this apparent paradox it is necessary to trace the development of American federalism and of those competing traditions which have been most influential in deciding how intergovernmental relations have evolved over the years.

Centralized or Devolved Powers: The Enduring Debate

The extent of the federal government's powers was a major debating point among the founding fathers at the Constitutional Convention in Philadelphia. This had two distinct dimensions. One involved the powers of the president in relation to Congress. Although both are federal institutions, the precise balance between the two certainly concerns the states, for if Congress were ascendant, representation of the states (via territorial representation in the Senate) would be enhanced. A powerful House of Representatives would also increase the representation of local interests. Neither the supporters of Alexander Hamilton (who favoured a strong executive) nor James Madison (who wanted a stronger Congress) actually triumphed. Instead, as we know, a compromise system of checks and balances or 'separate institutions, sharing powers' was accepted. Congress was given substantial powers, however, and as was shown in Chapter Four, it has been a fragmenting and often decentralizing influence throughout American history – even though Madison himself was a centralizer rather than decentralizer. The second controversy was more directly related to federalism: to what extent should federal as opposed to state institutions be responsible for carrying out the people's wishes? As with so many aspects of the Constitution, the document gives little guidance on which level of government should do what. Congress is specifically given the power to levy taxes, regulate interstate commerce, declare war, raise armies and regulate currency and credit. But none of these powers is unambiguous. What does the regulation of interstate commerce mean, for example? Read carefully, the Constitution guarantees to the states just four things: a republican form of government, protection against invasion and domestic violence, integrity of state territorial boundaries and equal representation in the Senate. The Tenth Amendment also promises that the powers delegated to the federal government by the Constitution 'are reserved to the states respectively, or the people'. What the states *actually* do is a matter for interpretation.

Small wonder that defining state and federal power has been a matter of constant dispute, and very early in the history of the republic it assumed the status of major controversy. During the presidency of Thomas Jefferson, decentralist influences gained ground. Jefferson's yearning to keep hold of a rural, essentially pre-industrial America was translated into an emphasis on state and, especially, local power. Put simply, the more local the level of government, the more responsive and accountable it would be to the people. In most respects, Jeffersonian democracy conformed nicely to the reality of early nineteenth-century America. Federal governments did very little; state governments were generally confined to providing frameworks of law within which local governments operated. The real stuff of public policy was conducted by local authorities. It was they who were responsible for elementary education, public order, road maintenance and the few other services which governments were expected to provide. Following the tradition of the New England townships, which represented the earliest attempts at local democracy in the United States,[1] the Jeffersonians hoped to prevent the emergence of centralized political power.

Very soon, however, it became apparent that costs were associated with a largely decentralized polity and society. The competing Madisonian tradition argued that the abuse of freedom was more likely in small constituencies. Hence Madison's plea in favour of what he called the Compound Republic:

Extend the sphere, and you take in a greater variety of parties and interests; you make it less probable that a majority of the whole will have a common motive to invade the rights of other citizens or if such a motive exists, it will be more difficult for all who feel it to discover their own strength and to act in unison with each other. In the extent and proper structure of the Union, therefore, we behold a republican remedy for the diseases incident to republican government.[2]

Although Madison was writing in the context of the framing of the Constitution, his idea of the compound Republic has remained influential ever since. In sum, too much local autonomy can result in the abuse of minority rights. Ergo, the federal government should always retain a check on state power. Madison showed great prescience in his fears regarding the abuse of minority rights. Southern states resolutely defended slavery on the grounds of 'state rights' and even after the passage of the Thirteenth and Fourteenth Amendments, 'Jim Crow' laws, effectively instituting an *apartheid* regime in the South, were protected by a compliant Supreme Court under the banner of state rights. Obviously, the proper extent of federal power was central to the dispute that caused the Civil War, but in one sense this was a side issue to the question that dominated federal–state relations from 1819 to 1937: the federal government's economic powers.

The first Supreme Court cases in this area tended to favour the federal government. Hence, *McCulloch* v. *Maryland* effectively sanctioned the creation of a national bank. Chief Justice John Marshall was unequivocal in his support of national supremacy:

The states have no power, by taxation or otherwise, to retard, impede, burden, or in any manner control, the operations of the Constitutional laws enacted by Congress to carry into execution the powers vested in the general government. This, we think, is the unavoidable consequence of that supremacy which the Constitution has declared.[3]

Later, in 1824, the Marshall Court endorsed the notion of national supremacy by a liberal interpretation of the interstate commerce clause (*Gibbons* v. *Ogden* involving the right of the federal government to run a ferry between New Jersey and

New York). But this period of a slowly encroaching federal government was short-lived. The South, determined not only to uphold slavery, but also to protect its vulnerable agricultural sector from foreign competition, began to win influence in Washington and particularly in the Supreme Court under Chief Justice Taney (1836–64). No sooner was national supremacy imposed by the Civil War than state rights were once again reasserted during the last twenty years of the nineteenth century. Between 1880 and 1937 the Court repeatedly defended the states against federal economic legislation. It took a constitutional amendment (the Sixteenth in 1913) to sanction a national graduated income tax, and a major constitutional crisis (the Roosevelt Court-packing plan) to overcome the Court's determined stand against key items of New Deal legislation.

Most of the debate on the proper role of the states in relation to the federal government centred on the concept of dual sovereignty. While this is the identifying feature of federalism, no one, at least as far as the American system is concerned, is sure of what precisely it means. In theory, dual sovereignty suggests that both state and federal governments have constitutionally guaranteed powers, but these may be shared, equally or unequally. As pointed out, the Constitution provides no clear guidance on this question.[4] States righters are convinced that only in certain areas – defence, foreign policy, currency control – should the federal government dominate. In other areas of domestic policy the states should be left alone, or at least should not be dictated to by Congress and the president. Increasingly during the twentieth century the states righters have been on the defensive and the national supremacists on the ascendant. To understand why this is so it is necessary to move away from sometimes arcane legal arguments for or against federalism, towards an understanding of the American system as a complex system of intergovernmental relations based on fiscal dependence and interdependence.

The Era of Intergovernmental Dependence 1937–78

In 1937 the Supreme Court effectively capitulated to the national supremacists in the area of economic policy. From then until about 1978 the federal government played an ever greater role in virtually every aspect of state and local finances. Initially, federal grants consisted primarily of matching funds provided to finance the new welfare programmes introduced during the 1930s. Later, during the 1940s and 1950s, federal grants for urban renewal, highways, housing and other services began to appear. It was after 1960 that the dramatic rise in federal aid occurred, however. As can be seen from Table 18, grants to governments increased from 7.4 billion to 32 billion dollars between 1960 and 1978 (in constant dollars). By that year federal aid constituted some 17.4 per cent of the federal budget. Note also that aid to *individuals* increased even more sharply than aid to governments during these years, from 3.4 billion to 18.9 billion dollars. The distinction is a vital one, for grants to individuals (channelled through governments) are generally more difficult to control. Most consist of aid for the poor (*not* aid based on contributions from earnings for pensions and the like, which is generally labelled social security in the U.S.). Although unpopular with most Americans, these grants are linked to clear demographic and economic trends.

In addition to financial aid, the federal government increasingly monitored, controlled and regulated state law through new civil-rights and regulatory legislation. What accounts for the rapid rise in federal aid and control? We can identify four main reasons, one of which could be called ideological and three political or economic.

The rise of redistributive centralism

In stark contrast to the period before 1930, from 1937 there was a change in the national mood that accelerated during the 1950s and 1960s: acceptance that the states should bear the main burden of domestic policy gave way to a general perception that the states *could not* play this role. The depression had confirmed in the minds of many that the states simply could not cope. Add to this the continuing subordination of Black Americans in the southern states and the need for federal action seemed irresistible. Most importantly,

TABLE 18

Aid to state and local governments for selected fiscal years

	Year				Percentage change 1978–83
	1960	1970	1978	1983	
Aid in current dollars (billions)					
Grants-in-aid	7.0	24.0	77.9	93.0	+19.4
To governments	4.5	15.0	51.9	48.2	−7.4
To individuals	2.5	9.0	26.0	44.8	+72.3
Tax expenditures*	NA	10.8	19.3	46.8	+142.9
Interest exclusion	NA	2.3	6.1	20.4	+234.4
Tax deductibility	NA	8.5	13.2	26.2	+98.5
Aid in constant 1972 dollars (billions)					
Grants	10.8	27.0	49.5	39.3	−20.6
To governments	7.4	17.2	32.0	20.4	−36.3
To individuals	3.4	9.8	17.5	18.9	+10.8
Tax expenditures*	NA	12.3	12.1	19.8	+63.6
Interest exclusion	NA	2.6	3.8	8.6	+163.2
Tax deductibility	NA	9.7	8.3	11.1	+33.7
Grants as a percentage of:					
Total federal budget	7.6	12.3	17.4	11.7	−32.8
Domestic federal budget	15.9	21.1	22.9	16.1	−29.7
State and local revenues	11.6	16.0	21.0	18.3	−12.9

Source: George E. Peterson, 'Federalism and the States', in John L. Palmer and Isabel V. Sawhill (eds.), *The Reagan Record* (Washington, DC: Urban Institute, 1984) Table 7.2.

* State and local governments receive indirect subsidies, as citizens can deduct state and local taxes from their federal tax bills. For full notes and sources, see original.

the experience of the depression and the Second World War showed that federal action could work; that, indeed, inequalities and injustices could be removed. Many commentators point to a retreat from federal action during Eisenhower's Republican administration. Yet the New Deal coalition was very much intact during the 1950s. Congress remained largely Democratic, and there was relatively little ideological aversion to an enhanced federal role. Moreover, underlying the whole decade was the continuing shame of the South. Few doubted that only federal action could solve the problem. By the early 1960s something approaching a national consensus existed on the need for federal action. Political and social theory supported the prevailing view. Borrowing heavily from Madisonian notions of the Compound Republic, critics argued forcefully that the states represented all that was regressive and backward; only the federal government with its national constituency and national leadership provided by Democratic presidents could solve the injustices of society. As Grant McConnell put it:

The effect of a small constituency is to enhance the power of local élites, whatever their character or sources of power . . . [T]he claims that small units ensure democracy are erroneous . . . Decentralization to local units does not make for democracy; indeed in the sense that democratic values centre about liberty and equality, the tendency inherent in small units to stratification of power relationships and to protection of established patterns of domination and subordination is almost alien to equality.[5]

Justifications for federal intervention were reinforced by the Black rebellion of the 1960s and by what was seen as an increasing incidence of urban poverty and decay. By the end of the decade, Congress had legislated in almost every area of social and economic life. Civil-rights laws were enacted; welfare-eligibility criteria were expanded; urban renewal and housing aid were increased; elementary and secondary education received federal subsidies for the first time; local police forces became eligible for aid; mass transit schemes burgeoned thanks to federal help. And so it went on. In almost every instance the motives behind the legislation were to redistribute resources from wealthier areas, individuals or social groups to poorer recipients. However, as we shall see, the reality during implementation was rather different.

Surprisingly, the advent of the Nixon administration changed rather little. Congress remained resolutely Democratic and committed to what I have called redistributive centralism. Nixon proved very much a pragmatist in domestic policy and although the motives behind his revenue-sharing plan[6] were decentralist, the net effect of the scheme was simply to add another grant programme to the hundreds which already existed. At an eventual six billion dollars, revenue sharing constituted a substantial increment to federal aid.

If anything, Watergate increased the tendency towards redistributive centralism. The mid-term elections of 1974 produced a fiercely Democratic House, intent on higher levels of domestic spending. In the face of this, President Gerald Ford could do little. Federal aid increased rapidly in 1975 and 1976 – much of it designed to compensate for the damaging effects of the oil-crisis recession on certain states and localities.

State and local fiscal stress

States and localities have, periodically, experienced fiscal stress throughout the history of the republic. Rarely, however, has there been pressure for higher-level governments to bail them out. All this changed during the 1960s and 1970s, in part because of the nationalization of politics noted above,[7] but also because, objectively, the fiscal condition of many cities and states had deteriorated badly. Initially, attention was focused on the plight of the cities. As more affluent members of the population fled to the suburbs, so the tax base of numerous older cities in the North and East deteriorated. Worse still, the remaining population tended to be dependent older people and welfare recipients and their children. Not only did they contribute little in taxes, they also needed more in the way of medical, social, educational and housing services. Public order was also a problem in many locales. As a result, the gap between revenue and expenditure widened sharply (Table 19). These figures are based on estimates made in the late 1960s, which in the event proved pessimistic. The revenue gap was wider in many cases but the level of federal funding was high enough to help close the gap. In some cases (Cleveland, Detroit, Buffalo), dependence took extreme forms, with the federal government paying for more than half the cost of local services. New York City, of course, almost went bankrupt in 1975 and was eventually bailed out by a reluctant New York State and the federal government. The Table is significant, however, in that it shows just how much the federal government was expected to do in the late 1960s.

TABLE 19

*Estimated annual revenue gaps and recommended
funding sources for 1966–75, selected cities
(in billions of dollars)**

Year	Estimated gap	Federal Government	States	Increases in city charges	Increases in net city debt
				Funding sources	
1966	4.5	1.0	–	0.5	3.0
1967	8.0	3.0	1.0	1.0	3.0
1968	12.0	6.0	2.0	1.0	3.0
1969	16.5	8.0	3.0	1.5	4.0
1970	22.0	10.0	4.0	2.0	6.0
1971	28.5	13.0	5.0	2.5	8.0
1972	34.5	16.0	6.0	3.5	9.0
1973	40.0	19.0	8.0	4.0	9.0
1974	45.5	23.0	9.0	4.5	9.0
1975	50.5	26.0	11.0	4.5	9.0
Total	262.0	125.0	49.0	25.0	63.0

Source: Dennis R. Judd and Francis N. Kopel, 'The Search for National Urban Policy from Kennedy to Carter', in Theodore J. Lowi and Alan Stone (eds.), *Nationalizing Government: Public Policies in America* (Beverly Hills: Sage, 1978) Table 7.3.

* These figures are estimates made in 1967 for the largest cities.

A major additional cause of local fiscal plight, which affected a wide variety of governments including many small cities
and suburbs, was the inelasticity of state and local taxes. Most
localities depended on property taxes, which are subject only
to periodic reviews. When inflation was high and increasing,
as was very much the case from the late 1960s on, local revenues simply could not keep pace. In a rather different sense,
the same was true for state governments. Their main income
sources are sales taxes. During recessions or down turns in
the economy, state incomes decline suddenly and dramatically as people consume less. Small wonder, then, that during
the 1970s a number of states began to feel the pinch, thus
increasing the pressure on the federal government to provide
an increasing amount of aid. State fiscal flexibility is further
reduced by the prohibition in many state constitutions
against deficit spending. Unlike federal governments, therefore, states find it difficult to spend their way out of trouble.
As with the cities, those states most adversely affected by
structural economic change – industrial states such as Michigan and New York – suffered the most. Even so, most states
experienced some problem or other. Even affluent California
went through a fiscal crisis, with state expenditure outstripping income from taxes.

Interest-group pluralism

Concomitant with the changed public philosophy on the federal role was a burgeoning Washington-based constellation of
interest groups eager for as big a share of the pie as possible.
Some interest groups represented particular social groups
such as the poor, Blacks or the elderly. Their targets were
governments of all varieties, but because of the pervasive
influence of redistributive centralism, the federal government
was usually the main object of their attention. Scholars have
argued long and hard about the extent of such groups'
influence. Most agree that although they hardly transformed
the political landscape, they did help increase federal spending by arguing for the expansion of eligibility criteria and
take-up rates in a wide range of programmes.[8] Less controversy surrounds the influence of those groups working for

improvements in environmental and consumer protection, occupational safety and the extension of civil and equal rights to women and minorities. Group activity in these areas was almost certainly instrumental in speeding up the passage of legislation. Often, such laws had important implications for federal–state relations. The fiscal repercussions were usually slight, but by superseding numerous state laws, a new federal supremacy in the general area of regulation was established. The Supreme Court consistently endorsed this supremacy until, in 1976, it struck down Congress's extension of the Fair Labor Standards Act to state employees (*National League of Cities* v. *Usery*). However, the logic of the 1976 decision was never extended to other areas and, as was noted in the last chapter, the Court firmly re-established federal supremacy in 1985 in *Garcia* v. *San Antonio Metropolitan Transit Authority*.

Other interest groups represented governments themselves and state, local, county and special district officials became more systematically organized to lobby for aid. Hence, by the mid-1970s the 'Big Seven' as they came to be known – the National League of Cities, the U.S. Conference of Mayors, the National Governors' Conference, the National Legislative Conference, the Council of State Governments, the National Association of Counties and the International City Management Association – worked hard to defend their particular member governments. Some commentators went so far as to argue that this new intergovernmental nexus represented a potent force for increased spending in the U.S., labelling the phenomenon 'topocracy', or rule by government officials. Samuel Beer saw no end to the pressures for increased spending.[9]

While it is virtually impossible actually to measure the influence of interest groups, there can be no doubting the rise of Washington-based lobbying during the 1960s and 1970s. By the time of the Carter administration, lower-level governments *were* better organized and all had their champions in Congress and within the relevant executive departments (Housing and Urban Development, Transportation, Health and Human Services, Commerce, Justice and Interior). Crucially, the lobbying efforts of the intergovernmental lobby tended to reduce the redistributive element in many aid pro-grammes. As we saw in Chapter Four, logrolling in Congress usually results in most constituencies benefiting from any federal largesse available. This is what tended to happen with the new federal programmes. Urban renewal money intended for larger cities ended up going primarily to small and medium-sized towns. Law-enforcement assistance was also spread thinly, as was transportation aid.

National fiscal stability

During the 1960s there was little sense of national fiscal crisis. Increased domestic and defence spending was paid for out of the natural growth of the economy or out of slowly increasing taxation. As can be seen from Table 20, federal spending did increase quite sharply from 1969 to 1978, but even so, this was not a matter of acute national concern – and this at a time when economic growth *was* faltering. Table 20 also shows that the growth in federal spending would have been much greater had there not been a sharp relative decline in defence spending. Domestic federal expenditure – much of it in the

TABLE 20

*Federal domestic and defence spending from own funds as
a percentage of G.N.P. 1959–84*

Year	Total	Defence	Domestic	Domestic spending on social security
1959	18.6	9.3	8.0	2.1
1969	20.0	8.1	10.5	3.6
1974	20.9	6.4	14.1	5.0
1978	21.3	4.6	15.0	5.5
1980	22.9	5.0	15.9	6.0
1982	24.9	5.9	16.3	6.8
1984	24.0	6.1	14.8	6.7

Source: Advisory Commission on Intergovernmental Relations, *Significant Features of Fiscal Federalism 1984* (Washington, DC: 1984) Table 6.

form of intergovernmental transfers and social security – rose particularly rapidly during these years.

To be fair to Presidents Nixon and Ford, national economic problems were mounting in the early and mid 1970s, but either they were not perceived to be serious (in the case of Nixon), or (in the case of Ford) there was little the president could do about them because of an overwhelmingly Democratic Congress. In sum, until the mid–late 1970s the federal government could, in one way or another, afford to continue to increase subventions to state and local governments.

Fiscal Retrenchment and the New Federalism 1979–86

From the late 1970s onwards the intergovernmental policy agenda changed dramatically. Each of the four factors discussed above either ceased to apply or applied in quite different ways. As an ideology, redistributive centralism was already beginning to wane in influence as early as the mid 1970s. Because of his political support from the cities and minorities, Jimmy Carter could hardly declare his dislike for the notion, although as a fiscal conservative he firmly believed that governments should pay out only what they could afford. As an ex-governor of Georgia – an economically growing and fiscally sound state – he favoured state autonomy and disliked the new assumption that cities and states were dependent.

At the same time, middle-income state and local taxpayers were beginning to resent what appeared to be sudden and rapid hikes in local and state taxes. As suggested earlier and as Table 19 on p. 185 shows, the states, in particular, were increasingly expected to help out local governments. Localities were in turn required to increase taxes to help pay for the burgeoning services. Moreover, increases in property taxes following periodic valuations seem sudden and dramatic during periods of high inflation. They certainly give the impression of being unreasonable, even if, in relation to the value of properties, they are not. The end result of all this pressure was what came to be known as 'the tax revolt'. Beginning in California in 1978 with Proposition 13, which limited property taxes in the state to 1 per cent of their 1975–6 values, a number of states followed suit by limiting and reducing property taxes and state income and sales taxes. The revolt reached its peak during 1979, when more than twenty states acted to reduce taxes.[10] Generally it was the more populist western states which implemented the most Draconian measures – although Massachusetts introduced what was probably the most radical reduction, Proposition 2½, in 1981. At national, state and local levels, therefore, the mood was changing from one where some redistribution to poorer areas was broadly accepted, to a new public philosophy of fiscal responsibility and resigned acceptance that inequalities were unavoidable.

Some cities continued to experience fiscal stress, of course, and to receive intergovernmental aid. But the new philosophy obliged many to cut services, reduce public employment and raise service charges rather than seek yet more help from other governments. Underlying all of these changes was a growing sense of national fiscal crisis. Jimmy Carter promised to balance the federal budget but failed to do so. Indeed the deficit increased under his presidency, and has continued to do so under his successor, Ronald Reagan. The deficit problem had profound consequences for intergovernmental relations. Put simply, of all the items on the national budget, grants to state and local governments are politically the most vulnerable. Payments direct to individuals (items such as social security payments and medicare) are well protected because the number of recipients is large and the mass of the population contributes directly through payroll taxes to benefits payable later in life. Defence spending was also well protected during the 1979–84 period and, indeed, increased considerably in real terms (see Table 20 on p. 188). Grants to individuals payable through state and local governments – mainly welfare and medicaid – are vulnerable to cuts, but it is difficult to reduce the number of eligible recipients. As Table 18 on p. 182 shows, such grants did increase in real terms between 1978 and 1983. In stark contrast, grants to state and local governments (for such things as urban renewal, housing, transport, revenue sharing, education, social services) fell by a dramatic 36 per cent in real terms in this five-year period. Why should this be so? The main reason is that many of these items affect capital spending, which has relatively few immediate beneficiaries. Also, the new public philosophy of self-sufficiency rather than dependence was easiest to implement in areas where, traditionally, local and state governments had dominated. It was, after all, only in the previous twenty or thirty years that the federal government had become involved in such things as education, urban renewal and social services. One thing is certain: the dramatic cuts of the early 1980s put paid to those theories claiming that a 'topocracy' would ensure ever higher levels of federal aid. The intergovernmental lobby has simply not been as influential or effective during the late 1970s and early 1980s as before.

With the advent of the Reagan administration, the trend away from redistribution and towards self-sufficiency accelerated. But Ronald Reagan brought another dimension to intergovernmental relations. Very early in his presidency he declared an intention to restore the institution of American federalism. His motives were both ideological and political. Ideologically, the president was averse to centralized government. As a former governor of California, he firmly believed that most domestic policies should be the responsibility of state governments. Only they could respond effectively to the wishes of citizens. The federal government was too remote and insufficiently accountable to the people to handle the complex mix of social and economic policies needed in a modern industrial country. Ronald Reagan's distaste for big government extended to all levels. Not only should the federal government devolve responsibility to the states, it should also stop subsidizing them. By implication at least, the level of funding, and therefore of services provided by the states, would decline as federal subsidies were phased out. In the regulatory area a similar disengagement by the federal government was planned. Hence less government at all levels was the president's aim.

Politically, reducing the federal government's role had a number of potential advantages. It would, first of all, help solve the thorny problem of the deficit. More importantly, it would reduce the need to take all the difficult distributional decisions that the existing intergovernmental system demanded of the federal government. As Budget Director David Stockman put it in 1981,

We are overloaded at the national level. We simply can't make wise decisions on the thousands of issues that come before us. There has to be a better division of labour and a redelegation of decision-making to lower levels of government.[11]

Silvio Conte, a ranking Republican on the House Appropriations Committee, put it in more overtly political terms:

It's far easier for people to come to Washington to get their social programmes. It would be a hell of a lot tougher if we diffuse them, and send them out to the states. All their friends and connections are in Washington.[12]

The political message is clear: governing in Washington is easier when other states have to decide who gets what out of the welfare, educational, regulatory, medical and other social services. The same is true of infrastructure and capital grants-in-aid for state and, particularly, local governments.

The Reagan administration introduced a number of radical reforms in line with this new philosophy. During 1981, the administration proposed the consolidation of eighty-three categorical programmes (grants tied to specific functions such as urban renewal and elementary education) into six human-services block grants. Block grants were favoured because they gave the states greater discretion over spending and because they reduce the close federal/state/local administrative and interest-group links associated with categorical programmes. In addition, a 25 per cent reduction in federal spending was proposed for fiscal year 1982. Predictably, most states and localities were hostile to the cuts, and with interest groups lobbying hard in Congress to protect pet categorical grants, the movement towards block grants was slow. These reforms paled into insignificance compared with the reforms proposed in 1982, however. As the centrepiece of the 1982 State of the Union Message, they constituted what would have amounted to a transformation of federal state relations. The proposals have been summarized as follows:

(i) A 'swap' of the three main welfare programmes funded by the states and federal governments on a matching basis. The states would assume full responsibility for Aid for Families with Dependent Children (A.F.D.C., the main welfare programme) and food stamps, while the federal government took over medicaid (medical care for the poor). So the existing federal cost of A.F.D.C. and food stamps (some $16.5 billion) would be absorbed by the states, while the federal government would take on the full cost of medicaid ($19.1 billion).

(ii) A 'turnback' to the states of some forty social, community-development and transport programmes together, initially, with the revenues to pay for them. Beginning in fiscal year 1984 a new federal trust fund would be created, financed by taxes on oil windfall profits, tobacco, gasoline, alcohol and telephones. Totalling $28 billion in 1984, this trust-fund money could be drawn on by the states up until 1987, when state taxes would gradually replace federal revenues so that by fiscal year 1991 the states would be virtually 'self-sufficient' in these programme areas. One estimate put the total amount of federal aid contributing to state and local aid at 3–4 per cent for that year, compared with 25 per cent in 1980. Also, part of the trust fund would be used to compensate those states who were net losers as a result of the swap.

A relatively small number of programmes were specifically excluded from the package, including the funding of interstate highways, higher education, and education for pre-schoolers, the disadvantaged and handicapped.

(iii) States were to be given a choice as to how they adapted to self-sufficiency. They could either continue to participate in existing categorical programmes – in which case the relevant federal agencies would be reimbursed from the trust fund – or they could receive their trust money as a single federal grant. The administration favoured the latter and, in theory at least, so would most states, for this new super revenue-sharing programme would give considerable discretion to state administrations. Indeed, the only proviso was that any existing monies going direct to local governments (such as mass transit) would have to continue to do so.[13]

In the event, the more radical of the reforms came to little. The welfare/medicaid swap was quickly dropped by the administration following massive opposition from states and localities, and the phasing out of federal grants via the trust fund was also rejected. However, the broad objectives of the above proposals have remained during the second Reagan administration. As already stressed, substantial cuts did occur. By 1986 the federal government was doing much less in the way of supporting the states and localities. The move to block grants and away from categorical grants has also continued. In the fields of regulation and civil rights the administration has also made serious efforts to reduce the federal role – not so much to strengthen the states as to weaken enforcement generally. Very often, however, this has meant attempting to leave the detail of implementation to state governments. As was noted earlier, resistance to change in this area from the courts and from bureaucrats in departments and agencies such as the Justice Department and the Environmental Protection Agency has limited the scope of administration policy.[14]   So although the specific objectives of the Reagan administration have not been achieved, the president has effectively shifted the policy agenda away from an acceptance of state dependence and towards a more devolved system where the states have to look out for themselves. Federal aid and direction continues, of course, but it is given more reluctantly and more selectively. Fortunately for Ronald Reagan, the economic recovery after 1983 greatly helped state and local finances. Inflation was low but incomes were rising rapidly. As a result, revenue from sales and property taxes increased quite rapidly and helped to pay for some of the new responsibilities lower-level governments had assumed.

However, the president's 1985 tax plan, which proposed ending the right of citizens to deduct their state and local taxes from their federal tax bill, will put further pressure on lower-level governments. In effect, ending the deductions will increase voters' state and local taxes by around 20 per cent, thus ensuring a renewed quest among the citizenry for 'value for money' in local services. State and local revenues will not, of course, increase by one penny.

The Future of American Federalism

Does all this mean a revival of the institution of federalism? Not necessarily. A downturn in the economy could once again increase the pressure for federal aid. Those states and cities which benefited little from the 1983–6 upturn have been, in any case, highly reluctant partners in the New Federalism. And amid all the talk of a revived federalism, those forces which were steadily nationalizing American society have not mysteriously vanished. As Chapter Seven showed, on such issues as abortion, economic policy, conditions of employment and criminal procedural rights, the Supreme Court has been undermining rather than strengthening federalism, through the application of national standards. In some respects the Reagan administration itself has been as much a centralizing as a decentralizing influence. Consider the question of banking deregulation. Few would dispute that American banking laws are archaic and inefficient – largely because individual states have put limits on branch banking and on the activities of out-of-state banks.[15] Successful deregulation must mean the application of national standards and thus a further weakening of state autonomy. Even in the area of moral standards, President Reagan has been, when it suited him, a nationalizer. During 1985 those states where the minimum drinking age was below twenty-one were obliged to raise it in order to deter drunken driving by young people. A threatened withdrawal of a proportion of federal highway grants ensured compliance by most states.

In the area of economic policy in particular, when the states have attempted to assert themselves – as with so-called unitary taxation or the taxing of corporations' profits outside as well as within state boundaries – they have been quickly condemned by Washington and an increasingly nationalized media.

The need for national rules and standards will prevent a return to the sort of autonomy and variety characteristic of nineteenth-century American federalism. It is also doubtful, however, that a more nationalized system will banish for ever the realization of the sort of responsive, accountable and democratic state governments that Ronald Reagan's New Federalism promised. As we established, the president was not motivated entirely by a desire to advance democracy. He was as much acting in a politically expedient manner, hoping to off-load difficult decisions on unwilling state governments. But even if the decentralization plan had worked, would it have brought governments closer to the people? Possibly. It depends very much on which governments and which people. For one thing, the president's plan (and notably those parts of it which were successfully implemented) strengthened *state* rather than *local* governments. Almost all the reforms were designed to remove those direct federal/local links which had grown up during the 1960s and 1970s. Instead, state governments would assume the centre of the stage by being given responsibility for administering federal grants and enforcing regulations. In effect they would have to manage the difficult business of cutting local services and deciding who gets what in a wide range of programmes. A centralization of power within states was likely, therefore. In many states this would have the effect of weakening the government/citizen link. Such states as California, New York or Ohio, which have large populations and bureaucracies, are several light-years away from the Jeffersonian ideal of small-town governments seeing to the limited needs of small-town citizens.

Even if it is accepted that decentralization to the states is likely to produce more responsive government than federally administered programmes, who would benefit and who lose? As we saw in Chapter Six, the disadvantaged have benefited much less than we would expect from *federal* social programmes. All the evidence points to a much more uneven distributive pattern when the *states* run these programmes. Poorer states would, of course, have relatively little to redistribute.[16] But even richer states are reluctant to engage in the sort of progressive programmes which national constituencies encourage. During 1983 the Washington-based Urban Institute made a systematic study of the costs and benefits of the New Federalism. Its broad conclusions were as follows:

Based on existing structures of decision-making in the states, a thoroughgoing decentralization of federal decision-making would result in a pattern of policy output which would vary significantly across the states. In particular, the interests of the poor, labour, pupils and teachers would be poorly served in states with low *per capita* income, states with a high percentage of their population in poverty, and states in which minorities constitute a high percentage of the population. Not only would the interests of these groups be poorly served in these states compared to the wealthier, low minority states, but, with the exception of teachers, their interests would also be weak *relative to other groups within these states*. The interests of business would be best served (and be stronger relative to other groups) in these same states.[17]

What these conclusions confirm is that sometimes dramatic variations in the political cultures of states continue to apply. Some states are conservative and moralistic while others are liberal and pragmatic. The typology of state political cultures pioneered by Daniel Elazar in the 1960s is still an approximate guide to variations among the states.[18] Federal aid and economic growth have altered the character of some states, especially those in the South, but not in ways that have homogenized political life, even if great uniformity in commercial and economic life exists.

This accepted, state government is almost certainly less corrupt and provincial than it used to be. Both politicians and officials are more professionalized and conscious of the need for high administrative standards.[19] It would be wrong to suppose that this leads them to reject federal direction and grants. On the contrary, most state officials are quite happy with an enhanced federal role – provided it does not go too far in undermining state autonomy.[20] The great paradox of the 1980s, therefore, is this: while structural economic and social forces continue to nationalize American society and therefore focus the political attention of organized interests on Washington, and while the states themselves are happy to participate in what could be characterized as a revival of Madison's Compound Republic, administrations in Washington have been intent on a substantial decentralization, the benefits of which are hard to identify. Put simply, federal, state and local governments in the U.S. are now essentially *interdependent* rather than simply dominant and dependent. Any reform which fails to recognize this fact is likely to founder, as did President Reagan's New Federalism, for the most part, during 1981–6.

CHAPTER NINE

American Government: Reform and Reality

No political system is perfect. Most regimes are fragile in the extreme, lasting no more than a few decades or years. Others may be longer-lived but fail the tests of justice, equality or democracy. Some simply fail to provide citizens with basic protection against violence and disorder, or with the minimum of food and shelter necessary for human survival. By these very elemental measures, the American system of government has been successful. The basic constitutional structure has remained unchanged for more than 200 years. Few regimes are as stable and none more successful at generating wealth. Violence is endemic in American society but only infrequently is it translated into politically motivated civil disorder. Inequalities in wealth and income are considerable – probably greater, in fact, than in any comparable country. While this problem should not be underestimated – and we will return to it later – the unequal distribution of income and wealth has only rarely led to social movements threatening the regime. Measuring justice and democracy is notoriously difficult, of course, but the U.S. probably scores quite high on both counts compared with most countries. No one questions the availability of the institutional mechanisms for democracy in America nor the opportunities for participation in politics. In the sense that public discourse is relatively free from state control and basic rights are protected by the courts, the U.S. also does much more to promote justice and equity than most countries.

If the system appears to work quite well in terms of both efficiency and more normative measures of performance, why is so much criticism aimed at how Americans govern themselves? Preceding chapters provide some of the answers. For one thing, the United States has responsibilities beyond its borders. As Chapter Two stressed, in both economic and military terms the U.S. helps determine the fate of numerous other countries. Since around 1970 evidence has mounted suggesting that the country is less able to take on this awesome role. At least some of the reasons for reduced performance in this area relate to domestic political events. For another thing, in terms of Americans' own expectations, the system appears to have worked less well over the last twenty years than in the previous twenty years. In particular, critics argue that trust in government has declined and that the parties no longer play the role of key coalition-builders and mediators between contrasting social groups. Congress serves the people's but not the public interest. The presidential nomination system often pre-selects inappropriate candidates for office. Washington is apparently awash with the politics of interest-group opportunism rather than with the politics of party programmes. A 'rootless activism' characterizes Supreme Court decision-making. The states are unsure of their proper role in an increasingly nationalized system of government. And so it goes on.

At the normative level the criticisms are just as loud and clear. Racial and ethnic discrimination continues to plague American public life. Black Americans, indeed, often appear to be excluded from the benefits of the great democratic experiment. A cultural 'loose boundedness' prevails in the United States, so that individuals, and especially children, fail to learn basic cues on how to participate fully in the political system.[1] Government/business and government/labour relations are conducted in a confrontational environment which reduces economic efficiency. The same spirit of confrontation helps clog the American court systems with interminable civil suits on almost every aspect of social and economic life. A military industrial complex encourages corruption, 'weapons fetishism' and starves social programmes of much needed cash.

Although many of these criticisms must be understood in the context of American values and the growing proclivity of Americans to indulge in self-examination, some of them are valid. More important, outside the United States there is an increasing tendency to assume that the country is, at best, badly led[2] or, at worst, downright hostile to the rest of the world. As repeatedly stressed, given America's pivotal role in world affairs, such perceptions must be a cause for deep concern. Three key questions can be raised in this context. First, to what extent do America's political problems stem from the failure of political institutions as opposed to other factors? Second, what institutional reforms, if any, are likely to improve the situation? Third, if institutional relationships are not at the heart of the problem, how can the American polity and the American people come to terms with those broader structural forces which have so clearly undermined the essentially sanguine view of U.S. government prevalent until the 1960s?

Are Institutions to Blame?

In some respects it is easier to blame institutions than broader social and economic forces for political failures. Institutions are, after all, easily observable and, in most instances, amenable to reform. The 'social structure' or the 'U.S. world role' cannot be changed overnight. It is highly unlikely they can ever be consciously directed by any political authority. Electoral, party, and constitutional systems are frequently and sometimes successfully reformed, however. There is hardly any part of the U.S. political system that has not been the target of reformers. What are the currently popular reform proposals? Are they feasible? Would they make a difference?

Without doubt the most problematical constitutional relationship is that between president and Congress. This has always been true, of course, but as we saw, the two institutions have found it especially hard to work well together over the last twenty years. The most radical reform proposal is simply to abandon the separation-of-powers mechanism and replace it with a parliamentary system. At a stroke the most formidable obstacle to efficient policy-making would be overcome; parties would receive an immediate boost, because, as in the British system, they would provide the natural connective tissue between president (or prime minister?) and the legislature. In spite of some support among academics,[3] the likelihood of this proposal receiving general support is so remote that we must dismiss it completely. As a central tenet of the Constitution, the separation of powers is almost sacred. And which existing members of Congress or state legislatures would even contemplate support for such a dramatic centralization of power? Almost certainly none. And as if to seal the fate of the reform, the system that had always been held up as the best example of parliamentary government – the British – has arguably performed even less efficiently than the American system over recent years.[4]

A rather less radical proposal is to synchronize congressional and presidential terms and require voters to select one or other party at ballots, thus ensuring that both major branches are always in the hands of the same party at the same time. This may involve either raising the House and presidential terms to six years (the reformers' ideal choice), or standardizing the terms at four years. Although a slightly more attractive alternative, the proposal does assume that the parties are sufficiently coherent to overcome the conflicts that the present system produces. Yet some of the worst failures of presidential/congressional liaison (during the Kennedy and Carter presidencies, for example) have occurred when the two branches have been controlled by the same party. Again, the proposal is too outrageously radical to be even remotely feasible.

The institution of a single six-year term for the president is much more realistic. Indeed, just such a proposal has been introduced to Congress as a constitutional amendment more than a hundred times. Jimmy Carter, Lyndon Johnson and eight other presidents have backed it. If anything, support for the change has grown in recent years, as media-based campaigns have grown in length and intensity. After all, how can any chief executive manage to achieve major objectives in what effectively turns out to be a three-year term (the fourth being reserved for campaigning)? Clearly the rationale behind the six-year term is to make the office less overtly political. This may or may not be a good thing. The new school of political economists condemns policies tailored to winning elections as sure recipes for inflation and economic dislocation.[5] Others argue that the presidency *should* be political. If implementing policies that please the people is not the very essence of democracy, then what is? Interestingly, demands for a six-year term have waned somewhat since the re-election of Ronald Reagan. As the first effective two-term president since Eisenhower (if we disregard Nixon's incomplete second term), he has, temporarily at least, dampened the enthusiasm of those who were convinced that all modern presidents were fated to short, dispiriting stays in the White House.

A related proposal is the introduction of a four-year term for members of the House of Representatives. As we noted, members of the lower house are presently condemned to per-petual election campaigning. With four years between elec-tions instead of two – preferably co-ordinated with the presidential term – representatives would have more time for constructive policy-making. Unlike the party slate reform discussed earlier, rather fewer objections to this proposal can be raised. The most telling is the fact that, like it or not, four-year terms for representatives would make the system less democratic. In a society where more rather than less democ-racy has been the recent theme, a fundamental change in the potential for responsiveness among members of the 'people's branch' is most unlikely.

The presidential selection process attracts as many reform proposals as does the separation of powers. Almost no one disputes the flaws in the present system. Equally, almost no one agrees on how exactly the nomination process should be reformed. Within the Democratic Party, the Hunt Com-mission reforms were partly implemented in 1984. The rep-resentation of party and elected officials at the convention was increased and the number of primaries reduced (see Chapter Five, pp. 94–5). But attempts to shorten the primary season came to little. Unfortunately for the reformers, fiercely independent state legislatures – not the parties themselves – decide on the timing of primaries (although the Supreme Court has deemed that national party rules prevail over state rules in other respects), so major changes in the sequence of primaries are unlikely. Much has been said about the merits of national and regional primaries. Both would simplify and shorten the nomination process. In the case of a national pri-mary, the whole nomination contest would be over in one election. Naturally, this would favour incumbent presidents and well-known challengers. It would almost certainly prevent the nomination of virtual unknowns such as Jimmy Carter in 1976. By giving an advantage to candidates with established records, public and peer-group review would be strengthened. Candidates intent on manipulating the public via numerous primaries, each blown up for mass consumption by the media, would fall by the wayside.

Although the national primary has many merits, it is not obvious that it would shorten the campaign. Candidates would continue to jostle for position months or years before the election. Americans are fond of contrasting their election campaigns with the British. With official notice of only three weeks, the British, so the argument goes, have a much superior system. In reality, British governments begin their electioneering at least a year before the election. And because they can choose when, exactly, an election is held, the degree of public manipulation is probably greater than in the U.S.

Again, the national primary is unlikely to be instituted. It would not require a constitutional amendment (there is nothing in the Constitution about parties or primaries), but Congress is lukewarm about enacting the change. A major problem is that public disquiet with the lengthy and theatrical primary season is greatest during an election year. To change the system at that time would obviously favour one candidate or another. As Representative Morris Udall of Arizona has put it: 'The impetus to get something done only occurs in a year when you can't do anything about it'.[6]

These are, in summary, the major reforms involving the separation of powers and the electoral system currently under discussion. Of the numerous others, the majority are either relatively minor or simply not feasible. Reform of the electoral college is rarely far from the surface, for example. As presently constituted, its winner-take-all mechanism could lead to the election of a president by a minority of voters. Membership of the college also favours smaller, rural states. But as with the national primary idea, real concern is only likely to arise during an election year, or when the system actually produces a minority president. Less dramatic are changes affecting the president's cabinet, the White House staff and the internal organization of Congress. In all these instances, reforms or natural evolutionary developments have been proceeding apace for many decades. It would be difficult to say, however, that in part or in whole they have significantly improved the efficiency or responsiveness of the institutions. The same is true of federalism. Changes there certainly have been, but none, including Ronald Reagan's much vaunted New Federalism, has perceptibly improved the strained relationship between the federal government and the states.

What of the Supreme Court? Literally hundreds of Court-curbing bills – most designed to limit the Court's jurisdiction – have been introduced in Congress over the last thirty years. None have succeeded, and none are likely to. Satisfactory or not, the Supreme Court is now firmly established as the final authority on the Constitution. As we discovered, its decisions are often controversial, and the justices are frequently confused or uncertain in their jurisprudence. But nothing they have done (or not done) in recent history compares with the crises provoked by the *Dred Scott* case and the rejection of New Deal legislation in the 1930s. Even then, major changes in the constitutional role of the Court proved unnecessary – although in the case of *Dred Scott* a bloody civil war intervened and effectively pre-empted a constitutional change.

We can conclude, therefore, that major institutional reform of American national government is either impractical, or, if implemented, would have uncertain and not necessarily positive results. Of course the abandonment – or even a substantial modification – of the separation of powers would have profound consequences. But in the context of the America of the 1980s any such change is simply inconceivable. Put another way, the apparent deterioration in American political life and institutions stems not from institutional relationships *per se*, but from other, deeper social and economic forces, which are far less amenable to change or reform. This is not to say that such forces are not affected by institutions, or that institutional/constitutional reforms would be neutral in their effects. We have more than enough evidence from other countries to demonstrate just how effective reforms can or could be. France's endemic governmental instability was instantly cured by the creation of the Fifth Republic. The reform of

Britain's archaic and patently undemocratic electoral system would surely transform the political landscape of that country. But equivalent changes are simply not going to happen in the United States. Indeed, the only constitutional reform that has come close to fruition in recent years is the balanced-budget amendment, which, if successful, would have truly destructive consequences. No national government should be prohibited from borrowing, or have its freedom to borrow seriously restricted. The suggestion is little short of absurd. Fortunately, those populist forces responsible for the movement are unlikely to get their way – even though President Reagan (rather disingenuously) gave his support to the amendment in 1982.[7]

If institutional reforms are not the answer – indeed how can they be if the problem is essentially non-institutional in nature – how can the American polity adapt more successfully to the unique social and economic circumstances of the late 1980s? Recall that three developments were identified in Chapter One, each of which has no precedent in American history. The U.S. role in the world has been transformed; the country has acquired a powerful national state; and social and political fragmentation has assumed a new, possibly damaging dimension. In the light of the discussion so far, what can be said about the prospects of adaptation to these changes?

America's World Role: The Need for Consistency and Flexibility

The U.S. world role is now highly complex and multi-dimensional. No simple recipe for adaptation exists, therefore. Consider the differences between and within military, foreign and foreign economic policy. Most scholars agree that the institutions of foreign-policy crisis management are, if not adequate, then certainly superior to those responsible for longer-term policy-making.[8] The president and key members of the National Security Council can and do take decisions quickly and relatively efficiently. The longer the crisis drags on, however, the greater the number of actors and interests involved. Uncertainty and indecision increase correspondingly. An immediate hostage crisis (in Iran or Beirut) extends into a major political impasse where the president becomes ever more vulnerable to criticism from Congress, the media and the public at large. On broader foreign-policy questions it is not at all obvious what the best interest of the United States is. In Europe, Africa, Central America, the Middle and Far East, American policy is fraught with difficulties and contradictions. In all these regions, strictly domestic political interests influence U.S. strategy. The domestic/foreign interaction is as great in the realm of defence policy. Weapons systems have their corporate and political backers. And once adopted — as in the case of the B1 bomber, the MX missile and the 'Star Wars' Strategic Defence Initiative — America's whole defence strategy is altered. Of course this happens in most countries, but in few are the societal pressures on the foreign-policy makers as great as in the U.S. Congressional involvement complicates the picture further. Congress *is* part of the foreign-policy-making process. Indeed beyond short-term crises, congressional approval is vital for virtually every foreign-policy decision. As a result, foreign powers often receive confusing and contradictory messages from the U.S. In some countries, members of national assemblies and parliaments may visit other countries and provide alternatives to the official foreign-policy line. But in which country do legislators go overseas and provide foreign-policy perspectives that are distinct from the executive's position but are in no sense unofficial? A travelling senator could, after all, be chairman of the Senate Foreign Relations Committee, with major responsibilities for the ratification of treaties.

If anything, the increasingly important area of foreign economic policy is even more fraught with policy confusions. Monetary, fiscal and trade policy are the responsibility of numerous institutions, from a number of congressional committees to the Board of Governors of the Federal Reserve System, the Departments of Commerce, Treasury and State, the president and the office of the Special Trade Representative. In such an overtly political and bureaucratic context, consistent policy-making is extremely hard to achieve.

It hardly needs stating that America's status as a declining *hegemon* has aggravated these problems over the last ten or fifteen years. Given that major institutional reforms are either irrelevant or impractical, what, if anything, can be done to improve this situation? In his recent book on co-operation in the world political economy, Robert Keohane provides at least partial answers to this question. Drawing on an extensive body of theoretical work on public choice and international relations, Keohane concludes that modern states, and especially the United States, have much to gain from co-operating in international regimes. Regimes can embrace everything from trade to arms control. As Keohane puts it:

. . . governments should seek reliability of action with the provision of high-quality information to their partners. International regimes facilitate both of these objectives by providing rules that constitute standards for evaluating state behaviour and by facilitating the establishment of contacts among governments that help to provide information not merely about policies but about intentions and values. Both the value of a reputation for reliability and the gains to be made from providing high-quality information to others challenge the traditional *Realpolitik* ideal of the autonomous, hierarchical state that keeps its options open and its decision-making processes closed.[9]

Ideally then, policy-making in modern states should neither be completely closed or so open as to give out inconsistent messages. No one could accuse the U.S. of having a closed system; almost everyone agrees that it is so open that rational policy-making is difficult to achieve. Fruitful membership of international regimes also requires governments to be pragmatic rather than ideological, and to be understanding of and empathetic to other countries' problems rather than critical or contemptuous of them. By this measure the Reagan administrations have been a regressive rather than progressive influence. Only in the area of trade relations have the administrations pursued a fairly consistent liberal or free-trade line. On exchange rates, arms control, defence and foreign policy generally, inconsistency and even confusion have abounded. In the vital area of arms control, for example, fundamental disagreements emerged between control supporters such as Secretary of State George Shultz and National Security Adviser Robert McFarlane on the one hand and opponents of control led by Defense Secretary Caspar

Weinberger on the other. Where President Reagan stands is not obvious.

As was stressed in Chapter Three, the president has also rekindled American exceptionalism and thus tapped a deep-seated atavistic belief in the American people that they and their system are morally superior to other states and peoples. Such claims are, of course, the very antithesis of what is needed to nurture international co-operation.

What is needed from American leaders is flexibility tied to a commitment to bilateral and multilateral institutions and co-operation. Such an approach requires great leadership skills not only abroad but also at home. Ronald Reagan has been only too aware of the maxim that 'What is a virtue internationally may be a vice domestically, and what is a virtue domestically – a restraint on executive power – may become a vice internationally.'[10] In sum, he has sacrificed international co-operation for domestic electoral advantage. We must hope that future presidents will follow the more constructive strategy of educating American leaders and the public at large into the need for a pragmatic but consistent leadership role. Unfortunately, such leaders are likely to emerge only as a result of some chastening event or events, which themselves may bring new perils in international relations.

The New American State: Big Government is Here to Stay

If exceptionalism is one strand in the American ideology, anti-statism is another. In spite of the huge responsibilities assumed by the federal government over the last fifty years, American political culture has never quite come to terms with the fact of big government. Yet the two biggest items on the federal budget – defence and social security – are as likely to get bigger as smaller. Of the remaining items, welfare and aid to state and local governments are more vulnerable, but as we saw in Chapter Eight, these too have their political champions and efforts to remove the federal government from these arenas have proved less than successful.

Similarly, in spite of the Reagan administrations' efforts

to deregulate American society, as many pressures exist to standardize and regulate it as to allow market freedom and discretion. Previous chapters have noted how banking deregulation must involve federal intervention, which amounts to the supersession of state regulations and the institution of federal ones. In education, occupational and road safety, health care and environmental protection, the trend is towards national standards of practice, which only the federal government can enforce. None of this is to deny the value of much of the deregulation that has occurred. The point is, rather, that the use of federal power in this and other areas of domestic policy should be adaptive and coherent rather than ideological and rigid. The central paradox of the Reagan era has been the federal government's commitment to free-market ideology, while beneath the surface the executive branch has been as busy undermining as strengthening market forces. On distributional questions the Reagan administration has also pursued contradictory policies. Ideologically and emotionally, most members of the administration are averse to the redistribution of resources towards the needy. Indeed they have made considerable efforts to reduce the government's redistributive role. Yet they can hardly declare their belief in more inequality, or deny that the federal government has any proper role to play in social policy. Some economists and political scientists have recognized the contradictions inherent in the Reagan position. Robert Reich, for example, has pleaded for a less ideological approach to social and economic choices, arguing instead for more pragmatic and adaptive policies:

... we will need political institutions capable of generating large-scale compromise and adaptation. Some of these institutions will be at local and regional levels. But we will also need a national bargaining arena for allocating the burdens and benefits of major adjustment strategies.[11]

Reich is referring mainly to industrial policy, but the implication is clear: in domestic policy the federal government has a crucial role to play in managing economic and social change. President, Congress and the Court are the only central institutions of the American state, and while accepting an important role for state and local governments, nationalizing forces will continue to oblige federal institutions to take the centre of the stage. This is not necessarily to argue for greater government spending and more regulation and planning. It may or may not involve these options. Unfortunately Reich, along with other liberal economists, fails to tell us how a combative Congress, a capricious Court and an ideological president can be persuaded to play a mediating and consensual rather than antagonistic and competitive role in American society. Moreover, proselytizing on the benefits of compromise and adaptiveness hardly has the media and public appeal of pleas to a return to the market and freedom. Jimmy Carter and Walter Mondale discovered this to their cost.

But to repeat the point, American national government – and especially the executive – cannot disengage from society, so eventually the choice will have to be made. Can the United States continue to live with the paradox of a government vested with vast responsibilities while its political leaders preach the merits of minimal government? Or can the American people come to terms with the fact of big government? In effect, is American political culture capable of such a profound but necessary adjustment?

Social and Political Fragmentation Can Have Advantages As Well As Disadvantages

Like most other commentaries on modern American politics, this book has dwelt on the disadvantages of fragmentation. We have also concluded that although institutional factors can be important, fragmentation in American political life has origins which lie deep in the social structure. So far, the argument of the book has been at least partly in agreement with the general chorus of political scientists with their 'promise of disharmony'[12] which further social fragmentation will bring. But as repeatedly pointed out in earlier chapters, fragmentation is synonymous with the decline of party, region, class and ethnicity. It is a very different phenomenon indeed from the fragmentation associated with Northern Ireland or the Lebanon. People have less, not more, commitment to rigid political preferences. Single issues may arouse them, but their position on any one issue relates in no coherent or ideological way to their position on other issues. Such a development does not preclude extremist political action, as the bombing of abortion clinics and some of the opposition tactics to the Vietnam War show. But such actions are much less serious than when the fate of whole social groups is bound up in a single, inclusive ideology. This has almost never been the case in the United States, of course, and disquiet with recent developments is a reaction to a move away from the quite weak class-based politics of the New Deal coalition.

How is this loosely-held-together politics of the 1980s compatible with the new conservative ideology associated with the Reagan administrations? The two are not so irreconcilable when it is recalled that first, President Reagan has repeatedly appealed to 'basic American values' such as freedom, individualism and strength abroad. Part of his success, therefore, is attributable to his tapping of values which Americans have always held dear – and which his immediate predecessors were seen to betray.[13] Second, polls have consistently shown little evidence of a substantial shift to the right in the United States. State, local and congressional elections confirm this. There has been some move to a conservative position, but nothing that resembles a 'conservative movement' or a 'realignment' in favour of right-wing Republicans. Public support for Reagan was for the man, not for a new market ideology.[14] Put another way, 'basic American values' could be sufficiently flexible to accommodate less ideologically right-wing presidents. Certainly the historical record strongly supports the view that pragmatic, adaptive presidents can succeed both in winning elections and in maintaining public support over long periods. The presidency of Franklin Roosevelt alone is proof enough of this.

It could be, then, that the loosely-held-together political coalitions of the 1980s are a suitable vehicle for the adaptive policies discussed earlier. Certainly compromise and bargaining in an open, political context are anything but alien to American politics. But as was argued, there is a need both for pragmatism and consistency of direction. We have already concluded that the Reagan administrations have been much more single-minded than most, but this has hardly helped prevent the adoption of contradictory and confused policies – especially abroad. Reagan's policies have had another consequence, which, in the context of social fragmentation, could be just as serious. By consistently speaking to and for middle- and upper-class Americans, the Reagan administrations further alienated from the mainstream of American life what is fast becoming an underclass. As Piven and Cloward and Kenneth Dolbeare have argued, such alienation, especially among Blacks, could produce a class-based realignment of politics.[15] They are probably wrong, however, in thinking that the disadvantaged could ever become a part of a winning electoral coalition. It is more likely that they will be condemned to the status of a permanently deprived and dangerously frustrated minority. In the longer term this could have serious consequences for American politics and the nature of American society. An administration more sensitive to the needs of all Americans might be better able to exploit some of the advantages of the new social fragmentation – namely the very absence of deeply rooted social cleavages and political commitments.

Conclusions: Governing Without the State?

One riposte to the foregoing critique of American government is that, whatever its faults, the U.S. political system suffers from problems that are no worse than those experienced by other comparable countries. Indeed by some measures, the American system performs rather better than, say, the British. This should not lead us to be complacent, however, because whatever the similarities between the U.S. and other states, America is truly distinctive in a number of crucial respects. Above all, the United States remains easily the most powerful nation on earth. In economic, diplomatic and military affairs more countries depend on American leadership, guidance and sheer power than on any other. American uniqueness is compounded by the extraordinary fact that great power is exercised in the context of a political culture which is essentially anti-statist in nature. In earlier chapters we repeatedly noted the reluctance of American politicians and the public to accept a prominent role for the state. Academics in the United States usually view the public interest as an aggregate of individual or group interests. American ideology – individualism, equality of opportunity, freedom, democracy – goes beyond this, but as was established, the origins of such a creed lie in society rather than in governments. Hence the country with one of the most powerful central governments in world history lacks a philosophy which locates the state in political discourse. Even when strong pressures for an enhanced federal government exist, as was the case with the New Deal, the Second World War and the Great Society, the resulting increase in Washington's role has been accepted only reluctantly or even as a temporary, short-term expedient. Of course many individuals and interests do accept the need for big government, but only because they see no alternative, not because government in itself is a good thing. Put another way, Americans cannot conceive of the state as a neutral and autonomous arbiter providing a hierarchy of values which are relatively distinct from societal interests. Instead, states are either inherently corrupt and self-serving, or are a sort of public cornucopia for influential interest groups. In Europe and Japan, while critics of the state are often vocal, the prevailing public philosophy does accept some role for a neutral and autonomous state.

This failure of the American public philosophy partly accounts for the pre-eminence of the presidency in politics. With Congress and state and local governments so apparently infused with societal influence, and federal civil servants held in such wide contempt, only the presidency and the courts remain to provide some form of independent leadership. As we saw, the courts usually play a reactive rather than a leadership role, and the adversarial, common-law tradition in any case gives primacy to society rather than to the state. Presidents, on the other hand, are expected both to lead and to be the embodiment of 'Americanism'. What is the responsibility of a vast legal and institutional state apparatus in many countries is, in the U.S., the job of just one man. As we saw, this anthropomorphic view of the state puts impossible burdens on the chief executive.

Ronald Reagan is often attributed with having restored the American presidency to its rightful status. He has shown, so the argument runs, great leadership qualities in his handling of domestic and foreign affairs. Earlier chapters suggested that, in comparison with his predecessors, Ronald Reagan has, by some criteria, performed well. He has helped restore American confidence, his liaison with Congress (at least in his first term) was of a much higher quality than any of his three predecessors; he is a good executive in the managerial sense; he secured a famous re-election victory in 1984. Yet when placed in the context of our discussion of the American state, Ronald Reagan has changed little. Preaching American exceptionalism has not made it easier for the U.S. to carry out a coherent world role. Challenging the need for big government while being obliged to strengthen some aspects of the state has not helped Americans to come to terms with the need for extensive federal action. Appealing to a majority of affluent Americans while ignoring the disadvantaged minority is in many respects a cynical exploitation of the new social fragmentation. What the Reagan experience has shown is that a strong president can profoundly affect the national mood. Congress, the states, organized interests, the media and the public at large were all affected by the president's easy optimism and by his ideological commitments. As we established, there has been no sudden or dramatic shift to the right in the United States. But the policy agenda and the nature of political discourse has changed. Domestic and foreign-policy liberals have been put on the defensive. Whoever the candidates happen to be, it will be Reagan policies and the Reagan record which will set the scene for the 1988 presidential election.

The pre-eminence of the president and the relative absence of what, in other countries, is called 'the state' produces a curious, and ultimately unsatisfactory mix of costs and benefits. The costs of a weak state are an inability to think strategically, plan ahead and produce comprehensive and coherent policy. The benefits are that society can place limits on the domestic and foreign role of government; as a result the potential for serious errors and the abuse of power may be reduced. Society, or at least those forces in society that have most influence, may endorse such abuses, however. Presidents are subject to a similar calculus, with the important qualification that they *can* act more independently and they *can* provide moral leadership for society. Given the slight prospects of institutional and other reforms, much will continue to depend on the personal qualities and capacities of presidents. With the probable exception of Ronald Reagan, few recent incumbents have emerged from the experience with enhanced reputations. More often their personal standing and that of the office has been reduced. All the signs are that the structural problems associated with the job will get worse rather than better over the next twenty years. One man (or woman?) will therefore continue both to embody the American national state and to struggle, often forlornly, to make policy and represent the public interest in a hostile and capricious institutional environment.

Notes

CHAPTER ONE

1. For critiques of Reaganism see Kenneth Dolleare, *Democracy at Risk: The Politics of Economic Renewal* (Chatham, NJ: Chatham House, 1984); Robert Lekachman, *Greed Is Not Enough: Reaganomics* (New York: Pantheon, 1982); Frances Fox Piven and Richard Cloward, *The New Class War: Reagan's Attack on the Welfare State and Its Consequences* (New York: Pantheon, 1982). Supporters of President Reagan's reforms express themselves mainly in newspapers and magazines, but see Ezra Solomon, *Beyond the Turning Point: The U.S. Economy in the 1980s* (San Francisco: W. H. Freeman, 1982); and Peter Duignan and Alvin Rabushka (eds.), *The United States in the 1980's* (Stanford: Hoover Institution Press, 1980).

2. Figures from Bruce Russett, 'The Mysterious Case of Vanishing Hegemony: Is Mark Twain Really Dead?', *International Organization*, 39, 2, Table 1.

3. Quoted in John E. Owens, 'The Regulation of Financial Institutions and Services in the United States: From Regulation to Deregulation' in Andrew Cox (ed.), *The State, Finance and Industry* (Brighton: Harvester, 1986) pp. 174, 177.

4. The classic statement of these positions can be found in the tenth anniversary issue of *The Public Interest*, published as *The New American Commonwealth 1976* (New York: Basic Books, 1976).

CHAPTER TWO

1. The major proponents of hegemony theory are Charles P. Kindleberger, Robert Gilpin, Stephen Krasner and Robert Keohane. See in particular Kindleberger's *The World in Depression 1929–1939* (Berkeley: University of California Press, 1973); Gilpin's *U.S. Power and the Multinational Corporation: The Political Economy of Foreign Direct Investment* (New York: Basic Books, 1975); Krasner's 'State Power and the Structure of International Trade', *World Politics* 28 (April 1976) pp. 317–47; and Keohane's 'The Theory of Hegemonic Stability and Changes in International Economic Regimes, 1967–1977', in Ole R. Holsti, Randolph M. Siverson and Alexander George (eds.), *Change in the International System* (Boulder, Colo.: Westview Press, 1980).

2. Based on calculations in the O.E.C.D. National Accounts Series, *Main Economic Indicators* (Brussels, various years).

3. The O.E.C.D. represents twenty-four western, mainly industrial countries. Reference to O.E.C.D. membership is a useful shorthand for the developed industrial West.

4. O.E.C.D. Economic Surveys, *Japan and the United Kingdom* (1982).

5. United Nations, *Monthly Bulletin of Statistics* (selected years).

6. Quoted in Melvyn B. Krauss, *The New Protectionism: The Welfare State and International Trade* (Oxford: Basil Blackwell, 1979) pp. xix–xx.

7. See Arthur A. Stein, 'The Hegemon's Dilemma: Great Britain, the United States, and the International Economic Order', *International Organization* 38, 2 (Spring 1984) pp. 382–3.

8. For a good account of the recent changes in international banking see Michael Moffitt, *The World's Money: International Banking from Bretton Woods to the Brink of Insolvency* (London: Michael Joseph, 1984).

9. Stein, 'The Hegemon's Dilemma', pp. 383–5.

10. Quoted in Austin Ranney, *Channels of Power: The Impact of Television on American Politics* (New York: Basic Books, 1983) p. 129.

11. Quoted in Michael Balfour, *The Adversaries: America, Russia and the Open World, 1941–1962* (London: Routledge Kegan Paul, 1981) p. 71.

12. Quoted in Stephen E. Ambrose, *Rise to Globalism: American Foreign Policy 1938–70* (Harmondsworth, Middx: Penguin, 1973) p. 10.

13. For good comparisons of U.S. and Soviet power, see Institute of Strategic Studies, *The Military Balance* (London, various years).

14. Mary Kaldor, *The Baroque Arsenal* (Harmondsworth, Middx: Penguin, 1981).

15. Economic historians have long argued that Britain's decline began as early as this. See Clive Trebilcock, *The Industrialization of the Continental Powers, 1780–1914* (Cambridge: Cambridge University Press, 1981) Chapter 6.

16. That hegemonic powers produce a stable international order and their decline marks a move towards instability has become the accepted wisdom in international economic relations. (For references see note 1 above.) Whether decline inevitably leads to the sort of unstable order characteristic of the 1914–39 period is not established, however. It could be that a world with greatly strengthened multinational institutions (not only the U.N., O.E.C.D., World Bank, International Monetary Fund, but also multinational corporations) will cope more successfully than during the inter-war period.

CHAPTER THREE

1. For a critique and defence of the concept of political culture see Gabriel Almond and Sydney Verba (eds.), *The Civic Culture Revisited* (Boston: Little, Brown, 1980).

2. For an example of the Marxist approach see Ira Katznelson and Mark Kesselman, *The Politics of Power* (New York: Harcourt Brace Jovanovich, second edition, 1979).

3. Antonio Gramsci, 'The Intellectuals' in Quintin Hoare and Geoffrey N. Smith (trans.), *The Prison Notebooks: Selections* (New York: International Publishers, 1971) p. 305.

4. Quoted in Seymour Martin Lipset, 'Socialism in America', in Paul Kurtz (ed.), *Sidney Hook: Philosopher of Democracy and Humanism* (Buffalo, NY: Prometheus Books 1983) p. 55.

5. Louis Hartz, *The Liberal Tradition in America* (New York: Harcourt Brace Jovanovich, 1955).

6. Samuel Huntington, *American Politics: The Promise of Disharmony* (Cambridge, MA: Harvard University Press, 1982) p. 25.

7. Even in their predictions of the future of capitalism Marxists and pluralists diverge much less than they used to. Few sophisticated Marxists now foresee the imminent demise of capitalism amid chaos and disorder. They are as likely to predict a slow, unsteady transition to corporation or state capitalism.

8. Indeed, by some measures inequalities of wealth and income are greater than in other Western societies. For a statistical review see Ira C. Magaziner and Robert B. Reich, *Minding America's Business* (New York: Harcourt Brace Jovanovich, 1982) Chapter 2.

9. For a discussion, see Kenneth A. F. Dyson, *The State Tradition in Western Europe* (Oxford: Martin Robertson, 1984) Chapter 8.

10. This has institutional as well as ideological origins. A first-past-the-post electoral system, restrictive voter-registration laws and federalism make it very difficult for small parties to win national support. Socialist parties have, in fact, achieved some success at the local and state levels, especially in the mid-West between 1900 and 1940.

11. A large number of Americans have opposed the specific teaching and proselytizing of communism and atheism. As many as 50 per cent of a 1962 sample survey agreed that 'a book that contains wrong political views cannot be a good book and does not deserve to be published'. Herbert McClosky, 'Consensus and Ideology in American Politics', *American Political Science Review* 8 (1964) Table 3.

12. See James A. Davis, 'Communism, conformity, cohorts and categories: American tolerance in 1954 and 1972/3', *American Journal of Sociology* 81 (November 1975) p. 506.

13. Recalls allow the electorate to recall an official from office on the presentation of a minimum number of signatures. Initiatives are similar devices which enable the electorate to pass a proposal directly, bypass-

ing the state or local legislature. The most famous of recent initiatives have been Proposition 13 in California (1979) and Proposition 2½ in Massachusetts (1980), both of which put severe limits on local property taxes.

14. For example, a famous 1960 study of public attitudes in five countries found that 82 per cent of the American sample declared that they had most pride in U.S. government and political institutions – far more than for other itemized responses, such as pride in the economic system, the characteristics of the people or the country's social/welfare system. Political institutions were given pride of place by 46 per cent of Britons, 30 per cent of Mexicans and just 7 per cent and 3 per cent of West Germans and Italians respectively. Gabriel A. Almond and Sidney Verba, *The Civic Culture: Political Attitudes and Democracy in Five Nations* (New York: Little, Brown, 1965) Table 1.

15. For a discussion, see Norman H. Nie, Sidney Verba and John R. Petrocik, *The Changing American Voter* (Cambridge, MA: Harvard University Press, enlarged edition 1979) Chapters 3 and 4.

16. Reynolds Farley, *Blacks and Whites: Narrowing the Gap* (Cambridge, MA: Harvard University Press, 1984) p. 199.

17. See Richard Merelman, *Making Something of Ourselves: On Culture and Politics in the United States* (Berkeley: University of California Press, 1984).

18. For an account of the rise and decline of Western agrarian populism see Grant McConnell, *The Decline of Agrarian Democracy* (Berkeley: University of California Press, 1983).

19. Michael Barone and Grant Ujifusa, 'Social Change and the American Voter', *Dialogue* 65, 3 (1984).

20. Daniel Bell, 'The End of American Exceptionalism', *The Public Interest* (Fall 1975) p. 167.

21. Quoted in Wayne Shannon, 'Mr Reagan Goes to Washington Teaching Exceptional America', *Public Opinion* (December/January 1982) pp. 15–16.

22. Shannon, 'Mr Reagan Goes to Washington', pp. 15–16.

23. Quoted in *The Times* (25 August 1984) p. 5.

24. Walter Dean Burnham, 'The Eclipse of the Democratic Party – Revisited', *Society* (July/August 1984) p. 40.

25. *Public Opinion* (June/July 1981) pp. 26–7.

CHAPTER FOUR

1. Judicial review was established in the celebrated *Marbury v. Madison* case (1803), when Chief Justice John Marshall established the precedent that the Supreme Court could declare any act of Congress unconstitutional. By the mid-nineteenth century the court was accepted as the

final arbiter of the Constitution, so enabling it to overturn executive, legislative and state laws and policies.

2. Property qualifications continued to apply in most states, although in some (Rhode Island, Massachusetts) something like universal male suffrage did exist. The Constitution decreed that the voting qualifications applicable in the individual states would be the basis for voting in national elections.

3. For a review of Parliament's role see Ian Budge, David McKay *et al.*, *The New British Political System* (London and New York: Longman, 1985) Chapter 3.

4. David Mayhew, *Congress: The Electoral Connection* (New Haven, CT: Yale University Press, 1974) Chapter 1.

5. 'Pork-barrel politics' was the colloquial name for bringing home the 'pork', or material benefits, to constituents in late-nineteenth-century America. It remains in general use to describe the ways in which members win federal grants and contracts for their districts.

6. James L. Sundquist, *The Decline and Resurgence of Congress* (Washington, DC: Brookings Institution, 1981) pp. 369–72.

7. Sundquist, *The Decline and Resurgence of Congress*, p. 371.

8. Jeane J. Kirkpatrick, *The New Presidential Elite: Men and Women in National Politics* (New York: Russell Sage Foundation, 1976).

9. Thomas E. Mann, 'Elections and Change in Congress', in Thomas E. Mann and Norman J. Ornstein (eds.), *The New Congress* (Washington, DC: American Enterprise Institute, 1981) p. 46.

10. Norman J. Ornstein, 'The Open Congress Meets the President', in Anthony King (ed.), *Both Ends of the Avenue: The Presidency, the Executive Branch and Congress in the 1980s* (Washington, DC: American Enterprise Institute, 1983) p. 189.

11. This section depends heavily on Ornstein, 'The Open Congress Meets the President', pp. 195–204.

12. Austin Ranney, *Channels of Power: The Impact of Television on American Politics* (New York: Basic Books, 1983).

13. Quoted in Ranney, *Channels of Power*, p. 150.

14. See James Buchanan and Richard Wagner, *Democracy in Deficit* (New York: Academic Press, 1977); Morris Fiorina, *Congress: Keystone of the Washington Establishment* (New Haven, CT: Yale University Press, 1977).

15. For an account of the 'old-style' budgetary process, see Aaron Wildavsky, *The Politics of the Budgetary Process* (Boston: Little, Brown, third edition, 1979).

16. See Allen Schick, 'How the Budget was Won and Lost', in Norman J. Ornstein, *President and Congress: Assessing Reagan's First Year* (Washington, DC: American Enterprise Institute, 1982) pp. 16–19.

17. Schick, 'How the Budget was Won and Lost', pp. 23–4.

18. For a discussion see Allen Schick, 'The Budget as an Instrument of Presidential Policy', in Lester Salomon and Michael Lund (eds.), *The Reagan Presidency and the Governing of America* (Washington, DC: Urban Institute, 1985).

19. For accounts see Sundquist, *The Decline and Resurgence of Congress*, pp. 431–5, and Michael J. Malkin, 'Rhetoric and Leadership: A Look Backward at the Carter National Energy Plan', in King, *Both Ends of the Avenue*, pp. 212–45.

20. The Federal Reserve System is the equivalent of central banks in other countries. However, it is a 'decentralized' central bank, with twelve regional districts governed by a board in Washington. This board, and especially its chairman, has considerable independent political clout. Presidents appoint the chairmen, but thereafter they often go their own way on the vital questions of monetary policy.

21. The U.S. Constitution separates church from state and requires Congress to 'make no law respecting an establishment of religion'. Over the last thirty years much dispute has surrounded this clause and particularly whether it prohibits the reading of (Christian) school prayers in schools receiving federal funds.

22. John Ferejohn, 'Congress and Redistribution', in Allen Schick (ed.), *Making Economic Policy in Congress* (Washington, DC: American Enterprise Institute, 1983) pp. 150–52.

23. Ferejohn, 'Congress and Redistribution', p. 151.

24. One of the most curious features of the early 1970s was the rapid increase in welfare spending during the Republican Nixon and Ford administrations. One reason was a Democratic Congress hostile to these presidents. Another was the continuing influence of Keynesian economics, which, in response to faltering economic growth, led politicians to take classical demand-boosting measures. By the late 1970s such thinking was rejected as inflationary and ultimately destructive.

25. Significantly, Supplementary Security Income – welfare aid for those old people on social security – was not cut severely. This reflects the special political place reserved for the old in American politics. Few politicians want to risk being identified with denying benefits to pensioners.

26. Stephen D. Krasner, 'United States Commercial and Monetary Policy', in Peter J. Katzenstein (ed.), *Between Power and Plenty: Foreign Economic Policies of Advanced Industrial States* (Madison, WI: University of Wisconsin Press, 1978).

CHAPTER FIVE

1. Or so numerous commentators have inferred from readings of the *Federalist Papers*. See, for example, Garry Wills, *Inventing America* (New York: Doubleday, 1978).

2. Much criticism has been directed at the electoral college, largely because it is a winner-takes-all system. The smallest plurality for a

candidate in a state wins *all* of the state's electoral college votes. It is possible, therefore, to win the presidency with a minority of the vote.

3. After Clinton Rossiter's celebrated analysis of presidential power in *The American Presidency* (New York: Harcourt Brace Jovanovich, 1960).

4. See Anthony King, 'How not to Select Presidential Candidates: A From Europe', in Austin Ranney (ed.), *The American Elections of 1980* (Washington, DC: American Enterprise Institute, 1981) pp. 303–28. See also Nelson Polsby, *Consequences of Party Reform* (New York: Oxford University Press, 1983).

5. The South was, of course, an exception to this rule for many years, the Democrats being very much a regional party. For an analysis of the development of American parties, see William Nisbet Chambers and Walter Dean Burnham (eds.), *The American Party Systems: Stages of Political Development* (New York: Oxford University Press, 1975).

6. See Austin Ranney's *Channels of Power: The Impact of Television on American Politics* (New York: Basic Books, 1983).

7. For a graphic account of these events, see Norman Mailer, *Miami and the Siege of Chicago* (London: Weidenfeld & Nicolson, 1968).

8. Howard L. Reiter, *The New Age of Presidential Nominations* (Philadelphia: University of Pennsylvania Press, 1985).

9. For full details of the 1974 act and *Buckley* v. *Valeo* see Michael Malbin (ed.), *Money and Politics in the U.S.* (Washington, DC: American Enterprise Institute, 1984).

10. See Michael Foley, 'The American Presidency: Changing Patterns in Leadership Recruitment', *Workpapers in American Politics* (American Politics Group of the Political Studies Association, 1983, available from the University of Bristol).

11. Richard Tanner Johnson, *Managing the White House: An Intimate Study of the Presidency* (New York: Harper & Row, 1974). For a reappraisal of the Eisenhower presidency, see Fred Greenstein, *The Hidden Hand Presidency: Eisenhower as Leader* (New York: Basic Books, 1982).

12. Although this too is changing. Recent prime ministers have often depended on 'kitchen cabinets' or informal groups of senior ministers for advice.

13. For a full account see Paul R. Portney, 'Natural Resources and the Environment', in John L. Palmer and Isabel V. Sawhill (eds.), *The Reagan Record: An Assessment of America's Changing Domestic Priorities* (Washington, DC: Urban Institute, 1984).

14. Hugh Heclo, 'The Changing Presidential Office', in Arnold J. Meltsner (ed.), *Politics and the Oval Office: Towards Presidential Governance* (San Francisco: Institute for Contemporary Studies, 1981).

15. The 1973 War Powers Act requires presidents, in the absence of a declaration of war, to inform Congress of any hostile use of American troops abroad. After sixty days, Congressional approval is required to continue military action. Congress can extend the action for a further thirty days, after which the withdrawal of forces can be ordered by a concurrent res-

olution. These congressional actions are not subject to a presidential veto.

16. Norman J. Ornstein, 'The Open Congress Meets the President', in Anthony King (ed.), *Both Ends of the Avenue: The Presidency, the Executive Branch and Congress in the 1980s* (Washington, DC: American Enterprise Institute, 1983) p. 204.

17. For a full account see Nigel Bowles, 'The Decline and Fall of Lyndon Johnson's Congressional Liaison – A Study of Presidential Neglect', paper before the American Politics Group of the Political Studies Association, University of Exeter 3–5 January, 1985.

18. Reported in Austin Ranney, *Channels of Power*, p. 139.

19. Quoted in Sam Kernell, *Going Public* (Washington, DC: Congressional Quarterly Press) p. 120.

20. See William Schneider, 'Elite and Public Opinion: The Alliance's New Fissure', *Public Opinion* (February/March, 1983) p. 5.

21. William Schneider, 'Elite and Public Opinion', pp. 6–7.

22. Arnold J. Meltsner, 'Politics and Governance', in Meltsner (ed.), *Politics and the Oval Office*, p. 301.

23. James David Barber, *The Presidential Character* (Englewood Cliffs, NJ: Prentice Hall, second edition, 1977).

24. As reported in *Time* (19 December 1983) p. 35.

25. Terry Moe, in John E. Chubb and Paul E. Peterson (eds.), *The New Direction in American Politics* (Washington, DC: Brookings Institution, 1985) p. 235.

26. Theodore J. Lowi, *The Personal President: Power Invested, Promise Unfulfilled* (Ithaca, NY: Cornell University Press, 1985).

CHAPTER SIX

1. Alexis de Tocqueville, *Democracy in America* (New York: New American Library, 1956) p. 95.

2. Sidney Verba and Norman H. Nie, *Participation in America: Political Democracy and Social Equality* (New York: Harper & Row, 1972) p. 31.

3. For a review see Congressional Quarterly, *The Washington Lobby* (Washington, DC: third edition, 1979) pp. 141–7.

4. Quoted in Jeffrey M. Berry, *The Interest Group Society* (Boston: Little, Brown, 1984) p. 160.

5. Berry, *The Interest Group Society*, p. 165.

6. David B. Truman, *The Governmental Process* (New York: Alfred Knopf, 1951).

7. The most eloquent statement of this position by an erstwhile pluralist is Charles E. Lindblom's *Politics and Markets, The World's Political Systems* (New York: Basic Books, 1977).

8. For a good summary see Kenneth Prewitt and Alan Stone, *The Ruling*

Elites: Elite Theory, Power and American Democracy (New York: Harper & Row, 1973).

9. The classic statement of this position is by Peter Bachrach and Morton Baratz, 'Decisions and Non-decisions', *American Political Science Review* 57 (September 1963) pp. 632–42.

10. E. E. Schattsneider, *The Semi-Sovereign People* (New York: Holt, Rinehart & Winston, 1960); Grant McConnell, *Private Power and American Democracy* (New York: Alfred Knopf, 1967).

11. Among the boldest statements of the iron-triangle position are Douglass Cater's *Power in Washington* (New York: Random House, 1964) and J. Leiper Freeman's *The Political Process* (New York: Random House, 1965).

12. For a general review of rational-choice theory see Kenneth A. Shepsle, 'Theories of Collective Choice' in *Political Science Annual* 5 (New York: Bobbs-Merrill, 1974).

13. See the special tenth-anniversary issue of *The Public Interest*, 'The American Commonwealth, 1976' for a sample of 'overload' perspectives, especially the essays by Samuel Huntington and Daniel Bell.

14. *National Journal* (15 December 1984) p. 2380.

15. Benjamin I. Page, *Who Gets What from Government* (Berkeley: University of California Press, 1983).

16. Page, *Who Gets What from Government*, Chapter 2.

17. Page, *Who Gets What from Government*, p. 58.

18. See Harold L. Wilensky, *The Welfare State and Equality* (Berkeley: University of California Press, 1985) Chapter 1.

19. See Christopher Jencks et al., *Who gets ahead? The Determinants of Economic Success in America* (New York: Basic Books, 1979).

20. Mancur Olson, *The Logic of Collective Action* (Cambridge, MA: Harvard University Press, 1965). See also his *Rise and Decline of Nations* (New Haven, CT: Yale University Press, 1982).

21. Graham K. Wilson, *Interest Groups in the United States* (London and New York: Oxford University Press, 1981) Chapter 7.

22. Lester C. Thurow, *The Zero Sum Society* (Harmondsworth, Middx: Penguin, 1981).

23. Page, *Who Gets What from Government*, pp. 172–3.

24. This is of course the charge levelled at the first generation of regulatory agencies who encouraged such practices. See, for example, Robert Fellmeth, *The Interstate Commerce Commission* (New York: Grossman, 1970).

25. Page, *Who Gets What from Government*, p. 31.

26. Arthur M. Okun, *Equality and Efficiency: The Big Tradeoff* (Washington, DC: Brookings Institution, 1975).

CHAPTER SEVEN

1. Alexis de Tocqueville, *Democracy in America* (New York: New American Library, 1956) p. 74.

2. *Marbury* v. *Madison*, the most famous Supreme Court case of all, involved the attempt by William Marbury to compel the secretary of state, James Madison, to grant a commission making Marbury a justice of the peace. Chief Justice Marshall would no doubt have favoured Marbury, as he disliked Jefferson, the new president, who had just taken office and was attempting to 'purge' the judiciary of defeated Federalists. Had he done so, the court would almost certainly have been ignored. Instead, in a brilliant judicial sleight of hand he declared that although Jefferson and Madison had acted illegally, the Court could not issue a writ enforcing the commissions. Why not? Because such writs were sanctioned by the 1789 Judiciary Act, which had expanded the Court's original jurisdiction. Such legislation was unconstitutional, the Court argued. Thus, Marshall asserted the power of judicial review while conceding the Marbury case to the Jeffersonians.

3. *Colegrove* v. *Green*, 328 U.S. 549 (1946).

4. *New York Times* v. *U.S.*, 403 U.S. 713 (1971).

5. Section Eight of Article I gives Congress the power to regulate interstate commerce, but the pre-1937 Court interpreted this in a very limited way. Any commerce conducted within a state was deemed not a matter for the federal government. Much federal regulation of industry and commerce was accordingly unconstitutional. More bizarre was the Court's extension of the due process clause of the Fourteenth Amendment to corporations. When treated under law as individuals rather than corporate entities, giant companies were immune from federal laws restricting their operations. This doctrine came to be known as 'substantive due process'.

6. The best short account of these decisions is by Henry Abraham, *Freedom and the Court* (New York: Oxford University Press, third edition, 1977).

7. For a discussion see Paul Bender, 'Privacy', in Norman Dorsen (ed.), *Our Endangered Rights* (New York: Pavilion, 1984) pp. 243–6.

8. Reported in the *Economist*, 'The Long Right Arm of the Law' (14 July 1984) pp. 35–6.

9. Reported in the *Economist* (14 July 1984) p. 36.

10. Reported in the *Economist* (16 June 1984) p. 30.

11. Paul Brest, 'Race Discrimination', in Vincent Blasi (ed.), *The Burger Court: The Counter Revolution that Wasn't* (New Haven, CT: Yale University Press, 1983) p. 113.

12. Quoted in Paul Brest, 'Race Discrimination', p. 118.

13. Reported in the *Economist* (16 June 1984) p. 31.

14. For a graphic account of this decision-making process, see Bob

Woodward and Scott Armstrong, *The Brethren* (New York: Simon & Schuster, 1980) pp. 229–40.

15. For a discussion see article by Vincent Blasi, 'The Rootless Activism of the Burger Court' in Blasi, *The Burger Court*.

16. Michael Horan, 'Adjusting the Separation of Powers: The Legislative Veto and Supreme Court's Decision in the *Chadha* Case', paper before the tenth annual conference of the American Politics Group, Political Studies Association, University of Durham, 1984.

17. Reported in *The New York Times* (20 February 1985) p. 13.

18. *Congressional Quarterly* (8 December 1984) p. 3076.

19. Reported by Gerald Gunther in 'Congressional Power to Curtail Federal Court Jurisdiction: An Opinionated Guide to the Ongoing Debate', *Stanford Law Review* 36, 4 (April 1984) p. 895.

20. For a graphic account of the painfully slow implementation of the *Brown* decision in the South, see Jack W. Peltason, *Fifty-eight Lonely Men* (New York: Harcourt Brace Jovanovich, 1961).

21. Quoted in Gunther, 'Congressional Power to Curtail Federal Court Jurisdiction', p. 895.

CHAPTER EIGHT

1. For a discussion see Sam Bass Warner, *The Urban Wilderness: A History of the American City* (New York: Harper & Row, 1972).

2. 'The Federalist, No. 10' in Alexander Hamilton and others, *Federalist Papers* (New York: New American Library, 1961) p. 83.

3. *McCulloch v. Maryland* (1819).

4. Some federal constitutions delineate powers more precisely. The West German constitution, for example, prohibits direct federal legislation in most domestic policy areas. Labour-market policies are excluded, however, and the federal government has broad fiscal powers which can be used to influence *Land* policies.

5. Quoted in Advisory Commission for Intergovernmental Relations, *An Agenda for American Federalism: Restoring Confidence and Competence* (Washington, DC, 1981) p. 80.

6. Revenue sharing was a block or general grant introduced in 1972 providing states with the freedom to distribute monies as they wished. The idea was to move away from categorical or specific 'strings-attached' grants which increased the power of federal administrators.

7. For a general discussion of the nationalization phenomenon see Theodore J. Lowi and Alan Stone (eds.), *Nationalizing Government: Public Policies in America* (Beverly Hills: Sage, 1978).

8. For the contrasting arguments see Frances Fox Piven and Richard Cloward, *Poor Peoples' Movements* (New York: Pantheon, 1977).

9. Samuel Beer, 'Federalism, Nationalism and Democracy in America', *American Political Science Review* (March 1978) pp. 9–21.

10. For a general summary see Roger L. Kemp, *Coping with Proposition Thirteen* (Lexington, MA: Lexington Books, 1980) Chapter 1.

11. Quoted in George Peterson, 'The State and Local Sector', in John L. Palmer and Isabel V. Sawhill (eds.), *The Reagan Experiment: An Examination of Economic and Social Policies under the Reagan Administration* (Washington, DC: Urban Institute, 1982) p. 165.

12. *The New York Times* (21 June 1981) Section 4, p. 4.

13. David H. McKay, 'Theory and Practice in Public Policy: The Case of the New Federalism', *Political Studies* (June 1985) pp. 187–8.

14. See Paul R. Portney, 'Natural Resources and the Environment', and D. Lee Bowden and John L. Palmer, 'Social Policy', in John L. Palmer and Isabel V. Sawhill (eds.), *The Reagan Record: An Assessment of America's Changing Domestic Priorities* (Washington, DC: Urban Institute, 1984).

15. For an extensive review see John E. Owens, 'The Regulation of Financial Institutions and Services in the United States: From Regulation to Deregulation', in Andrew Cox (ed.), *The State, Finance and Industry* (Brighton: Harvester, forthcoming 1986).

16. The pattern of welfare benefits, which are currently organized on a federal/state matching basis, confirms this point. In 1979, for example, Hawaii provided benefits for a family of four of up to 96 per cent of the locally defined poverty level, compared with just 49 per cent in Mississippi. Generally the southern and south-western states provide low benefits, while the northern and north-eastern states provide higher benefits. See *The Federal Role in the Federal System: The Dynamics of Growth, Public Assistance, the Growth of a Federal Function* (Washington, DC: Advisory Commission for Intergovernmental Relations, 1980).

17. H. Wolman and F. Teitelbaum, 'Interest Groups and Interests in the Reagan Era', in *Project on Changing Domestic Priorities*, Urban Institute discussion paper, September 1983, p. 77.

18. Daniel Elazar, *American Federalism: A View from the States* (New York: Crowell, second edition, 1972).

19. See David H. McKay, 'Fiscal Federalism, Professionalism and the Transformation of American State Government', *Public Administration* 60 (Spring 1982) pp. 10–22.

20. See Deil S. Wright, *Understanding Intergovernmental Relations* (Monterey, CA: Brooks/Cole, second edition, 1982) pp. 260 et seq.

CHAPTER NINE

1. For a forceful argument along these lines see Richard Merelman, *Making Something of Ourselves: On Culture and Politics in the United States* (Berkeley: University of California Press, 1984).

2. This is the broad conclusion of European opinion polls. See, for example, Ivor Crewe, 'Britain Evaluates Ronald Reagan', *Public Opinion* (October/November 1984) pp. 46–9.

3. See in particular Charles M. Hardin, *Presidential Power and Accountability: Toward a New Constitution* (Chicago: University of Chicago Press, 1974). Leading political scientists who have proposed a major reform of this sort include James David Barber and Walter Dean Burnham. American political scientists have also organized a Committee on the Constitutional System (C.C.S.) to discuss reform proposals.

4. For a recent American critique of British politics, see Samuel H. Beer, *Britain Against Itself: The Political Contradictions of Collectivism* (New York: Norton, 1982).

5. For a general summary of these arguments, see James E. Alt and K. Alec Chrystal, *Political Economics* (Brighton: Harvester, 1983) Chapters 5–7.

6. Quoted in Godfrey Hodgson, *All Things to All Men: The False Promise of the Modern American Presidency* (Harmondsworth, Middx: Penguin, 1984) p. 251.

7. By 1985 the balanced-budget amendment had been endorsed by thirty-three states – two short of ratification. As presently worded, the amendment would leave some discretion to Congress on how, exactly, the budget should be balanced.

8. For a general discussion, see John Spanier and Eric M. Uslaner, *American Foreign Policy Making and the Democratic Dilemmas* (New York: Holt, Rinehart & Winston, fourth edition, 1985) Chapter 7.

9. Robert O. Keohane, *After Hegemony: Co-operation and Discord in the World Political Economy* (Princeton, NJ: Princeton University Press, 1984) p. 259.

10. Spanier and Uslaner, *American Foreign Policy Making and the Democratic Dilemmas* p. 261.

11. Robert B. Reich, *The Next American Frontier: A Provocative Programme for Economic Renewal* (Harmondsworth, Middx: Penguin, 1983) p. 276.

12. After the title of Samuel P. Huntington's *American Politics: Promise of Disharmony* (Cambridge, MA: Harvard University Press, 1982).

13. For a discussion, see Gerald Pomper and colleagues, *The Election of 1984* (Chatham, NJ: Chatham House, 1985) Chapters 2 and 7.

14. Between July 1975 and November 1984 Gallup polls indicated that people characterizing themselves as left-of-centre increased from 10 per cent to 16 per cent of the population, centrists remained steady at 41 per cent and right-of-centre identifiers increased from 30 per cent to 32 per cent. Don't knows and no opinions decreased from 19 per cent to 11 per cent. *Public Opinion* (April/May 1985) p. 35.

15. Frances Fox Piven and Richard A. Cloward, *The New Class War: Reagan's Attack on the Welfare State and Its Consequences* (New York: Pantheon, 1982). Kenneth M. Dolbeare, *Democracy at Risk: The Politics of Economic Renewal* (Chatham, NJ: Chatham House, 1984).

Further Reading

CHAPTER TWO

For a good analytical account of the problems associated with declining American power see Robert Keohane, *After Hegemony: Co-operation and Discord in the World Political Economy* (Princeton, NJ: Princeton University Press, 1984). On the U.S. economy, see Robert B. Reich, *The Next American Frontier* (Harmondsworth, Middx: Penguin, 1983). For changes in U.S. foreign policy, see John Spanier and Eric M. Uslaner, *American Foreign Policy Making and the Democratic Dilemmas* (New York: Holt, Rinehart & Winston, fourth edition, 1985).

CHAPTER THREE

No single volume describes the social and political changes of the last forty years, although William Issel's *Social Change in the United States, 1945–1983* (London: Macmillan, 1985) provides an overview of developments in some areas. For a pessimistic view of the political consequences of social fragmentation, see Samuel P. Huntington, *American Politics: The Promise of Disharmony* (Cambridge, MA: Harvard University Press, 1982). On recent changes in political parties, see Martin P. Wattenberg, *The Decline of American Political Parties, 1952–1980* (Cambridge, MA: Harvard University Press, 1984). Kenneth Dolbeare's *Democracy at Risk: The Politics of Economic Renewal* (Chatham, NJ: Chatham House, 1984) argues that recent social and economic changes will bring a new class alignment in American politics.

CHAPTER FOUR

For a general account of recent changes in Congress, see James L. Sundquist, *The Decline and Resurgence of Congress* (Washington, DC: Brookings Institution, 1981). Congressional/presidential relations are covered by Anthony King (ed.) in *Both Ends of the Avenue: The Presidency, the Executive Branch and Congress in the 1980s* (Washington, DC: American Enterprise Institute, 1983). Two classic accounts of the legislator/constituency link exist: Richard Fenno's *Home Style* (Boston: Little, Brown, 1978) and David Mayhew's *Congress: The Electoral Connection* (New Haven, CT: Yale University Press, 1974). For a stimulating account of the relationship between senators and the media, see Stephen Hess, *The Ultimate Insiders* (Washington, DC: Brookings Institution, 1986).

CHAPTER FIVE

Numerous texts on the presidency and biographies of individual presidents exist. Among the better texts are Louis Koenig's, *The Chief Executive* (New York: Harcourt Brace Jovanovich, fourth edition, 1981) and Thomas E. Cronin's *The State of the Presidency* (Boston: Little, Brown, second edition, 1980). See also Godfrey Hodgson's more historical treatment in *All Things to All Men* (Harmondsworth, Middx: Penguin, 1984). Recent presidential elections are covered in the series edited by Gerald Pomper, the most recent of which is *The Election of 1984: Reports and Interpretations* (Chatham, NJ: Chatham House, 1985). Among the better biographies of modern presidents are James MacGregor Burns, *Roosevelt: The Lion and the Fox* (New York: Harcourt Brace Jovanovich, 1956) and *Roosevelt, the Soldier of Freedom* (New York: Harcourt Brace Jovanovich, 1970); Robert J. Donovan, *Conflict and Crisis: The Presidency of Harry S. Truman* (New York: Norton, 1977); Arthur M. Schlesinger, *A Thousand Days: John F. Kennedy in the White House* (Boston: Houghton Mifflin, 1965). On the Nixon era, see Jonathan Schell, *The Time of Illusion* (New York: Vintage, 1975). Ronnie Dugger's *On Reagan* (New York: McGraw-Hill, 1984) is a critical account of Ronald Reagan's policies. A good essay on recent developments in the office is Theodore J. Lowi's *The Personal President: Power Invested, Promise Unfulfilled* (Ithaca, NY: Cornell University Press, 1985). Samuel Kernell's *Going Public: New Strategies of Presidential Leadership* (Washington, DC: Congressional Quarterly Press, 1986) is the best account of presidents using the public as a resource.

CHAPTER SIX

Charles E. Lindblom's *Politics and Markets, the World's Political Systems* (New York: Basic Books, 1977) is now the classic criticism of pluralism. A good general text on interest groups written from a pluralist perspective is Jeffrey M. Berry, *The Interest Group Society* (Boston: Little, Brown, 1984). See also Graham K. Wilson, *Interest Groups in the United States* (Oxford: Oxford University Press, 1981). A public-choice perspective is provided by Mancur Olson in *The Rise and Decline of Nations* (New Haven, CT: Yale University Press, 1982).

CHAPTER SEVEN

The volume edited by Vincent Blasi, *The Burger Court: The Counter Revolution that Wasn't* (New Haven, CT: Yale University Press, 1983), provides a balanced account of the performance of the Burger Court. A critique of the Burger Court's civil-rights and liberties record is provided by Norman Dorsen (ed.), *Our Endangered Rights* (New York: Pavilion, 1984). The political role of the Court is analysed in Richard Hodder Williams, *The Politics of the U.S. Supreme Court* (London: Allen & Unwin, 1980). The American Enterprise Institute publishes a series entitled *Significant Cases of the Supreme Court*, by each judicial term. Henry J. Abraham's *The Judicial Process: An Introductory Analysis of the United States, England and France* (New York: Oxford University Press, fourth edition, 1980) remains one of the best introductions to the subject.

CHAPTER EIGHT

The best descriptive introduction to the subject is Deil S. Wright's *Understanding Intergovernmental Relations* (Monterey, CA: Brooks/Cole, second edition, 1982). For a good account of fiscal federalism see Roy Bahl, *Financing State and Local Government in the 1980s* (New York: Oxford University Press, 1984). A justification of Reagan's New Federalism is given in Charles E. Barfield, *Rethinking Federalism: Block Grants and Federal, State and Local Responsibilities* (Washington, DC: American Enterprise Institute, 1981). Comprehensive accounts of intergovernmental relations generally are published by the Advisory Commission for Intergovernmental Relations (A.C.I.R.) in Washington.

CHAPTER NINE

Two edited collections on the current state of American political institutions and policies stand out as exceptional: John E. Chubb and Paul E. Peterson (eds.), *The New Direction in American Politics* (Washington, DC: Brookings Institution, 1985); Lester M. Salomon and Michael S. Lund (eds.), *The Reagan Presidency and the Governing of America* (Washington, DC: Urban Institute, 1985).

Index